FRENCH AND FRANCOPHONE STUDIES

Stolen Limelight

Also in Series

FRENCH AND FRANCOPHONE STUDIES

Stolen Limelight

Gender, Display and Displacement In Modern Fiction in French

Margaret E. Gray

UNIVERSITY OF WALES PRESS
2022

www.uwp.co.uk

British Library Cataloguing-in-Publication Data
A catalogue record for this book is available from the British Library.

ISBN   978-1-78683-860-5
eISBN 978-1-78683-861-2

Front Cover: Larry Rivers (1923–2002) VAGA @ ARS, NY. I Like Olympia in Blackface, 1970. Oil on wood, plastic, plexiglas. 182 x 194 x 170 cm. AM 1976-1231. Photograph: Philippe Migeat. Musée National d'Art Moderne, Centre Georges Pompidou, Paris, France. Digital image copyright CNAC/MNAM, Dist. RMN Grand-Palais/ Art Resource, NY.

Typeset by Gary Evans
Printed and bound by CPI Group (UK) Ltd, Croydon, CR0 4YY

For Off-the-Deep-End Oz,
with whom it all began

For Joseph and Nathan,
with whom it almost ended

And in memory of my mother
Hazel Ward Burton Gray
1931–2020

Contents

Series Editors' Preface

This series showcases the work of new and established scholars working within the fields of French and francophone studies. It publishes introductory texts aimed at a student readership, as well as research-orientated monographs at the cutting edge of their discipline area. The series aims to highlight shifting patterns of research in French and francophone studies, to re-evaluate traditional representations of French and francophone identities and to encourage the exchange of ideas and perspectives across a wide range of discipline areas. The emphasis throughout the series will be on the ways in which French and francophone communities across the world are evolving into the twenty-first century.

Hanna Diamond and Claire Gorrara

Je t'ai longtemps, longtemps, gardé
Sur ma table et j'ai retardé
Le moment de te laisser suivre
Un chemin brumeux ignoré …
Va-t'en, mon livre.

[I have, for a long, long time, kept you
On my table and I've delayed
The moment of letting you follow
A misty unknown path …
Off with you, my book.][1]

Jules Supervielle

Preface

Time and again – that is, for a long time – rather than going to bed early, I used to work on Proust. And then one fine day, resolved to be post-Proust and finding myself in a small brasserie on the rue de Vaugirard with a gentleman of my acquaintance, I was eating a potato omelette and talking about my various post-Proust projects. It came to me that they all had something in common; I was halfway through a book before I realised it. And yet, in its sudden illumination of such an organic, inadvertent link binding disparate pieces into an unexpected whole, this resolutely post-Proustian endeavour had been neatly anticipated by the Proustian narrator himself. In his description, such a retrospectively established federation results in an 'unité qui s'ignorait, donc vitale et non logique, qui n'a pas proscrit la variété, refroidi l'exécution' ['unity unaware of itself, thus vital and not logical, a unity that has not forbidden variety, nor chilled execution']. Pointing to Wagner's Ring cycle and the many works of Balzac's vast *Comédie humaine* ['Human Comedy'], the Proustian narrator views each collection as emerging from a moment of belated discovery on the part of its creator, each enthused by such a sudden intuition: an illumination uniting 'des morceaux qui n'ont plus qu'à se rejoindre' ['fragments that have only to join each other'].[2] I was less post-Proust than I had imagined, and yet, somehow, found this not only comforting, but affirming. How could I ever have wished it otherwise?

My appreciation extends well beyond the potato-omelette gentleman of that long-ago lunch, and the two beloved sons who were to follow. Audiences hearing various early versions of these pages at an array of conferences on both sides of the Atlantic provided helpful reactions, as did an invitation to speak at the University of London's (then-named) Institute of Germanic and Romance Studies; a September week at the Rockefeller Foundation's Bellagio Center on Lake Como was both blissful and inspiring. More specifically, sustaining me through this project were the constant friendship and support of my Indiana University/Bloomington departmental friends and colleagues; my Bloomington friends beyond the department; fellow Proustians Emily Eells, David Ellison, Eddie Hughes, Adam Watt and others; my through-thick-and-thin Aix-en-Provence friends and colleagues Jeannine Féral and Patricia Reffay; my childhood friend and college roommate, Christie King. Susan Harrow's kind invitation to speak at the fabled Gregynog allowed me to push further certain arguments in my introduction, while Sianne Ngai's visit to campus under the auspices of our Center for Theoretical Inquiry in the Humanities prompted insights for the conclusion. My lasting, profound gratitude goes to the peer reviewer for the Press, Prof. Diana Holmes, whose probing, judicious and insightful reading greatly improved these pages; their pernicious remaining faults can only be my own. I owe much to the unfailing support, encouragement, attentiveness and professionalism of the Press's own Sarah Lewis, Head of Commissioning. But as Virginia Woolf wrote, 'the list threatens to grow too long and is already far too distinguished. For while it rouses in me memories of the pleasantest kind it will inevitably wake expectations in the reader which the book itself can only disappoint. Therefore I will conclude'.[3]

All translations from the French are my own.

Introduction

Who has not, in a favoured moment, succeeded – whether deliberately or inadvertently – in 'stealing the limelight'? The implications of such an act of display – with its illicitness, its verve, its vertiginous reversal of power, its subversiveness – are explored in this book. Across a range of twentieth-century novels in French and their selected film adaptations, narrative management of the effects of 'stolen limelight' is analysed: the manipulation within a fiction of the heightened visibility associated with such display. Such acts appear to solicit attention; to provoke reaction of some kind from the reader or embedded spectator, of whatever sort – whether veneration, desire, admiration, shock, horror or any of a range of responses. Yet, curiously, these scenarios of display can become effective strategies of displacement; they may ultimately work to neutralise, even occult, the very subject whose attention they appear so energetically to solicit. Essentially, then, the pages that follow attempt to account for display *as* displacement. Such transgressive 'stolen limelight' ultimately disempowers a threat: one that, in the narratives analysed here, takes gendered form. In these gendered contexts, display becomes linked to struggle, resistance or repression.

As a transgressive yet enviable act – enviable perhaps precisely *because* transgressive – 'stealing the limelight' inspires both scorn and admiration, disdain and reverence, censure and celebration; it is an act to which we cannot remain indifferent. Necessarily disruptive, shocking in its audacity and nerve, it is also revered for its upsets, for the improbability of its triumphs. Its reversals are freighted with surprise, produced as they are by a surge of unexpected energy from an unlikely source – a source that intercepts, arrogates and redirects the spectator's or reader's attention. 'Stealing the limelight' creates a larger-than-life glare or focus, producing a sort of hypervisibility. Attendant upon such hypervisibility are implications of performativity, of the stage and artifice, of the mechanics of framing and stylisation. At times, these dynamics veer into caricature or into the grotesque, the monstrous: spectacular extremes that, in the curious paradox of display as displacement that will be explored here, work towards an effacing effect.[1] For what appears to confirm the viewing subject's primacy – what appears to be organised and arranged for the reader or embedded viewer's consumption (again, however shocked, horrified or pleasurable such consumption might be) – works instead, as I argue, to displace this subject. Display and its reversals inflect and inform our reading practices, even as these practices designate sites of instability within narrative. Understanding the work of gendered and gendering practices within the creation and shaping of narrative display allows us to trace the power of visual dynamics within these texts.

By way of illustration, we might turn to an act of stolen limelight depicted in a 1970 sculpture by American artist Larry Rivers: a work offering a racially inflected send-up of Manet's renowned 'Olympia'.[2] Rivers reverses the women's races to feature a new Black Olympia under the gaze of a white maid. The original Olympia, Manet's reclining white prostitute cynically returning the viewer's gaze, now recedes as background prop, or even a mere paper-doll outline – her sharp gaze and features now vague, effaced. Guiding our gaze, and emphasising the shift in limelight, Rivers stages Manet's Black maid – demoted with her white mistress to the background – as still focused, askance, on Olympia. However, her scandalised gaze seems fixed not on her own white mistress, as in Manet's painting, but – in a diagonal traverse of the scene – on the new Black Olympia. As the viewer encounters this Black maid's eyes in the sculpture's background, we find ourselves following her gaze across the work, right back to the Black, not white, Olympia – as though to keep reminding us of the Black Olympia's transgressive yet decisive accomplishment in monopolising our attention. Could this background maid's focused gaze and scandalised expression (the most detailed feature of the work, whose three other human faces lack similar definition) be serving to emphasise for us just how successfully the new Black Olympia has arrogated display? And yet, the new Olympia does not appear to be basking in her illicit, stolen visibility; rather, she has become somehow indifferent to the viewer so intently fixed and positioned by her white predecessor in Manet's painting. One eye is effaced; the remaining eye seems set in a vague, blank stare. Cast indifferently beyond the viewer, this Black Olympia's almost mechanical gaze seems, in its glazed, inhuman indifference, to displace the spectator from 'his' former power and privilege as the interlocutor who is also, most likely, the customer whose gift of flowers is being displayed to her mistress by the maid. Rather, this customer/viewer is displaced, virtually discarded; 'his' stature, despite the effort to anchor and ensure – indeed to *buy* – his importance with the gift of flowers, collapses before the new Olympia's glassy indifference. Rivers' sculpture thus captures the dynamic of display as displacement; its reversals and energy are focused, heightened and intensified by the Black maid's sharp and shocked reaction. Following hers, our own gaze is cued to replicate its mix of disapproval and admiration, its reluctant avowal of the power at work in the Black Olympia's upstaging of her white predecessor.

Narrative manipulation of such tensions and reversals is the subject of this book. Opening with a discussion of 'stolen limelight' as transgression, I turn to practices of spectation and their pertinence for the gendered narrative dynamics to be studied. Analyses of techniques of framing, display and still-life from art-historical and museum contexts help to identify such aspects within narrative: aspects that work to create distance between the beholder and the beheld. Behaviours of display such as hysteria, mourning and mania, illuminated by psychoanalytic theory, allow us to understand the visibility that they bring to narrative, as do literary theories of melodrama. Gender theory – arguing for the social construction of gender identity, as, precisely, display – helps us study the ways in which such display informs narrative dynamics. Spectating practices analysed by film theory provide assistance in understanding readerly response to such display. Enlisting these various approaches, I ask what narrative tensions are produced when gendered display becomes excessively, sometimes monstrously, visible. Such hypervisibility disturbs codes and conventions; it ruptures boundaries, releasing possibilities for resistance, oppression, subversion or repression.

These dynamics take place in various ways, occurring most obviously as an unexpected reversal or redirection of visibility, as in the appropriation of another's display. They may also be at work in the unjust or illicit (hence, 'stolen') forcing of monstrous visibility upon an innocent victim, so as to disempower its perceived threat; securely distanced through such spotlighting, such a threat is safely pinpointed and paralysed. In this way, stolen or illicit limelight becomes glare – and available for purposes of isolation, neutralisation and suppression. Throughout my corpus, whatever the specific effect of such gendered, 'stolen' (illicit, unauthorised, unexpected) display – whether it resists, overturns, neutralises, suppresses or otherwise counters a force construed as threatening – it becomes a forceful oppositional tactic.

Yet, the impact of 'stolen limelight' as it interests me here is not limited to the displacement or occulting of the viewing subject or reader. Speaking from her experience of working in Western Australian light, landscape painter Barbara Bolt emphasises the destructive power of blinding 'glare', suggesting that it is 'inconceivable to practice under European notions of light in the "glare" of the Australian sun. Too much light on matter sheds no light on the matter … the "glare" of the sun fractures the nexus between light, form, knowledge and subjectivity'.[3] Taking Bolt's notion of fractured 'form, knowledge and subjectivity', we might understand this powerfully annihilating effect of glare as a different sort of stolen limelight. Engaging the idea of limelight via the past participle – as in limelight that has been stolen – allows for the uncoupling of subject and object, the detachment of thieving act from object stolen. With this shift, we move from subject to object, allowing us to focus, as well, on the effects produced by the act – rather than solely on the act itself. An equally transgressive move, the directing of glare upon 'form, knowledge, subjectivity', works in different ways towards purposes of resistance, repression. In such circumstances, rather than arrogating power to itself, the energy of glare – as in Bolt's argument – works to disempower its object. In such instances, stolen limelight works as the hostile manipulation of visibility: the glare forced unjustly upon an innocent or unwilling object for purposes of containment and control. It becomes the unwelcome limelight of the interrogation lamp, the glare of surveillance and domination: the pinpointing spear of light that fixes and paralyses its victim, thus neutralising any threat that it might bear. Such widened focus – not only on the act, but on its victim; not only on the theft itself of 'limelight', but on the object 'stolen' or disfigured by such glare – enlarges the field of meaning commanded by limelight. Hypervisibility becomes invested with dynamic new combinations and tensions, opening onto scenarios in which it is turned upon an innocent or reluctant object by an unscrupulous force – rendering that object *other*, alien: indeed – at times – excessive, monstrous. In such instances, we might understand the notion of 'stolen' as designating an illicit, unjust, unfounded visibility forced upon its object.

Increasingly, in cultures so heavily inflected by the visual, attention has turned to 'the modes whereby texts engage with visual culture' in what has been called the 'New Ekphrastic Poetics'.[4] In her discussion of this 'visual turn' in literary criticism – a 'turn' that she proposes, consonant with the visual lexicon, as a 'swerve' – Harrow particularly signals the 'destabilizing of tropes of viewing' through such dynamics as 'interrupted visual-textual traffic'.[5] Launched by Judith Butler, for instance, influential work on what we might call the 'interruption of gender', has tended to privilege the more spectacular, campy, 'queer' aspects of gender – such as drag – in efforts to demonstrate the stylised acts that make up all gender identity.[6] Following the same trend towards the more visible, narrative itself as a dynamic has been somewhat eclipsed by performance and performativity – that is, spectacles promoted by image-saturated cultures, with attendant emphasis on viewing practices, mechanisms and pleasures, and their impact on interpretive discourses. In such an image-governed age, mourned Naomi Schor as early as the 1990s, narrative has lost its centrality, just as gender has lost its stability as a category through which to understand difference.[7] Schor deplored the loss of what feminist critics of the 1970s and 1980s considered the 'two pillars of feminist criticism': narrative and gender. If feminist criticism were to survive, or to rise from its own ashes, claimed Schor, then gender (however reorganised) and narrative (however under attack) had to be retained.[8] If interest in narrative has been superseded by attention to performativity, and the gendered subject dismantled by gender construction – particularly 'queer' genders – it is time to take what we have learned from these developments and apply them to what has been left behind – narrative itself – in order to learn how to see (i.e., to read) what Harrow calls 'the visuality of text'.[9]

By way of launching an investigation of such 'visuality', we might engage Stephen Greenblatt's distinction between museum practices inducing 'resonance' and those inducing 'wonder'. Arguing that resonance-based exhibiting seeks to place its artefacts in cultural, historical context, Greenblatt suggests that such practices effectively create narratives embedding the artefacts displayed. On the other hand, continues Greenblatt, wonder-based exhibiting fosters an 'enchanted' absorption 'from which everything but the object is excluded, when intensity of regard blocks out all circumambient images, stills all murmuring voices'.[10] Whereas resonance-based exhibiting emphasises context or narrative, wonder-based exhibiting fosters arrest, absorption, isolation: dynamics that work against the ordering, successive project of narrative. We might associate Greenblatt's 'enchanted … wonder' with Svetlana Alpers's 'museum effect', which involves 'turning all objects into works of art'. In this way, Alpers's 'museum effect' is 'a way of seeing'.[11] Borrowing a phrase from Alpers, I would like to use the idea of 'crafted visibility' to describe the 'stolen limelight' dynamics to be studied here. What happens when arresting, absorbing effects (Greenblatt's enchantment and wonder) erupt within the narrative 'resonance' – or ordering – crafted by fictions? What energies are released by the conflict engaged in the encounter of these two 'way[s] of seeing': the isolating way, and the contextualising way?

What follows, then, is an effort to engage narrative via the visual. How might advances over the past two decades – involving such issues in visibility as the gaze, spectatorship, performance, the simulacrum, mimesis, display – be diverted to the study of narrative? Applying performativity to narrative would seem to be a perverse move, in that the performative works to disrupt, to destabilise – whereas narrative is necessarily a work of linking: however stretched and contested that linking may be. But it is precisely because the performative carries disruptive potential that its effects within narrative deserve our interest. Associated with display and spectacle, the performative seeks visibility; and visibility, commanding fascination, bathed in the glare of limelight, works to suspend temporal progression and narrative movement. In what follows, I ask how narratives manage the disruptions brought by the excess, or hypervisibility, of display; how narratives both construe such energies and stifle them; how such energies ultimately elude narrative control. What happens when gendered energies become linked in some way to the excessively, sometimes monstrously, visible? And how do narratives negotiate such tensions, such threats? Although narrative itself arises precisely out of tension, as Peter Brooks has argued, its unleashed energies seek appropriate binding, or resolution, in a return to quiescence.[12] Meanwhile, however, whatever forms they take and however they express themselves, such energies of display can become disruptive, threatening. As they acquire heightened visibility, they disturb codes and conventions; they rupture boundaries. In this way, they are often tied to struggle and resistance, even as they call forth punitive and repressive reactions. This book will explore gendered display as, on the one hand, the action taken by a subject, linked to strategies of resistance – and on the other, the action performed upon an object, victimised by strategies of repression.

For, in the perverse paradox mentioned earlier, the transgressive visibility of stolen or unfounded limelight can be projected in ways that work to isolate its object, rendering it 'other', alien, even monstrous, as we will see in the case of Mauriac's heroine, Thérèse Desqueyroux. Such stolen limelight may be inadvertent: the accidental or unknowing manipulation of visibility that becomes chance display, as we see in Colette's novel when the young heroine unwittingly manipulates a set of gendered tropes that confound the masculinist gaze. A surprise usurpation is also at work in Japrisot's fiction, where the coded-as-virile model of the detective quest, ostentatiously displayed by the narrative, is infiltrated and ultimately overturned by a very different genre: the love story, and a homoerotic one, at that. Unaware of the rich, transgendered implications of this surreptitiously homoerotic macho detective 'transfer' narrative, one of its male characters scornfully dismisses it as 'une histoire de filles' ['girl stuff']. With Gide's 1909 novel, we will see how the notion of limelight backfires in the self-denying, self-effacing theatrics of Alissa and her sister Juliette. Their frantic efforts to elude the limelight of visibility are consonant with techniques of muteness, found in melodrama, that serve to focus attention precisely on self-eclipsing silence. Limelight is here inadvertently, accidentally, stolen, despite – or because of – the two sisters' frantic efforts to efface themselves. In Oyono's narrative of colonial domination, the 'feminisation' of colonial power becomes one of the few forms of resistance available to a young native houseboy. Yet the houseboy Toundi's resistance project founders, undone by his own desire for the white commander's unscrupulous wife. Instead, it takes a native woman's gaze to hijack the wife's lime-lit display and turn it back evaluatively upon the white woman, coldly and clinically exposing her pathology. In Duras's narrative of scandalous display produced by the transgressive affair of the young Frenchwoman and her Chinese lover, we will trace a daughter's struggle to displace a more engulfing, more threatening feminine energy: that of her mad, destroyed mother.

One might notice that, in general, variations of the hypervisible, when linked to gendered subjects, tend towards feminine figures culturally relegated to social margins, as in the narratives to be explored here. Mauriac's masculinised female 'monster', Colette's strangely innocent hyperfemininity, Gide's Protestant fanatic, Duras's teenage mistress of an older Chinese gentleman, Japrisot's lesbian murderess, Oyono's nymphomaniac, would seem to comprise a pantheon of caricatures.[13] We realise that this connection between hypervisibility and feminine extremes only makes intuitive sense; for the comforting, the everyday, the ordinary – de-eroticised and absorbed by the invisibility of habit, blanketed by routine – fades from visibility. Coded as the normal, natural, comfortable, safe space of familiarity, this is a space of nurture, intimately linked to creaturely comfort and domesticity, to safety.[14] For display to become not only visible as such, but glaringly hypervisible, bathed in limelight, it must set itself apart from familiarity and habit, becoming potentially thrillingly, dangerously, *other* than the ordinary: and, in this way, transgressive. This antipodal space – a space excitingly unstable, a space of artifice and seduction, of unfamiliarity – is the space of the artful, the manipulated, the non-natural. The fascination it commands links it to hypervisibility.

Now, when the boundaries dividing the comfortably invisible – such as the familiarly maternal, for instance – and its opposite, that is, the seductively visible and gendered, dividing the invisible and the hypervisible, the everyday and the dangerous – are suddenly scrambled, our confusion is acute. We discover that we no longer know just what we are looking at; we suddenly realise that what we are looking at is not what we *thought* we were looking at.[15] For, in the opposing regimes of habit and seduction, of life and art, we know what the rules are for each; we know the codes and conventions; but the liminal space between them is threatening precisely for the way in which it destabilises and scrambles the two.

The implications of these two modes – their safety, on the one hand; their danger, on the other – might help explain why the need to define the difference between the two has become so anxious. The very urgency of being able to draw a boundary between the true and the false, natural and artifice, real and fantastic – the need to be able to distinguish the two realms – is in itself revealing. Why should such distinctions be so important? Because any scrambling of these boundaries is transgressive, resistant; it carries a political bite and valence that disconcerts the established order, rather in the way Bakhtin's manipulation of the 'carnival' trope overturns orderly categories. The very anxiety invested in parsing out the disconcerting blurring of that boundary is symptomatic of its unsettling power. Indeed, the very boundary between 'real' and 'artificial' is contested in Butler's analysis of drag. Pointing to the disconcerting moment of not knowing whether we might be looking at a body that is male or female beneath its apparel, Butler argues that the idea of what part of the spectacle is assumed and what part is 'real' is nothing more than a convention, a fiction. Implicit in Butler's analysis is the suggestion that more interesting than what may or may not 'really' lie beneath the appearance of femininity is, instead, the *need* to know the difference.[16]

And yet, such anxious parsing-out of gendered identity has given way to alternatives that allow us to resituate such questions. One solution, of course, has been to dispute gender as a cultural, natural or essential given, seeing it instead as inseparable from its appearance. In her early (1929) analysis of femininity as construct, of 'womanliness as a masquerade', Joan Riviere analysed an intellectual woman compelled to follow each public act of competence with excessive ogling and coquetry. This masquerade, argued Riviere, was a defence: 'women who wish for masculinity may put on a mask of womanliness to avert anxiety and the retribution feared from men.'[17] 'The reader may now ask,' she concludes, 'how I define womanliness or where I draw the line between genuine womanliness and the "masquerade". My suggestion is not, however, that there is any such difference; whether radical or superficial, they are the same thing.'[18] Drawing on Riviere, Butler famously radicalised the claim that 'womanliness' and masquerade 'are the same thing'. Gendered appearance does not express a gendered essence; instead, as a 'stylized repetition of acts', gender is inseparable from its own performance.[19]

If gender is always already performance, as Butler argued, we lose the reassuring variations, the degrees, between the 'natural' and the performed – in a destabilising, disquieting collapse. However, while the 'natural' as the putative essence of gender may have been forever exploded by Butler, its appearance – we might say, the simulacrum of the natural – still carries effective bite and valence. We need to investigate such an artificial 'natural' within performance, and performance within the 'natural', so as to appreciate ways in which movement in and out of the limelight, in and out of hypervisibility, works towards differing agendas. Such an absolute, intimate intertwining of gender with its own appearance, or masquerade, allows us to discard obsolete, essentialising questions concerning its nature – and thus to situate this enquiry further along the use and practice of gender, further into its embeddedness and grittiness within contexts. This allows us to take up gendered constructs not as essence, but as representation – and as a particularly visible representation, at that. Indeed, in the novels to be considered here, it is the gendered construct that – whether deliberately, unwillingly or even unconsciously – acquires the limelight of an extra or heightened visibility.[20]

Just how does such excess become visible? How does it move from the invisible, to the hypervisible? We notice that the everyday is a web of contexts; from this web of the invisible, our habitual network of relationships, how do things become visible, standing out against the everyday? They become detached from context, through various mechanisms involving increased visibility: framing, display, theatre – isolating mechanisms implied by Greenblatt's notions of absorption, wonder and enchantment. One aspect of the hypervisible involves framing, for framing designates and sets apart. Such setting-apart in theatre, for example, begins with frames, for frames serve to separate the real from the non-real. Indeed, such framing has been argued as endemic to theatre.[21] We can put a frame around theatre, and say, 'this is not'; as Butler puts it, we can say, 'this is just an act', and we can make it into something entirely different from 'what is real'.[22] Display created by framing removes the familiar, 'natural' context, creating heightened focus or visibility. In isolating objects to promote aesthetic contemplation of them, display, argues Emma Barker, invites the viewer's projection of 'meanings and values' not necessarily based in the objects themselves.[23] Barker explores the implications of display lighting, arguing that spotlighting, for instance, can act to discourage the viewer's involvement with 'meanings and values' surrounding the object in its original context; instead, spotlighting – argues Barker – encourages 'self-consciousness on the part of viewers about the cultural distance between themselves and the objects on show'.[24] Such isolated, wonder-based viewing (in Greenblatt's term), in focusing attention on the object itself, divested of its context and bathed in hypervisibility, heightens the object's otherness – and fosters fascination in the viewer. Such a capacity in the spectator to distinguish the act, or representation, from the real, is crucial for the very function of representation. When an object depicted stands for its real counterpart, we are in a first order of representation, a comforting, habitual one. We *know* we are looking at representations of the real, not at the real itself; the boundary between the two is maintained. The knowledge of this difference produces a feeling of safety in us, for we cannot ourselves become whatever is depicted; these boundaries protect us from falling into the depicted space.[25]

By way of deepening our understanding of stolen limelight and its displays as they work within narrative, however, let us return to a space without frames, a disconcerting space somewhere between life and art, between the natural and the artificial: a theatrical space. Theatricality, we realise, is threatening precisely because it is *not* theatre, with theatre's frames, codes and conventions: the *Verneinung*, or 'deniability', that allows us to say, 'this is not real', and walk away. Theatricality is somehow in excess of theatre; as Hobson puts it, it is both theatre *and* something else. Such an idea of theatricality beyond the confines of theatre implies the transgression of a boundary between art and life; it establishes two distinct sites, bringing them into communication yet holding them apart in the very moment of transgression.[26] Theatricality disconcerts because it refuses to choose, and thus scrambles the difference between theatre and non-theatre. In confounding this difference, argues Litvak, theatricality 'signifies not a single, unitary style or content, but a set of shifting, contradictory energies'. Theatre itself evokes a more stable art form – as we realise even with post-Artauldian theatre, in which the staged event overflows the stage to involve the entire space itself and audience beyond; for the audience is present precisely for purposeful, deliberate 'theatre-going' reasons. Theatricality, however – maintains Litvak – is open-ended.[27] And such open-endedness becomes disconcerting – indeed, threatening. When the act that had defined theatre occurs without the frame of its conventions, there is no longer any distinction or separation between theatre and reality. 'On the street or in the bus,' writes Butler, 'the act becomes dangerous, if it does, precisely because there are no theatrical conventions to delimit the purely imaginary character of the act.'[28] We will be exploring the effects of such a 'disquieting' act 'on the street or in the bus' of narrative – when we find that the discursive frames shaping our readerly reactions are shifting and unsteady; that our narrative world, our textually defined normative 'real', is no longer safely distinct from a – perhaps scarcely perceptible – drift into a theatricalised, hyperreal, version of itself.

But in thinking about the subtle menace posed by such a blurred boundary, we are reminded that the scrambling of such demarcation between the conventions of theatre and the familiarity of the ordinary calls forth an entire history of anxiety. The eighteenth-century English masquerade, for example, specifically linked the scandal of such boundary-scrambling to class-bound, gendered norms. The masquerade was one of the few social functions that respectable women were free to attend unescorted; prostitutes were similarly able to disguise themselves as 'women of quality' at these events, in the hope of enticing customers. So rare a convergence of prostitutes and 'respectable' women within the same space was particularly anxiety-provoking, for any woman at a masquerade might be a disguised prostitute: 'at once hypersexualized, hypocritical, and an exploiter of innocent men'.[29] The masquerade, then, 'this realm of dream, dismay and laughter', as Castle demonstrates, 'is also, par excellence, the realm of women'.[30]

The scandal of such blurring of reality and simulation, or artifice, accompanies the notion of theatricality into the nineteenth century. For the Victorians, writes Nina Auerbach, theatricality was scandalously deceitful, implying as it does 'a fluidity of character that decomposes the uniform integrity of the self'. Auerbach points to a pervasive nineteenth-century fear of performance, motivated by 'a covert fear that any activity is destructive of character because all activity smacks of acting'. The source of such fear lay not in stage performances, argues Auerbach, but in the liminal space of theatricality: 'in the histrionic artifice of ordinary life.'[31] For these reasons, Auerbach suggests, intriguingly, that theatre – feared and distrusted by the Victorians as an emblem of the volatility of the self – represented not so much '[a] threat to the integrity of sincerity, but the theatricality of sincerity itself'.[32]

Such a threat does not end with the Victorians, however. Pointing to the link in Western culture between a 'theatrical self' and a certain subversiveness, Benston refers to a 'subversive desire, desire that would redirect meaning by resisting enclosure, exposing contradiction, and producing alternatives'.[33] In its effort to recover the subject as a reliable locus of meaning, modernity attempts, argues Benston, 'to contain the disruptive energies latent in unauthorized concepts of performance'.[34] Pursuing further the transgressive implications of unauthorised performance is to realise that, in straying into a space that hints at spectacle, theatricality invites our gaze. Yet, in that it is not pure theatre, but both theatre *and* something else – something exceeding the boundaries of theatre – it also shows itself to be aware of us, its spectators. It thus repositions us, pins us – no longer masterful viewing subjects, we suddenly become objects of another gaze. Theatricality thus produces 'a fractured reciprocity whereby beholder and beheld reverse positions in a way that renders a steady position of spectatorship impossible'.[35] 'Something is looking at my looking', is the way Bryson puts it in his discussion of Raphael's 1504 painting, 'Marriage of the Virgin'. Here, behind the wedding ceremony, is an architectural space organised around an open doorway at the centre of the temple. From this blank, central 'eye', radiating lines – carried by the steps and flagstones of the piazza – trace a widening movement that positions and fixes us as viewers, argues Bryson; even as our own attention is drawn to the activity of the marriage ceremony in the foreground, we are ourselves fixed, objectified as spectators by the centrally positioned yet distant blank temple doorway. 'Its gaze returns that of the viewer as its own object: something is looking at my looking: a gaze whose position I can never occupy.'[36]

Pursuing the disconcerting effect of theatricality, let us imagine an instant in which attention floats over the surfaces of daily life, to be arrested by the sense that what was ordinary is suddenly different, other, changed. This is the realm – for example – of the Freudian uncanny. For Freud, the *heimlich* is what we have been calling the quotidian: it is the intimate, the comfortable, 'arousing a sense of security as in one within the four walls of his house'.[37] Yet, when the *heimlich* becomes the uncanny, the familiar is suddenly strange. In our terms, it is as though, believing ourselves to be within the relaxed space of familiarity, we suddenly find ourselves in a more undefined, more strangely artificial, more unexpectedly spectacular space than we had realised. Our attention is solicited more intently than we would expect. Theatricality is characterised, as Freedman argues, by a sort of 'display of display'. Theatricality *'shows that it knows that it shows*, and so turns itself inside out in a series of frames framed by their contents'.[38] For even as display's spectacle enjoins the viewer to react, it also displaces the viewer with its excess, its glare; it somehow goes too far in soliciting our attention. The theatricality of display thus destroys intimacy, rupturing its relaxed comfort. Its exaggerated demand for attention insists upon a heightened spectating consciousness; it forces focus upon our vague inattention.[39] Such heightened visibility marking display evokes what Schechner calls 'twice-behaved' behaviour. 'Performance behavior isn't free and easy. Performance behavior is known and/or practiced behavior or "twice-behaved" behavior.'[40] It is a behaviour that forces limits and boundaries with its excess, demanding attention and spectatorship, transgressively stretching the spaces of the *heimlich*, the intimate and private, towards the public, formalised space of theatre.

Twice-behaved or theatrical behaviour, suggesting a form that is not quite what it seems – neither familiar, ordinary, quotidian, 'natural'; nor pure artifice, pure theatre – reminds us of another form, that of *trompe l'oeil*, whose capacity to arrest and disconcert the spectator is similarly pronounced. Bryson's analysis of Pompeiian 'xenia', the still-life frescoes depicting food brought by guests to their host, points to the play of these frescoes with representation. The xenia are actually anti-representational; 'when they refer most faithfully to the reality of the world,' argues Bryson, 'they at once shift away from that world into transitions and thresholds which culminate in the opposite of figuration – irrealisation, artifice, the simulacrum.'[41] These xenia thus hover in a theatrical space, destabilising the boundary between life and art. Faithfully appearing to reproduce the world exactly, to replicate its most familiar and daily aspect, they simultaneously cancel that servile reflection as they slip towards artifice. They are, as Bryson puts it, 'committed to the deletion or erasure of the depicted object at the exact moment when depiction takes place'.[42] In this way, *trompe l'oeil* creates an effect of vertigo or shock in the viewer. An important boundary is ruptured; we think that we are looking at the real, and suddenly discover we are looking at the artificial. And this instant of fascination and shock provokes a disconcerting loss of bearings, producing 'doubt on the human subject's place in the world', claims Bryson.[43] The painting 'Quince, Cabbage, Melon and Cucumber' by Juan Sánchez Cotán, for instance, so perfectly mimics the real that vision is jolted, mocked, displaced; as Bryson points out, '[h]anging on strings, the quince and the cabbage lack the weight known to the hand. Their weightlessness disowns such intimate knowledge'.[44]

Pertinently enough, *trompe l'oeil*, for its 'trickiness', its 'potential to mislead', has been specifically linked to things feminine.[45] Understanding the eye as a metonymic substitution for the 'I' of subjectivity, Mary Ann Doane suggests that what jolts and disconcerts in *trompe l'oeil* is that 'it demonstrates that the eye/"I" does not possess an unshakeable position of knowledge'. Doane goes on to argue that woman, for a masculinist subject, threatens as 'the *trompe l'oeil par excellence*'; the menace that she embodies becomes 'a trick against which the masculine subject must constantly be on guard'.[46] In this way, the play of *trompe l'oeil* links it to theatricality; opposed to theatre, *trompe l'oeil* works as a troublingly liminal space hovering between the 'natural' and the artificial: jolting, disconcerting, deceiving (*tromper*).

This 'trick' of still life and *trompe l'oeil* opens up a disconcerting instant, a destabilising hesitation in the spectator. In an instant of epistemological confusion, the spectator is no longer sure of *knowing* the object perceived; what seemed familiar is suddenly other, what was known is suddenly unknown. And this instant of uncertainty, this destabilising of the ground upon which rest the distinctions established by knowledge, implies a further, more threatening, instability: the blurring of the boundary between self and other. For such self/other scrambling, we might further pursue Freudian notions of the uncanny, or the return of repressed. The uncanny, we saw above, has to do with what was once familiar, *heimlich*, homely, domestic, quotidian; but which has undergone repression, and now returns – returns as both familiar, yet different. Taking the uncanny a step further, we realise that the intuited and troubling excess that defines theatricality may have to do with an element that strikes us as childish. This childish excess is familiar, suggesting as it does our early selves and the unrepressed flamboyance of childhood, a flamboyance that may pale into decorous adulthood; we think of the children we know prancing about, demanding that we watch them. Similarly, in gendered flamboyance, we recognise an uncanny, *unheimlich* reminder of that uncensored phase of license that characterises childhood. We might read this moment as a sort of reverse Lacanian mirror-phase; as adults, we suddenly perceive our former childish selves, in an instant that is both a recognition of self and an alienation of self. Our familiar selves are refracted to us disconcertingly in the mode of otherness, scrambling distinctions between selfhood and alterity. As something 'which is secretly familiar, which has undergone repression and then returned from it', the uncanny thus recalls to us our past, outgrown identities.[47] Analysing the uncanny effect produced by madness, as well as epilepsy, Freud suggests that 'the layman sees in them the working of forces hitherto unsuspected in his fellow-men, but at the same time he is dimly aware of them in remote corners of his own being'.[48] The uncanny is thus further associated with an unwilling recognition of the self, a reluctance to embrace a distasteful or threatening otherness within the familiar. Linking madness to the uncanny, Freud further argued, is the impression that madness produces of 'automatic, mechanical processes at work behind the ordinary appearance of mental activity'.[49] The spectacle of a theatrical self may produce an uncanny impression of yet another sort; for this imbrication of self and otherness also involves the disconcerting confusion between the human and the artificial, the mechanical. We might point to our hesitation as to whether an object is living or inanimate, as in the case, quoted by Freud, of the mechanical doll Olympia in the first act of Offenbach's *Tales of Hoffmann*. One thinks here, as well, of the live modelling in occasional department-store display windows, its human yet unsettlingly mechanical models commanding our uneasy fascination.[50]

Further associations with the uncanny may be useful in studying the slippery dynamics of 'stolen limelight'. Freud mentions the uncanniness of the double, 'being a creation dating back to a very early mental stage, long since surmounted – a stage, incidentally, at which it wore a more friendly aspect'.[51] Again, we recognise here the uncanny jolt produced by the double-as-self. The spectacle of a theatrical self may produce an uncanny impression because of this imbrication of self and otherness: the uncanniness of recognising a past, childlike self or double, paired with the allure of artifice, of what hesitates between real, natural and the construed. The uncanny arises here in the contemplation of the self as other, or the other as self, in an unsettling imbrication. And this doubleness, binding real and artificial in an impossible, arresting, coercive instant, ties into the institutionalised tradition of the eighteenth-century English masquerade – with the attendant risk, both riveting and threatening, of imposture that we noticed earlier. Here, pleasure 'attended on the experience of doubleness, the alienation of inner from outer, a fantasy of two bodies simultaneously and thrillingly present, self and other together, the two-in-one'.[52] Such doubleness thus plays upon, even as it transgresses, the distinctions separating 'self and other, the natural and the artificial, the familiar and the alien'.[53]

We have been thinking about the self and otherness, and their imbrication: the impression of uncanniness produced by the spectacle of alterity, a spectacle in which we also recognise ourselves. Such fissured self-recognition is also self-alienation, and accompanied by the vertigo and shock of witnessing our own displacements. Such vertigo produced by the suspension of regimes, argues Roger Caillois, is a pleasant bodily sensation: a sort of ecstatic, virtually hallucinatory plunge into an altered state, as when traditional, primitive rituals provoke shocks that brusquely, summarily, destroy reality.[54] One might also recall here Walter Benjamin's analysis of the erotic shock produced by Parisian crowds upon a poet plunging into the electricity of the crowd as though into a foreign element.[55] This shock might help explain our fascination with undefined spaces, spaces that hover between regimes, confusing perception, displacing boundaries, displacing our habitual, quotidian selves. We are teased and fascinated by the flamboyant, we are charmed and thrilled by it; yet, as we saw in its capacity to produce an impression of the uncanny, we are also unsettled, disconcerted. This shock produced by such a double-take is pleasurable – as in the pleasure of looking at a *trompe l'oeil* painting, the pleasure of Caillois's voluptuous vertigo – precisely for the thrill of its momentary panic, its fleeting loss of self.[56]

Having sketched out the notion of theatricality as disruptive of boundaries – between the habits of the quotidian and the codes of theatre, between spectator and spectacle, familiar and alien, self and other – we are reminded that issues of performance have occupied the centre stage of the critical stage, so to speak, for some time. Following upon the great modernist experimental prose narratives, performance – eclipsing narrative – has been read as *the* defining contemporary concern. Indeed, postmodernism itself has been characterised as 'a move from narrative to theater, from a spectator consciousness to a displaced and displacing performer consciousness, from the structure of story to the infinite play and display of discourse'.[57] From within this 'display of discourse', exemplifying, as Jean Comolli puts it, the 'frenzy of the visible',[58] we might usefully turn back again to the novel. If aspects of gendered constructions have come to be associated with a certain hypervisibility, as we saw in Doane's claims above, we might now become newly aware of narrative shaping, staging, management and exploitation of that visibility.

In what follows, we will be mindful of Lukàcs's vision of the novel as the genre that embodies time, and therefore repetition.[59] With repetition, the novel establishes habit, the ordinary, the everyday in its work as 'le zoo des pratiques quotidiennes' ['the zoo of everyday practices'], as Certeau puts it.[60] Yet, while the novel may be the genre of the everyday, it also engages the extraordinary; for within the ordinary, something becomes worthy of telling; narrative emerges out of change, irregularity. Something is different, arresting our attention, becoming commanding, insistent. Against the backdrop of the ordinary, something else takes shape. We think of certain narrative models that dramatise this emergence of difference from within the same: Kafka's Gregor Samsa awakening to find himself a giant cockroach, for instance, or the effort of Sartre's Roquentin to make sense of his persistent impression that something is different, something has changed.

Just as the liminal space between habit and display creates a disconcerting realm of explosive, transgressive energies, so certain novels produce theatrical effects in their negotiation of the ordinary and the other. In the narratives to be discussed in these pages, a situation is implicitly construed as known, familiar: the unhappy-marriage scenario crippling Mauriac's Thérèse; Colette's rehearsal of familiar gendered stereotypes in a coming-of-age setting; Japrisot's superlative detective novel with its ostensible quest for 'the' solution. In Duras's novel, we find a wilful adolescent; in Gide's, a driven Protestant fanatic; in Oyono's, the depiction of colonial tensions. Yet within the normative codes established by each narrative, we become aware of an element of excess: an energy that departs from its normative confines, a straying from the codes and conventions; something goes too far, becomes insistent, arresting our attention.[61] In these various narratives and through various devices, eruptions of gendered excess carry decisive consequences; for they suddenly scramble other, implicit distinctions. That is, once the distinctions between real and artificial, between natural and theatrical have been blurred, other boundaries are also scrambled. These are the boundaries between familiar and alien; self and other; spectator and spectacle. In flirting with these distinctions, gendered excess produces a jolt or shock in its observer, to disconcerting or destabilising effect. How novels manage such excess and its effects will be the focus of these pages.

Across a wide range of narratives in French and their film adaptations – from canonical texts by François Mauriac, Colette, André Gide and Marguerite Duras, to a detective fiction by Sébastien Japrisot, to a francophone African fiction by Ferdinand Oyono – we will chart the various effects of gendered display put towards purposes of displacement. While consisting entirely of twentieth-century novels in French, my corpus implicitly accounts for and respects the period's range and diversity. Gide's novel, with its context of ascetic Protestant fanaticism, is set during the century's early years preceding World War I. The 1920s bring us not only Colette's coming-of-age narrative but also Mauriac's portrait of the stifling, landed, Catholic bourgeoisie. France's colonial empire is represented not only in Duras's two narratives set in the French Indochina of the 1930s, but in Oyono's depiction of French rule in the Cameroon of the 1950s. Japrisot's detective novel of the 1960s widens the scope of my corpus in honouring a popular genre's advances into intellectual respectability. While Duras's *L'Amant* ['The Lover'] is set, as noted, during the colonial 1930s, techniques of voicing and fragmentation cast this autofiction within a *nouveau roman* context of the 1980s (continuing into the early 1990s, with its 1991 rewrite, *L'Amant de la Chine du Nord* ['The Lover from North China'], and 1992 film adaptation). In this diverse way, my corpus sketches a rough timeline through signal cultural, political and literary aspects of the twentieth century.

Yet such a varied corpus allows nonetheless for the emergence – across time periods, cultural contexts, thematic material, narrative styles and authorial identities – of a common dynamic traversing these disparate texts: the manipulation of gendered display resulting in effects of displacement. Feminine tropes in Colette's novel innocently sabotage normative masculine virility in a climactic closing episode. After serving to feminise the white colonists in Oyono's narrative, gendered agendas culminate and explode in a scene opposing two women as the white Commander's wife turns cold, evaluative scrutiny upon a Black potential maidservant – who deftly and covertly displaces colonial white superiority by returning the inspection. Gide's heavily embodied Juliette – whose Shakespearean name alone genders her decisively as feminine – spectacularly self-immolates, disappearing into a predictably corporealised and female destiny of voluminous maternity. Her theatrical return in the novel's closing scene throws light – literally and figuratively – on her self-imposed displacement, revealing its function as subtle display. The mannish interests of Mauriac's Thérèse are enrolled in the narration's effort to isolate and display her as monstrously unfeminine. Between-the-lines love between women emasculates the official and virile hunt for the truth in Japrisot's text. Undoing gendered oppositions in Duras's narrative becomes the text's strategy for safely displacing the mad mother's engulfing threat by transgendering her as the daughter's own Chinese lover.

In Part I – 'Embodied Display and Effects of Displacement' – I focus on corporeal displays in novels by Colette, Oyono and Gide; in each text, a richly gendered bodily display ultimately works (whether deliberately or inadvertently) to upset a balance of power. Expanding my argument, Part II – 'Narrating Display, Narrating Displacement' – moves from embodied displays as depicted within narrative, to more abstract dynamics of display and their effects of displacement in novels by Mauriac, Japrisot and Duras. In this way, through exploring constructions of both corporeal and narrative display, I hope to demonstrate that within a culture dominated by the image, visual practices necessarily cue literary interpretation. For some time now, we have been moving away from essentialising and philosophical questions on the nature of gender, towards more culturally entangled and fraught issues – such as the ways in which gender is manipulated or exploited. Meanwhile, the study of narrative has been eclipsed by interest in the visual, entailing the rise of non-print media as art form and object of study, with the attendant development of branches of theory to account for viewing practices, mechanisms and pleasures. In the pages that follow, I attempt to recover what has been overlooked and left behind, arguing for ways in which such dynamics of spectation and its reversals are at work in reading practices. Extending attention to scenarios of display across the relation between reader and text, between spectator and spectacle, provides access to a range of tensions – gendered, racial, cultural – at work within narrative. Understanding gendered displays as strategies of displacement opens up new possibilities for interpretation in a wide variety of narratives, those studied in these pages as well as those beyond.

Part I
Embodied Display and Effects of Displacement

Chapter One
Staging the Hyperfeminine: Colette

While Colette's coming-of-age novel, *Le blé en herbe* ['Ripening Seed'] decisively overturns normative masculinist projections of femininity in a climactic closing scene, such an outcome would not immediately seem likely.[1] Colette's voluminous production, on both stage and page, tends to indulge in extreme, exaggerated feminine images – as in the hype of her successful 'Claudine' novels, as well as the glare and scandal of her music-hall roles. In husband Willy's canny management of his ingénue wife as a virtual walking billboard for her 'Claudine' novels, we already see the shape of hyperbolised feminine display to come; Colette herself, overshadowed by her own mythic creation, Claudine, becomes the orchestrated puppet of a male gaze. 'A côté de moi' ['Next to me'] wrote Colette significantly when Willy, crafting his wife into a Claudine clone, lops off her long braids in a slashing, cropping image to which we will return – 'quelqu'un voyait beaucoup plus loin' ['someone saw a good deal further'].[2] Yet, in the subversive manipulation of feminine tropes that closes *Le blé en herbe*, Colette's narrative ultimately succeeds in confounding any male gaze putatively seeing 'a good deal further'. From exploited object, Colette's hyperfeminine display ultimately provokes the veritable consternation of the desiring, prurient male gaze. Seeking to read the index of its own impact, this gaze confronts, instead, the spectacle of its own exclusion: a scenario bespeaking utter indifference to its domination. Such manipulation of hyperfeminine tropes to displace – rather than affirm – the masculine gaze is prepared not only in Colette's earlier writing, but during the performing years between the 'Claudine' novels and the 1923 publication of *Le blé en herbe*: the first novel signed not 'Colette

Willy,' but, simply, 'Colette'. A full assessment of the freight of *Le blé en herbe*'s closing scene thus calls for its wider contextualisation within the feminine hype and clichés characterising Colette's life and work leading up to her first officially self-authored novel.

As a running experiment with images, caricatures, hyperboles and figuration, Colette's life itself was a long and intense engagement with gendered display – her image-production, highly crafted and stylised, extending to her own self-representations. In *Le pur et l'impur* ['The Pure and the Impure'], a narrating voice at times indistinguishable from Colette's own refers to 'un ancien aspect de moi-même, aspect public, dont j'ordonnais, avec ostentation, la légende, les détails extérieurs, le costume' ['an earlier me, a public one, whose legend, appearance, costume I myself ostentatiously arranged down to the last detail'].[3] The studied craft of these 'elaborate arrangements' invites us to go back to the early scenes and extremes of Colette's relationship to feminine tropes. Such displays – from *being* played as exploited Claudine pawn by Willy's manipulation; to Colette's own playing and performing *of* gendered tropes as actress and mime onstage; to her playing *with* these tropes in her texts – will then inform our return to Colette's writing, where we will find them re-textualised in the highly crafted balcony scene that closes *Le blé en herbe*. For in a gendered itinerary that anticipates Vinca's evolution in *Le blé en herbe*, the young heroine of Colette's early series of four rollicking novels – Claudine – is styled as a vigorous, independent tomboy, maturing into confident self-assurance. Colette's relationship to her own creation – from Claudine as literary character to Claudine as stage figure to Colette's own dispossession of and subordination to Claudine – provides insight into her manipulation of hyperfeminine tropes.

At the outset, Colette enjoyed the welcome distraction and anonymity of the reassuring 'mask' provided by the 'farce' of her Claudine novels: 'Rien ne rassure autant qu'un masque. La naissance et l'anonymat de 'Claudine' me divertissaient comme une farce un peu indélicate, que je poussais docilement au ton libre' ['Nothing is so reassuring as a mask. The birth and the anonymity of 'Claudine' entertained me like a slightly indelicate farce, which I obediently pushed towards a licentious tone'].[4] This farce, however, ends up eclipsing Colette herself, for when the 'Claudine' novels evolve into a stage production, it is the actress Polaire – not Colette – who is chosen to perform the title role. In Colette's own judgement, though, Polaire's obstinacy, her resistance, her very mistakes, created an 'unforgettable' Claudine: 'elle ne s'est trompée qu'heureusement. Elle montra, à réclamer le rôle, une obstination d'illuminée … "Non, Meussieur Vili, Claudine, c'est moi"' ['she was only wrong in the most fortunate ways. She demonstrated, in demanding the role, the stubbornness of a visionary … "No, Mister Vili, *I* am Claudine"'].[5] Colette admired the passion and ferocity with which Polaire took to the role, suggesting that Polaire lived only for her Claudine performances, and drooped between showtimes: 'Oh! moi, jeu [*sic*] ne dors guère, vous savez … j'attends. – Qui donc? – Personne. J'attends la représentation de demain' ['Oh! me, I scarcely sleep at all, you know … I'm waiting. – For whom, then? – No one. I'm waiting for tomorrow's performance'].[6] And Colette writes almost wistfully of Polaire's passionate embrace of the Claudine persona:

> Polaire croyait à Claudine, pensait à Claudine avec un sentiment profond et pur. Les reprises de la pièce, les représentations données hors de Paris lui inspirèrent des mots quasi mystiques: 'Je vais la retrouver, disait-elle'.
>
> [Polaire believed in Claudine, thought about Claudine with profound, pure feeling. The reprises of the play, the performances given outside Paris, inspired in her the almost mystical words: 'I'm going to find her'.][7]

Ultimately, Colette finds herself obliged to 'abdicate', as she puts it, her Claudine creation to Polaire: 'en l'écoutant, j'abdiquais secrètement, et je faisais hommage à Polaire d'avoir inventé Claudine' ['in listening to her, I secretly abdicated, and paid homage to Polaire for having invented Claudine'].[8] Colette goes so far as to claim – despite her own onstage eventual Claudine performances[9] – that Polaire was the only true Claudine: 'Il n'y eut qu'une interprète de qui le jeu trépidant, le brûlant visage, la voix parfois saccadée d'émotion écartaient toute idée d'école, de métier, de sensualité concertée, il n'y eut pas d'autre "vraie Claudine" que Polaire' ['there was only one actress whose vivacity, whose burning face, whose voice sometimes halting with emotion, eliminated all idea of acting, of method, of a belaboured and factitious sensuality; there was no other "true Claudine" than Polaire'].[10] It is Polaire's Claudine, rather than Colette's, who defines the character so decisively that every nightclub, every bar and seedy cabaret had its own imitation, a Claudine who struggled to emulate Polaire.[11] Even after Colette herself has gone upon the music-hall stage in mimodramas, playing non-Claudine roles of her own, she is described as strikingly resembling Polaire's little sister.[12]

Dispossessed of her own creation in this stampede to emulate Polaire's Claudine, Colette herself is subsequently swallowed up in Willy's marketing campaign; conscripted for publicity purposes, she is made over into a second-best Claudine. Following the bobbed hair that brought about Colette's resemblance to Polaire, Willy took to going about with these two specular Claudines in matched outfits – walking the two women, as Polaire complained, the way one might walk a pair of greyhounds, or Great Danes.[13] Polaire went so far as to claim that Willy himself even occasionally mistook the two women for each other.[14]

But Colette's displacement and doubling as Polaire's twin soon mushrooms into the aggressions of a crowd of clones. When Polaire, committed to her stage career, starts avoiding Willy's threesome outings and dinners, Willy contrives to find an understudy 'twin', multiplying what Colette called her 'occasional doubles'. They encroach, buy the same hat from her milliner, and one, Colette writes, had even appropriated her name – for, after various postal 'ricochets', a letter arrived from an enamoured supply officer.[15] Colette's ultimate impatience with such confusion – between herself and Claudine, herself and Polaire, herself and masqueraders of herself – might be read in her little scripted scene with an imagined Claudine. Hailed by Claudine's cheerful 'Hello, my double', 'Colette' shakes her head and answers:

> Je ne suis pas votre sosie. N'avez-vous point assez de ce malentendu qui nous accole l'une à l'autre, qui nous reflète l'une dans l'autre, qui nous masque l'une par l'autre? Vous êtes Claudine, et je suis Colette.
>
> [I am not your double. Haven't you had enough of this misunderstanding that throws us together, that reflects us in each other, that masks us, each by the other? You are Claudine, and I am Colette.][16]

In her flight from Willy's domination as impresario, Colette at last acquires more control over stage creations of her own: creations that, in her own mind, allow her to mask herself. As she writes, '[d]es mois passèrent, et des années' she writes, 'pendant lesquels, me donnant çà et là en spectacle, j'usais du droit de me taire sur moi-même' ['months passed, years, during which, performing myself here and there as spectacle, I exploited the right to be silent about myself'].[17] Such welcome self-silencing in the refuge of the stage, however, also leads to a virtual emptying-out of self, as when Colette suggests that even in off-stage moments she becomes nothing but a role. Catching sight of her bedraggled reflection in a window during the touring troupe's layover in the countryside, Colette writes of the cruelly specular, involuntary role she is reduced to playing: the role of a touring actress, even in her most off-stage, off-duty moments. Listing the various piteous creatures her discouraged reflection evokes, including a plucked bird and a governess fallen upon hard times, she concludes, 'Mon Dieu, j'ai l'air d'une actrice en tournée, et c'est assez dire' ['My god, I look like an actress on tour, and that says it all'].[18]

Yet such self-effacing or emptying is accompanied, in ironic contrast, by generalised visibility and scandal, beginning with Colette's role as the scantily dressed Paniska, companion of Pan in an outrageously impudent performance, in one critic's view.[19] Perhaps most well-known of the scandals that accompanied Colette's music-hall roles, however, was that provoked by 'Rêve d'Egypte' ['Egyptian Dream']. The opening-night performance culminated in a kiss between Colette, as a mummy come to life, and the Marquise de Belboeuf ('Missy') – Colette's companion following the rupture with Willy – in the role of an archaeologist enchanted by the mummy's charms.[20] Reactions ranged from indignation to outrage:

> Si des personnes ne comprennent pas que leurs associations d'un ordre trop spécial ne doivent pas être offertes à l'admiration publique, il est bon que Paris ne leur fasse parfois entendre, fût-ce par les moyens élémentaires du soufflet.

> [If people don't understand that their relations of a too-particular order mustn't be offered to public admiration, it is right that Paris should occasionally make them realise it, be it by the elementary means of boos and hisses.][21] [22]

In a later mimodrama, 'La Chair', elements of feminine display, seduction and manipulation are organised around a jealous triangle as the beautiful Yulka receives, in the absence of her husband, Hokartz, the attentions of a junior officer. Surprising the illicit lovers, Hokartz disarms and ejects the officer and might have turned on Yulka herself in his rage, but for 'la chair' [the flesh] which he passionately worships; with her garment ripped in the fray, Yulka's nudity now stands revealed in all its glory. As Hokartz hesitates, Yulka flees, and he kills himself in despair of ever again possessing such beauty.[23]

Yet, while some programmes, such as that of the Casino de l'Eldorado, similarly render the ripping of Yulka's clothes as accidental – 'Elle veut se protéger de ses bras, dans le mouvement qu'elle fait, et sous le geste brutal de Hokartz, son vêtement se déchire et elle apparaît nue' ['She tries to protect herself with her arm, but in her struggle, and under Hokartz's brutality, her garment rips and she appears nude'] – others argue for Yulka's ruse and coquetry. As her husband hesitates, runs one interpretation, 'La fine mouche s'en aperçoit et le brave. Connaissant le pouvoir de ses charmes, elle déchire tout à coup ses vêtements et jette à la face du jaloux, éperdu de rage, le défi de sa souveraine beauté soudainement dévoilée' ['The crafty beauty notices and defies him. Knowing the power of her charms, she suddenly rips her clothes and flings in his jealous, enraged face, the challenge of her sovereign beauty, suddenly revealed'].[24] As another programme puts it, 'Celle-ci connaît le pouvoir de ses charmes. Elle paraît devant lui la poitrine nue. Le mari vaincu renonce à sa vengeance et emploie son poignard à s'ouvrir les veines du bras' ['She knows the power of her charms. She appears before him, her chest bared. The defeated husband renounces revenge and uses his dagger to slit the veins of his arm'].[25] As thought to emphasise this power of 'la chair' ['the flesh'], Colette appeared onstage completely naked at one performance reserved for the press alone – scandalising, among others, Polaire.[26]

Such a shift in the interpretation of Yulka's role – from a terrified, victimised wife whose clothes are ripped by an enraged husband, to a crafty coquette who rends her own clothes so as to seduce him – figures another shift. This is the movement from Colette herself as victimised, masterminded publicity object, her hair slashed and cropped by Willy, to Colette as crafty, mastermind*ing* manipulator of feminine tropes in *Le blé en herbe*.[27] [28] Following upon these years of stylised feminine caricatures – first, as a walking 'Claudine' billboard; later, as music-hall mime and actress performing hyperfeminine roles – Colette's apprenticeship in such theatrics might be read as culminating in *Le blé en herbe*'s closing pages. Whereas the treatment of gender in the novel appears more fluid and flexible than the staged caricatures we have seen here, the novel's ending appears to relapse into stale feminine tropes. As I will argue, however, such display works to displace, rather than gratify, the prurient, normative, masculine gaze.

It is generally accepted that *Le blé en herbe* was inspired by the incestuous as well as adulterous relationship between Colette and her stepson Bertrand de Jouvenel.[29] Unrepentant, however, in a piece written just months before her death, Colette presented this novel as having to do with births, blossomings, and thresholds, claiming it to be her favourite: 'Aussi parmi mes livres, *Le blé en herbe*, qui tente de peindre l'amour naissant et le dur passage de l'enfance à l'adolescence, m'est-il peut-être le plus cher' ['Thus, among my books, *Le blé en herbe*, which tries to depict emerging love and the rough passage from childhood to adolescence, is perhaps dearest to me'].[30]

Colette's treatment of gender in *Le blé en herbe* appears initially to be more supple than the extremes and caricatures that define her stage career. Readers have pointed in particular to the masculinity of Madame Dalleray, the story's older *femme fatale*. They have also noted the feminisation undergone by the young hero, Phil, following his sexual initiation at the hands of Madame Dalleray. In a particularly notable example, Phil's own reflected image in a darkened window, his lips smeared with Madame Dalleray's lipstick, strikes him as that of a bruised young girl.[31] Yet we are now able to do more than merely point to these reversals. Feminist film theory argues for such gendered ambiguities not as essentialised – welded to the screen character – but instead, as inhering in the various positions occupied by these characters: positions established by the manipulation of a gaze that construes its subject as masculine and its object as feminine. In positioning and repositioning gender as shifting, unstable subject or object of a gaze, Colette's novel subscribes to a surprisingly contemporary vision of gender as culturally constructed and coded.

Indeed, the pertinence of feminist film theory for Colette's 1923 novel acquires further validity when we recall Colette's vivid interest in the cinema, expressed in a variety of short pieces: film reviews, dialogues, scripts, even a 'Little Manual for Aspiring Screenwriters' detailing the characteristics of such heavily gendered roles as the *femme fatale*, the energetic young hero, the jaded woman of the world.[32] A 1950 claim holds that 'Colette has a movie camera at the end of her pen'.[33] Just months before her death in 1954, in fact, a film version of *Le blé en herbe* appeared; unable to attend its première, Colette made a recording played to the audience before the screening.[34]

Colette's active and sustained interest in the cinema lends further legitimacy to an effort to read gender ambiguity and oscillation in *Le blé en herbe* through film theory. Beginning with Laura Mulvey's inaugural 1975 demonstration of the implicit inscription of spectator as narcissistic male voyeur, theorists have argued for the elaboration and manipulation of gender through specific camera and narrative devices.[35] Mulvey's analysis linked spectating pleasure to a certain male narcissistic identification with leading men, and to an equally male voyeuristic enjoyment of objectified, eroticised heroines.[36] Similarly, one enjoys a different but parallel pleasure in gazing upon women onscreen; the movie heroine satisfies a voyeuristic pleasure in serving as a spectacularised, sexualised feminine screen-object. Mulvey further argued that male roles in mainstream cinema tended to be stereotypically active, dynamic, driving the narrative's action forward, while female roles tended to ossify as static, erotic objects through camera practices freezing women in framed stills. Furthermore, in identifying male roles as active bearers of the gaze – supporting and figuring the collective gaze of audience spectatorship – and female roles as its objects, Mulvey uncovered the importance of positioning (whether behind or in front of the gaze) in gender construction. The demonstration of gender as culturally construed has been a particular success of film theory, a success that has rendered more visible similar strategies in texts.

Such gendered distinctions inform *Le blé en herbe*, which opens with the restless, adolescent Philippe fretting to his patient, submissive childhood friend Vinca about the remaining years before manhood. Set on the rocky Brittany coast, the novel teems with elaborate descriptions of the marine life of inlets and tidepools, fostering a 'naturalness' that infuses the sentimental idyll of the two adolescents. And yet, friends since infancy, Phil and Vinca seem destined to fall into the polarised gender roles of their parents' bourgeois marriages, particularly in scenes marked as social, as opposed to natural: scenes, for example, set within the summer house jointly rented by the two families. A woodcut illustration from a 1928 edition of *Le blé en herbe* suggests such social spaces as sites of gender definition and ossification. Within the house walls, Vinca demurely bends over the domestic chore of mending, while Philippe – asserting his masculine affiliation with the public, political sphere – relaxes, feet propped up, by reading the newspaper.[37]

The text goes on to express their relationship in terms of Phil's mastery and manipulation of a gaze particularly gendered as masculine. Watching Vinca walk, Philippe compares her, for instance, to her former, childlike self (p. 1185). But such masculinised spectation is not only carried out by Phil's focusing the readerly gaze upon Vinca as particularly feminised object. It is also, consonant with feminist film theories of spectatorship, accomplished by Phil's directing Vinca's admiring gaze upon himself – 'Vinca Regarde-moi!' ['Vinca! Look at me!'] (p. 1199) – and basking in its unquestioning adoration. Phil's narcissism is further certified by the text's later reference to 'le plaisir qu'il ressentait lorsque son amie le regardait. Il se savait beau à cette minute' ['the pleasure he felt when his friend looked at him. He knew himself to be handsome in that instant'] (p. 1206).

Through his manipulation of Vinca's worshipful gaze, Phil contemplates his own idealised image, further enacting masculine-gendering devices. For as Mulvey argued, the screen-hero's idealised, more complete, more perfect self, works as a sort of Lacanian mirror-phase for the male spectator, who narcissistically admires his 'on screen' variation as Hollywood leading man.[38] Culminating in his mastery of Vinca's gaze is a scene in which Phil draws a capital letter 'V', 'deforming' it, with a blue pencil, into a blue eye with long eyelashes: 'Vinca's eye'. Having appropriated Vinca's gaze in his drawing, Phil completes his possession by directing Vinca's real gaze to his accomplishment: 'Regarde, Vinca' ['Look, Vinca'] (p. 1209). Here Phil cements his control by directing Vinca's gaze to its own stylised figuration as *he* construes it in his drawing.

As the novel continues to assign ossified gender roles, the more liminal site of the veranda, open to the air and sea, offers a transitional space 'naturalising' Vinca's movement from tomboy companion towards an apparently inevitable destiny as bourgeois housewife. Here Vinca, in a ritualised feminine gesture, impeccably and adeptly, despite the capricious breeze, pours coffee for the adults. Her absurdly fluffy organdy dress, exaggerated through its replication on her little sister, prompts Phil's scorn: a short-lived scorn, however, for it is suddenly interrupted by his discovery that another, older, male gaze sees Vinca differently, exploding Phil's own vision of the scene. In the eyes of the visiting Parisian, we gather that the fluffy, matching dresses serve not to unite the sisters as little girls, but rather, to divide them into woman ('mother') and child. With her little sister designated as child, Vinca is positioned to occupy the space of womanliness in a subtle transformation operated by the visitor's gaze. Stunned by the visitor's ecstatic 'voyez-la! ['Look at her!'] as Vinca – holding a lace doily with her chin and blocking an overturning chair with her foot – deftly continues pouring coffee (p. 1190), Phil – confident of his tomboy companion, realises that he had not yet seen a young woman in her.

With the intervention of an older 'dame en blanc' ['woman in white'] who seduces Philippe for her own holiday diversion and pleasure, the idyll becomes a triangle, and the gender roles more elastic and vital, more dynamic: each character in the triangle in turn both masculinised and feminised in supple choreography. Outside the bourgeois household governed by Phil's and Vinca's respective parents, gender becomes destabilising, rather than confining. Phil's fledgling male mastery, for example, is threatened by the intrusion of a gaze he does not control, a virile gaze that looks back at him not in worshipful admiration, but with an intent and agenda of its own: the gaze of the older woman in white, Madame Dalleray, who looks him in the eyes, 'comme un homme' ['like a man'] (p. 1197), and later smiles at him with a 'virile smile' (p. 1233). Disconcerted to find himself the object of her virile laugh and masculinised gaze, Philippe is feminised, 'paralysé par une de ces crises de féminité qui saisissent un adolescent devant une femme' ['paralysed by one of those attacks of femininity that seize an adolescent in front of a woman'] (p.1197), a crisis marked by his fleeting faintness in front of her: 'Je ne sens plus mes bras … Je crois que je vais me trouver mal' ['I no longer feel my arms … I think I'm going to be sick'] (p. 1197). As Phil slips towards sexual initiation under the direction of Madame Dalleray, her control of *his* gaze increases. Accepting the offer of an orangeade, he enters her cool, dim villa, promptly losing his sight and any faint remaining vestiges of mastery; in the obscurity, he bumps into a piece of furniture, falls to a cushion, hears her laugh from an uncertain direction and nearly bursts into tears with anxiety (pp. 1212–13). Aptly capturing the atmosphere of Madame Dalleray's villa, Offord sees it as figuring the relationship between the older woman and Philippe; both the villa and the relationship, he writes, have 'brutal, sadistic, often painful characteristics'.[39] Eventually escaping to the familiar realm of his control of Vinca, Phil recovers his mastery and sight, a return to self-possession he expresses by kissing Vinca's 'charmants yeux bleus' ['charming blue eyes'] (p. 1214). Curiously, it is only following his sexual initiation under the guidance of Madame Dalleray, once this ritual has 'made him a man' – that Phil's feminisation is complete. On the way home afterwards, he cries; is ashamed; and then realises he is crying with pleasure (p. 1222). Furthermore, this coercive feminine colonisation continues when, rubbing his face, he realises that his hands are imbued with Madame Dalleray's perfume (p. 1224). Climactically, consulting 'sa nouvelle figure d'homme' ['his new man's face'] (p. 1225) back in his bedroom, Phil sees the traces of Madame Dalleray's lipstick on his own lips; and the text summarises his languid eyes, rouged lips and dishevelled black curls as 'des traits plaintifs, et moins pareils à ceux d'un homme qu'à ceux d'une jeune fille meurtrie' ['plaintive features, and less like those of a man than like those of a bruised young girl'] (p. 1225). Late the next morning, his feminisation continues as he emerges onto his balcony to the teasing of his own and Vinca's families amassed below. He is depicted as weak and pale, prudishly swathing himself up in his robe to go swimming. He is taken aback when Vinca crushes a tiny crab underfoot; bursts into violent sobs at her zestful and bloody efforts to extract an eel from its lair beneath a rock [p. 1228], later asking her pardon 'd'avoir été si "petite fille", si ridicule' ['for having been so little-girlish, so silly'] (p. 1231); is appalled at her vigorous cracking open of a lobster at lunch; and in a theatrically 'feminine' lapse, faints during a conversation with his father. Phil's fragile masculinity, we realise, is only as deep as the parts and pieces of a costume; although he had earlier rejected the toys of childhood, this was accomplished in a less-than-definitive way, by stowing them in a shed – for the text compares it to putting away 'les pièces d'un déguisement qui doit servir longtemps' ['the pieces of a disguise that must serve for a long time'] (p. 1199).[40] Such ineffective gestures to discard childhood mark a gendered identity that is as yet shallow and unstable. Returning from an errand on a hot day, Phil throws himself off his bicycle and onto his back; opening his eyes at the sound of her voice, he looks into Madame Dalleray's face to find the reflection of his own, 'inversé comme dans un miroir d'eau' ['inverted, as though in a mirror of water'] returned to him in feminised form. Later, the seduction scene at Madame Dalleray's villa will acquire in his memory a jarring and surrealist theatricality (p. 1215) as it takes on, for its passive, feminised recipient, the sharpness of a penetrating, phallic dart: 'un indiscernable orage de couleurs, de parfums, de lumières dont la source dissimulée épandait un dard aigu' ['an indiscernible storm of colours, of perfumes, of lights whose hidden source emitted a pointed dart'] (p. 1223).

In a symmetrical gender reversal, however, no sooner has the virile Madame Dalleray seduced Philippe for her own holiday diversion and pleasure, than cracks begin to show in her masculine façade of control and mastery. Originally moved by the erotic pleasure of her own 'corps de femme, voué à des rapts délicats, doué d'un génie spoliateur, d'une implacabilité passionnée, d'une enchanteresse et hypocrite pédagogie' ['woman's body, destined for delicate abductions, endowed with a despoiler's genius, with a passionate implacability, with an enchanted and hypocritical pedagogy'] (p. 1224),[41] the virilised Madame Dalleray proceeds to undergo an increasingly feminine-coded transformation.[42] Phil observes appreciatively that she is again dressed in white, her face made up (p. 1216). She cannot help asking Phil whether he loves her, a question coded as feminine as Madame Dalleray seeks to construe herself as the object of *his* gaze and desire – even as she is obliged to read, in his surprise and evasiveness, his answer (p. 1235). Her subsequent sudden and unannounced departure betrays a dismay and retreat, a sort of feminised, sentimental neediness. Such vulnerability makes it difficult to subscribe to claims for Madame Dalleray as an unchanging 'symbol of possessiveness and domination'.[43] No longer, it would seem, is Madame Dalleray following the virile male script of trivialising a pleasure-seeking seduction. When she departs, it is 'having realized', as Jouve puts it, 'that she is "the beggar" in the affair with young Philippe'.[44]

Meanwhile, following upon those of Phil and Madame Dalleray, a third gender reversal is undergone by Vinca. While Offord notes 'an emotional ambiguity about Vinca which is conveyed by reference to her displaying both adult and boyish characteristics', we might go further in parsing this ambiguity.[45] For Vinca's gaze begins to resist Phil's manipulation and acquire an independence of its own. When Phil gathers a bouquet for Madame Dalleray, the text indicates that this particular hollow in the dunes deserves to be called 'le miroir des yeux de Vinca' ['the mirror of Vinca's eyes'] for its blue flowers (p. 1216). The dune hollow's flowers, however, no longer the delicate and mild periwinkle originally giving Vinca her name, have become thistles bristling with thorns – and Phil slashes his hands gathering them, as though Vinca's gaze, no longer docile and manipulable, has matured into aggression. Thrown by Phil over the walls of Madame Dalleray's villa, his bouquet scrapes and cuts the cheek of Madame Dalleray herself. And indeed, Vinca's gaze has penetrated Phil's secret; no longer the original, admiring, pliable, docile look, her gaze is now aggressive, cutting. 'Elle l'éblouit, en lui jetant au visage le rayon bleu de ses yeux grands ouverts, dans un brusque et ferme regard' ['She dazzled him, throwing into his face the blue beam of her wide-open eyes, in a brusque and firm look'] (p. 1252). Ultimately, it is Vinca's gaze that tracks and covers Phil's as his own eyes seek, upon the nocturnal sea, the invisible white road leading to Madame Dalleray's villa (p. 1261). Vinca has now come to occupy the dominating, masterful position of power, her gaze as masculine and 'boyish' as her punch to Phil's jaw.[46]

Intriguingly, Vinca's boyish aggressiveness and abandon is registered in two stills printed by *Le figaro* just before Claude Autant-Lara's film version of *Le blé en herbe* opened in Paris in 1954. These shots are not included in the film itself, perhaps because the film conveys a far more limited and conventional depiction of gender than that evoked by the subtle shifts and complexities in Colette's novel: shifts suggested in these discarded stills – for they point to Vinca's masculinity in contrast to Phil's feminised timidity and hesitation. In the first, Phil and Vinca face each other against a rocky-shore background. Vinca's posture is very straight and tall, but she is smiling, obviously at ease and enjoying herself, in her loose, rolled-up summer-shore clothes. Curiously, as if to figure her eventual punch to Phil's jaw, she is extending a long lobster-hook towards Phil. Phil, in contrast to Vinca's confident posture, is leaning back, away from the lobster-hook that visibly disconcerts him, one arm beginning to lift as if in self-defence. Phil's stiffness and awkwardness is further emblematised in prissy schoolboy clothes, a white-collared shirt, sweater and knee-length cuffed shorts: an outfit that completes his contrast to Vinca's virilised, self-confident and relaxed demeanour.[47] Such gendered postures are further inscribed in the second still, where Phil – in the same schoolboy outfit – sits disconsolately on a rock, with an arm outstretched as though to protect himself from the inquisition of an aggressive Vinca bent towards him.[48]

Beyond these discarded stills and their implied gender suppleness, however, Colette's daring gender shifts are effaced by the normative efforts of Claude Autant-Lara's 1954 film adaptation. To be sure, the film's treatment of gender opens with promising ambiguity; although we begin with Phil manfully manoeuvring a kayak as the wind rises and those on shore run for cover, such virility overturns with the kayak, leaving Phil calling for Vinca as he struggles in the water. Floundering naked to shore, he finds a little girl's abandoned straw hat to cover himself minimally, and in this vulnerable, humiliating situation, makes his way home until, cowering behind a tree, he is discovered by Vinca's young rival, Margot.

Yet the film's opening and somewhat audacious feminisation of Phil is quickly compensated by Phil's assertive kissing of Margot, after she taunts him, smelling the sherry on his breath following his visit with Madame Dalleray: 'elle se contente de cela, la bonne femme?' ['she contents herself with that, the dame?']. Phil also kisses Vinca later the same evening, after they leave the cinema. Through such sexual initiatives, the feminisation undergone by Phil in the novel and at the film's opening is subsequently avoided in the film; lipstick traces, for example, are left on his cheek, not his mouth. He is given a bruise on the shoulder, the trace of a passionate night; the scene of his fainting is omitted, as is his bursting into tears at Vinca's ferocity in cracking open a lobster. Furthermore, whereas the novel depicts Phil's second encounter with the lady in white as accidental – a chance encounter while Phil takes a telegram addressed to his father's client to the post office – the film, instead, gives Phil the initiative in seeking out further contact with Madame Dalleray. He strides, unannounced and uninvited, into her villa, having volunteered to deliver a telegram addressed to her, surprising her (and ourselves) with his audacity.

Just as the film – beyond the opening scene – avoids any hint of Philippe's femininity, it also carefully suppresses Madame Dalleray's virility. In the novel's scene of their meeting, as we have seen, a prone Philippe in the sand suddenly finds himself the object of her virile gaze; in the film, however, the encounter softens and genders her as feminine, coiffed in a feminine style, with a flowing, white travel cape ruffling from her shoulders. She is shown in profile at her dressing table following lovemaking with Phil; when Phil asks whether she will miss him, she looks at herself in a full-length mirror as her answer betrays her neediness: 'pas encore' ['not yet']. When Phil next comes to her villa, she is shown wrapping herself in a fringed, flowing shawl, then descending an outdoor stairway in front of the camera. Her own sentimental vulnerability is betrayed in her resolute effort to convince Phil, her voice nearly breaking, that he is merely 'un souvenir de plage' ['a beach memory']; and after Phil's final departure, she is shown from behind, gazing forlornly out the window, to the strain of violins.[49]

Similarly, Vinca, even in her most assertive moments, is invariably styled as extremely feminine, 'charming' in Autant-Lara's summary of her role in his film: light often falling on her blonde hair, her whims and caprices part of such charm. Only once, perhaps, is she given a startlingly unfeminine gesture; in preparing a mouse-trap with a sliver of cheese, she deliberately snaps the trap shut under a startled Phil's nose. Yet such a move, rather than appearing masculine and virile, seems crafted to portray Vinca's childlike verve and mischievousness.

The film version of *Le blé en herbe*, then, proposes far more conventionally defined gender roles than those depicted in the novel itself.[50] Similarly, textual critics note such gender-bending roles in Colette, yet only to absorb them, ultimately, into conventionally gendered norms. Yannick Resch, for instance, ascribes the novel's gender-bending to a certain pathology: a reaction to threatened integrity.

> L'homme se pose comme féminin en se laissant admirer et aimer, la femme comme masculine en donnant et protégeant. Comportement qui est souligné par l'attitude des personnages dans la vie sociale – le personnage féminin se 'masculinise' d'autant plus ostensiblement que son intégrité est menacée. Il fume, boit, jure, conduit une voiture et, si son environnement l'enferme dans un univers proprement féminin, il s'en libère par une autonomie d'esprit qui joint la force critique à la lucidité.

[The man presents himself as feminine in allowing himself
to be admired and loved, the woman as masculine in giving
and protecting. Behaviour that is emphasised by the attitude
of the characters in their social lives: the feminine character
is 'masculinised' all the more obviously as her integrity is
threatened. She smokes, drinks, swears, drives a car, and, if
her environment sequesters her in a properly feminine
universe, she frees herself with an independence of mind that
joins critical strength to lucidity.][51]

In Resch's reading, masculinity in a female character is understood
as a defence, a reaction to threatened integrity. The effort to justify
such masculine behaviour only reinforces the transgression that it
represents, as though such departures from gendered norms must
have some sort of explanation – such as 'threatened integrity'.

As we have seen, however, Colette in *Le blé en herbe* certainly
seems to be undermining conventional gender ossification, with
her reversible gender roles. Adolescent Philippe, impatient for
manhood, is eventually feminised; virile Madame Dalleray is also
feminised in her sentimental neediness; and virginal Vinca
masculinised with her boyish fist-blows and aggressions, her zestful
fishing pursuits. Why not conclude here, with Colette's prescient,
subtle shifts and instabilities of gender, as the culmination of her
long experimentation, onstage and off, in gendered roles?

We may not wish to conclude just yet. For the problem with
such role reversals, as E. Ann Kaplan points out, is that the same old
polarities themselves that define gender remain intact.[52] The
position of power, action and dominance remains scripted as
masculine even when occupied by a woman, as by Madame
Dalleray; and the passive erotic-object position remains feminised,
even when occupied by a man, as by Philippe. Gender is
constructed and inheres, argues Kaplan, in the binary pairing and
dependence of the two positions upon each other. That is, the
masculine position, associated with action and domination, is
virtually dependent for self-definition upon the presence of
an Other, different, feminine or passive object-position. This
observation allows Kaplan to deplore what might otherwise be
understood as more subtle gender scripting, in which leading

women (such as, for our purposes, Madame Dalleray) aggressively construe men as *their* erotic objects. For Kaplan, this does not get us far enough; the positions themselves retain their gendering, whatever the sexes scripted into them. Women are allowed to play aggressive masculine roles, provided that men assume the erotic-object 'feminine' positions; but the structure of binary co-dependent gendering remains intact.

In light of Kaplan's argument, then, if we try to celebrate Colette's daring shifts of gender, to admire her prescience in laying bare cultural devices of gender-construction, we run into a snag. Colette indeed goes so far as to disrupt gender-essentialising by detaching gender from character and ascribing it instead to positions on either side of a gaze. But her treatment of gender seems in the end to succumb to Kaplan's criticism that essentialism has only been re-located, creeping back in to essentialise positions, rather than characters. Amidst all the ambiguities and shifts, the reversals of gender undergone by characters, does gender in Colette's novel ultimately fall back into ossification in remaining binarily co-dependent? Phil, Madame Dalleray and Vinca may engage in all the gender reversals that they and their author please; but it would seem that gender remains essentialised, masculine and feminine nonetheless defined and stultified by their opposed positions as binary 'others'.

Instead, however, I would like to suggest that Colette's destabilising treatment of gender culminates in a final scene that conclusively disrupts gender conventions. Gender-essentialising is decisively undone; gender-assignment is dislodged, not only from the particular character involved, but from the position occupied by that character.[53] In this 'morning after' scenario, the shifts and instabilities of gender roles, so dynamically explored earlier in the novel, seem at first to solidify into a traditionally gendered polarity. Phil, having relieved Vinca of her virginity the night before, slips out in the morning and watches for her to appear at her window. While waiting, Phil rehearses to himself a discourse of consolation and reassurance, for he remembers the cultural script – 'On assure qu'elles pleurent, après' ['it's said they cry, afterwards'] (p. 1268) – and expects confidently to reassure a devastated Vinca that nothing has really changed between them. Phil's masculinised, self-assured position is furthered by his voyeuristic post outside Vinca's window: a post from which his gaze, trained on the feminine emblem of the window frame, bears and supports the reader's.

When Vinca appears in the text's description of this scene, it is as in a stereotypically cinematic shot; within the very window frame itself, she is further framed for Phil and the reader by the shutters she folds against the wall (p. 1269). Construing Vinca as object of a combined gaze – that of Phil and that of the reader – Colette's depiction conforms to Mulvey's description of a film heroine as 'isolated, glamorous, on display, sexualised'.[54] Set off as framed, eroticised object of a desiring, voyeuristic male gaze, Vinca further inscribes clichéd femininity by such ritualised, culturally over-coded gestures as watering the fuchsia blossom on her balcony, combing her hair and singing (p. 1269). Moreover, the balcony setting alone suffices to stamp the scene with the cultural over-determination that marks a certain hyperfeminine display. For, adding to the portent of this closing scene is its implicit allusion to other balcony scenes, from Shakespeare's Juliet calling for her Romeo; to Rostand's Roxanne in *Cyrano de Bergerac*, drawn from her bedroom by an eloquence she mistakenly ascribes to Christian, rather than Cyrano; to perhaps the scene's most extreme formulation in Genet's *Le balcon* ['The Balcony'], set in a brothel, where, in ultimate feminine capitulation to male scripts, the prostitutes ritually enact their clients' fondest scenarios.

Are we to conclude, then, with the text's ultimate failure to overturn gendered polarities? Does Colette's novel succumb, in the end, to what has been studied as a 'double trajectory of gender identity,' that is, 'a radical questioning of gender accompanied by a conservative return to tradition'?[55] While the oscillations of gender so dynamically explored in *Le blé en herbe* seem in this closing scene to settle rigidly into the most weary of gendered binaries, the very extremes of these spectacular feminine tropes invite further scrutiny. We might ask, for instance, whether Vinca's reproduction of feminine clichés, understood as what has been called a kind of female mimicry, might appear to subscribe to gender clichés while in fact subverting them.[56] Such 'mimétisme', to use Irigaray's term, argues that deliberately assuming the role historically assigned to the feminine is to transform subordination into affirmation; '[j]ouer de la mimésis, c'est donc, pour une femme, tenter de retrouver le lieu de son exploitation par le discours, sans s'y laisser simplement réduire' ['playing the mimetic role, for a woman, is to try to locate the site of her exploitation by the discourse, without simply letting herself be reduced to it'].[57] This notion of a subversive hyperfeminine argues that ironic repetition empowers the feminine, allowing woman to designate the site of her exploitation without being reduced to it: to 'appropriate [representations of the feminine] ironically, manipulate them from an internal critical distance'.[58] In according her a measure of ironic distance, Irigaray's 'mimétisme' would seem to provide the feminine with a discourse of refusal. As Toril Moi puts it, 'Irigaray's subtle specula move (her mimicry *mirrors* that of all women) intends to *undo* the effects of phallocentric discourse simply by *overdoing* them' (pp. 139–43).[59]

There are two problems here, however, that might interfere with a reading of Vinca's feminine tropes as ironised mimicry. One difficulty is that Irigaray's 'mimétisme' necessarily posits an 'elsewhere' of femininity: 'Si les femmes miment si bien, c'est qu'elles ne se résorbent pas simplement dans cette fonction. *Elles restent aussi ailleurs*' ['If women play the hyperfeminine so well, it's that they are not simply reabsorbed by this function. *They also remain elsewhere*']. This fetishistic preserving of a 'pure femininity' in a vague 'elsewhere' reinscribes the old essentialist problem of just what, just where, femininity is, as though some absolute realm must be maintained. As Butler puts it, 'masquerade can be read as a denial of a feminine desire that presupposes some prior ontological femininity regularly unrepresented by the phallic economy'.[60] That is, masquerade can be read as mask, disguising a repressed feminine desire. And, as Butler indicates, this is Irigaray's position in claiming that the masquerade allows women to participate in man's desire, but at the cost of giving up their own.

The second difficulty here is the very energy that animates this ludic, ironic, stance. In energetically designating the site of exploitation, even in flaunting it, the hyperfeminine only more effectively, it seems, subscribes to this exploitation; for the very intentness of this miming activity perversely endorses the importance of patriarchal power. The irony of such miming is that it sacrifices, in a sense, an opportunity to make a statement *for* the feminine, in favour of making a statement *against* the masculine and its codes. What may lie beneath the mime, or instead of it, is eclipsed in the haste to attack patriarchal myths. For the feminine masquerade, as Riviere argued, anxiously seeks, through its theatrical tropes, to attract the male gaze and desire, in a sort of prostitution to the male script for femininity.[61] And Irigaray's conception of feminine mimicry, I would argue, too readily becomes an equivalent (though more covert, certainly) sell-out to the masculine. For the very energy that animates mimicry's ironies, its very attentiveness to male-scripted femininity, necessarily forces feminine mimicry into the cruel perversion of endorsing the importance of the masculine script. Devoting such energy to mocking its roles is only to re-endorse the very power of that script.[62]

There is a final point that troubles any embracing of the mimicry-as-gendered-sedition argument as a reading of Colette's closing scene. Crucial to these notions of feminine mimicry is precisely the presence of conscious, ironic distance. Yet Vinca's very innocence and spontaneity, her unconcern (as, unaware of Phil's gaze, she believes herself alone) make it difficult to ascribe an ironic cast to her balcony behaviour. What does appear to impose itself inevitably, however, is the text's apparent failure to overcome gender ossification in this final spectacular and wholesale sell-out to cliché.

In fact, though, this theatrically gendered scene in which Colette's gendered slippages and ambiguities seem to ossify in deplorably stultifying clichés, is the moment at which gender definition is most decisively undone. For the purpose of Phil's masculine, voyeuristic gaze is to admire, narcissistically, what he imagines to be the seismic impact his sexual initiation of Vinca has had upon her. Phil's gaze seeks in Vinca the consequence of his own mastery, the Lacanian mirror-phase image of a more perfect, idealised, virilised, self. Yet what Phil is forced to contemplate, instead, is the spectacle of his own insignificance. In contrast to his own 'foudroyante' ['earth-shaking'] as he puts it, reaction to *his* sexual initiation at the hands of Madame Dalleray, Vinca is quite matter-of-factly and unconcernedly going on with life. Phil observes the very banality of her behaviour with astonishment: 'Elle chante ... Il faut bien que j'en croie mes yeux et mes oreilles, elle chante. Et elle vient d'arroser le fuchsia' ['She's singing ... I have to believe my eyes and ears, she's singing. And she's just watered a fuchsia'] (p. 1269). Intriguingly, whereas Phil's disbelieving summary of the situation considers Vinca 'indemne' ['unscathed'] (p. 1270), one English translation chooses to emphasise Vinca's unaltered behaviour as 'unaffected';[63] for Vinca, it would seem, nothing has changed – even her song is the one that she sings every day (p. 1269). In the novel's closing lines, Phil contemplates 'sa propre petitesse, sa chute' ['his own insignificance, his fall'] in reflecting that all he has given Vinca is 'un peu de douleur, un peu de plaisir' ['a little pain, a little pleasure']: 'Je ne lui aurai donné que cela … que cela …' ['that's all I'll have given her, just that … nothing but that …'] (p. 1270).[64] In manuscript, the text went even further in emphasising Phil's distress at the scene, for Colette had originally used, then scratched out, the verb 'subir' ['to suffer, endure'] in indicating that Phil did not merely contemplate his own insignificance, but 'suffered' such contemplation.[65] In Phil's dismayed recognition of his own unimportance as '[n]i héros, ni bourreau' ['neither hero nor tormenter'] (p.1270), Vinca's femininity in this morning-after scenario is crushingly independent of – even indifferent to – his own newly discovered virility.

Interestingly, Autant-Lara's film does not respect the novel's placement of Phil in a removed, voyeuristic position. Rather, the film's very different morning-after scene follows fairly precisely not the text's version of the action itself, but rather its account of the watching Phil's *projected* scenario as he tries to absorb the implications of Vinca's nonchalance: 'Que je paraisse à la fenêtre voisine, que j'enjambe la balustrade pour la rejoindre et elle me jettera ses bras au cou' ['If I should appear at the neighbouring window, if I should stride across the balustrade to join her, she'd throw her arms around my neck'] (p. 1270). As described in the text, Phil's phantasmatic scenario preserves his astonished reaction at Vinca's own response to events, but with an important difference; it de-feminises Vinca somewhat, in re-infantilising her through childish gestures and exuberance. The film scene begins with Vinca opening the shutters on her balcony; but we see this act from an oblique angle, preventing the shutters from serving too obviously as a frame, and thus inhibiting our recognition of the balcony scene's familiar, hyperfeminine topos. As we see Vinca smiling into the sunlight, we expect the camera to shift to Phil's distant post of observation, detailing his dismayed, astonished expression. However, following Phil's little imagined script in the text, the film shows the next door along the balcony opening and Phil himself emerging, instead. Still following Phil's imagined scenario for the scene, Vinca laughs spontaneously, hugs and caresses him, then grabs his hand to drag him in while she brushes her teeth: a sisterly gesture whose very banality proclaims Vinca's girlishness. The film, we realise, chooses to follow Phil's imagined version of Vinca's reaction, in favouring youthful impishness over femininity; she is playful with Phil, and not depicted – as she is in the text – engaged in such highly coded, ritualised feminine gestures as watering flowers, brushing hair and singing. The film scene, as opposed to the novel's, thus seems less explicitly to fling nonchalant, indifferent womanliness in Phil's face, while allowing him to cling to a certain fragile agency in scripting Vinca's behaviour. Implicitly, then, the film restores Phil's authority, in enacting his own imagined scenario.

Vinca's display of hyperbolic femininity, however, far from being reduced (as in Phil's phantasm) to childish exuberance, far – as well – from seeking to construe itself as object of a male gaze and male desire, instead serves here a very different function. Revolutionising this use of the hyperfeminine is Vinca's innocent, unknowing, indifference – not only to Phil's hidden male gaze, but, more importantly, to his impact as male. This scenario must, then, be understood as surpassing models of the feminine masquerade and mimicry, for both are performed, either frantically or ironically, for the benefit of a male gaze. Vinca's hyperfeminine tropes, however, announce not only independence, but unwitting indifference to the power of this gaze. The most hackneyed feminine clichés here thwart masculine projections of the feminine, and hence become an effortless deflection of controlling normativity; for the feminine object of a fantasising male gaze, is no longer, as Mulvey would put it, 'styled accordingly'.[66] Instead, Vinca's innocent nonchalance is so disconcerting to Phil because it confounds the male script of 'woman as icon, displayed for the gaze and enjoyment of men'.[67] Vinca – however innocently and unknowingly, and all the more successfully *because* innocently and unknowingly – overturns the premise that what matters about the heroine is what she inspires *in the hero*: the love, fear, concern, provoked by her refracted image within him. It is the displacement of the expected topos of devasted lost virginity (Phil's confidence that 'they cry, afterwards') in favour of another, but unexpected topos (womanly assurance and nonchalance), that jars and disconcerts Phil's gaze.

Apparently reasserting clichéd femininity as it joins the topos of other balcony scenes, this scene rewrites it, instead; for we recall that it also reinscribes another liminal scene, the earlier one of Vinca pouring not water on a blossom, but coffee on the veranda. In the earlier coffee scene, Vinca's ritualised feminine gesture, fetishised by the ecstatic male gaze of the visiting Parisian, occurs in a transitional space. Neither altogether inside nor outside, the veranda becomes a liminal site of transformation, where, before Phil's stunned gaze, his tomboy companion enacts graceful womanliness (p.1190). The coffee-pouring gesture's ritualised femininity is re-inscribed in the text's closing scene as Vinca's flower-watering, just as the liminal, transitional space of the veranda is implicitly refigured in the similarly liminal space of the balcony. Such a subtle echo of the novel's earlier coffee-pouring gesture, implicitly rehearsed now within its final, flower-watering act, thus infuses the balcony with a charge of transformation. Just as Phil expected to see a child on the veranda and discovered, instead, womanliness at its most self-possessed in a transformed Vinca, so also, in the text's closing scene, he expected to behold in Vinca a display of virginal devastation in resounding validation of his own power and impact. Again, to his chagrin, Phil is made to confront yet another transformation, instead; this time, Vinca's womanliness at its most relaxed and nonchalant implicitly mocks his own masculine grandeur. Phil's gaze and expectations are decisively confounded by this charged scene of transformation. Even as it displays hyperfeminine clichés, the balcony episode becomes a volatile site of displacement, overturning gendered conventions.

As we have seen, Colette's *Le blé en herbe* manipulates gender in a particularly cinematic use of the gaze as normatively masculine, desiring, aggressive, construing its object as feminine. Over the course of the narrative, each character occupies gendered positions on either side of the gaze. These oscillations of shifting spectation and shifted gender culminate in a closing scene that scrambles gendered polarities.[68] Here, the most tired tropes coding the feminine – appearing on a balcony, singing, combing her hair, watering a blossom – are manipulated by the text as a refusal: the more effective for being spontaneous, 'naturalised' and unaware of any onlooking presence. For the narcissistic male-voyeur gaze seeking the index of its own impact, the very banality of these feminine gestures displays a disconcerting, innocent indifference to onlooking normative masculinity, obliging it to read its own insignificance. The novel's closing scene might thus be read as the culmination of a long evolution. From displaced, effaced author of the 'Claudine' series; to 'Claudine' clone, vulgarly paraded by Willy with an eye to book sales; to hyperfeminine caricature on music-hall stages; to its surprising, innocent and subversive display in the 1923 novel that she considered perhaps the dearest ('peut-être le plus cher')[69] to her of her oeuvre, an important evolution is accomplished in Colette's exploration of gendered tropes.

Study of such deft – if inadvertent, in Vinca's case – disempowering of a confident masculinist script through a display-as-displacement dynamic continues in the next chapter, where we will again find feminine elements of display at work in the undermining of normative masculinist paradigms in Oyono's *Une vie de boy* ['Houseboy']. As we will see, a gender-dismantling process of resistance in French-occupied colonial Cameroon culminates in an explosive scene between two women, a Black domestic servant and her potential white employer.

Chapter Two
'Stripped Naked': Dismantling Gender in Oyono's *Une vie de boy*

In Oyono's novel, set in 1950s French Cameroon, gender politics are at work in the native effort to feminise – and thus effectively disempower – French colonial domination.[1] Critical studies of the novel have favoured epistemological readings, arguing for the native gaze as instrument of knowledge; Toundi, the native houseboy, 'sees' and thus knows that the myth of white superiority is a sham. I argue, however, that the native gaze is so threatening to the myth of white colonial superiority not merely because it knows, but also because it unmans, or feminises. Betrayed by his own feelings, however, Toundi is unable to take the final step and relinquish the feminine ideal travestied by the white commander's beautiful but promiscuous wife. Instead, it takes a native *woman*'s gaze to complete the dismantling project of political resistance in a climactic and neglected scene, reversing Madame's seductive limelight to turn it clinically back upon her. In this explosive and heavily embodied episode, Madame evaluates the native Kalisia as a potential housemaid: a brutal inspection during which Kalisia, herself ostensibly on display, covertly assesses her assessor as Madame circles her – as she would a slave – in critical appraisal. Yet in effortlessly diagnosing Madame's nymphomania, Kalisia adroitly displaces Madame's own display by revealing its pathology. In this culminating scene played out between a native and a white woman, dynamics of spectacle and limelight are reversed; the adoring limelight enjoyed by the white commander's universally venerated wife becomes a chilly, diagnostic glare as a different gaze is trained upon her. While white male colonial power is undone in the novel by a feminising process, exalted white femininity is also dismantled in the novel's fraught gender dynamics.

In arguing for such a reading, I maintain that, for some time, it has no longer been obligatory for the Western reader to worry guiltily about cultural imperialism and appropriation when approaching a francophone African text. Rather, one now openly embraces the tensions and conflicts produced by the encounter of Western reader and francophone African text, understanding them not only as inevitable, but mutually enriching. What evolution has been accomplished? Formerly, the question of just how an African text could be read by the West tended to become stranded in the cultural divide between the two. How the West might 'know' the African Other 'in and of itself' was the anxious preoccupation; but the formerly fetishised francophone African text has subsequently been reconstrued, along with such acute epistemological anxieties. Epistemological imperatives, along with what Edward Said called the 'antiseptic, controlled quality' of their 'theoretical environments', gave way to a grittier awareness that such 'knowledge' is not essentialised, out there to be obtained, but the shifting refraction of power relations produced in the fraught encounter of observer and observed.[2] The scrutinised, laboratory-specimen African text was reconceived; part of a larger cultural encounter of different energies, Africa and the West were no longer seen to clash as 'reified opposites', as Christopher Miller put it, but to meet in 'a hall of mirrors in which cultural codes play off each other, corrupt each other, and enrich each other'.[3] Interestingly, a comparable move emphasising reciprocal enrichment of contrasts and differing specificities was launched the same year in the context of postcolonial theory when Edouard Glissant published his landmark work, *Poétique de la relation*.[4] Arguing for the pluralisation of Creole cultures, imaginaries, and poetics, Glissant proposes replacing 'créolité' with 'créolisation' for the dynamic interweave of composite cultures; rather than 'une entité bien définie à laquelle on s'identifie', 'créolisation' conceives identity as complex, 'rhizomatic', extensive, according to Glissant's idea of the intersection of self and other. He argued for the construction of 'une personnalité instable, mouvante, créatrice, fragile, au carrefour de soi et des autres'.[5] Whereas Miller uses a hall-of-mirrors image to describe the encounter of Western perspectives and African texts, Glissant uses that of a crossroads to capture notions of cross-cultural influence. Both Miller and Glissant – in varying contexts, colonial and postcolonial, Western, Creole and African – argue for more dynamic, 'unstable', conceptions of cross-cultural and inter-cultural presences, fertilisations and impacts.

This move – from a fetishised notion of knowledge of the African Other towards what Said would call a more worldly understanding of the encounter between Western reader and African text – might be emblematised on a more specific and local level. Epistemological preoccupations, for example, have tended to dominate criticism of Ferdinand Oyono's *Une vie de boy*, arguing that the native Toundi's fatal transgression is to *know* that white colonial superiority is a sham. But the difficulty with such epistemologically inflected readings – those that conclude somewhat abstractly with 'knowledge' as the explanation of Toundi's downfall – is that they fail to recognise the issues of power, manipulation and resistance played out in the guise of knowledge: issues that lend knowledge its gritty purchase and political edge. What critics have neglected is *why* this transgressive knowledge takes on such power as to render Toundi's destruction imperative for the whites. For what empowers Toundi's epistemological transgression – his 'knowing' – is a sexual and gendered transgression: the accession to a forbidden sexual and gendered status. As Moore points out, for the sake of his own safety, Toundi's must remain a 'threatless asexuality' for the white colonists.[6] Pursuing this claim, I argue that it is not merely that Toundi 'sees' through the charade of white superiority that makes him so menacing for the whites; rather, it is that he does so *as a man*.

It might be useful, though, before turning to the sexual and racial tensions that pass as 'knowledge' in *Une vie de boy*, to retrace in more detail the changed critical context that legitimises such analyses. The epistemological monopoly formerly shaping discussions of the 'Other' African text emerged inevitably in reaction to the imperialist, disfiguring abuses committed in the name of describing and depicting a 'true' Africa.[7] To correct such abuses, Miller, in his eagerness 'to let the Other have its true dimensions, to stretch and displace the categories of a Western approach and not simply be, in Baudelaire's phrase, 'an East of the West' ['un Orient de l'Occident'] – that is, 'to break the shell of self-reflexivity and Eurocentrism' – originally called for the displacement of 'theory' by anthropology in the study of African texts. African texts, suggested Miller, were to be approached via a 'literary anthropology', producing readings 'influenced by the "facts" of ethnography and … a willingness to adopt modes of interpretation that might come out of the culture in question'.[8]

One example of such an ethnoculturally specific approach is Jacques Bourgeacq's analysis of the eye motif as a site of power relations in *Une vie de boy*. 'Eyes', he writes, 'are a powerful force of both persuasion and knowledge.'[9] Set within the ethnocultural perspective of southern Cameroon, Bourgeacq's discussion implies that a Western perspective would be unable to disengage the raw power at work in the eye motif. 'What would be viewed by the Westerner as a psychological mechanism', claims Bourgeacq, 'is perceived in that part of Africa, at the metaphysical level, as a utilization and display of a concrete force'.[10] Such ethnocultural approaches, with their claims for 'a more complex, more revealing interpretation',[11] yield indisputably valuable readings. Understood from the perspective of African ritual practices, Toundi's death, argues Bourgeacq, is the story of a symbolic victory; for Toundi 'has a mind of his own: while he is being killed, he turns his killers into puppets, blind participants in a ritual scheme designed by their victim'.[12]

Yet such approaches must not be taken as the only legitimate readings. One difficulty they pose is the tricky ideology that arises when a Westerner – Bourgeacq himself, for example – manipulates such ethnoculturally specific approaches. What then becomes of the claim, implicit in Bourgeacq's analysis, that approaching the text from 'within its own context' produces superior interpretations? What must not be neglected is the question of *who* is approaching the text, and from what perspective of his, her or their own. Such questions arose within the practice of anthropology as it aroused suspicion for its reluctance to engage 'the problematic of the observer, remarkably under-analyzed in the revisionist anthropological currents'.[13] If African literature were to be approached from within its own anthropology, what would ensure that the Western manipulation or *reading* of that anthropology itself be any more authentic, more legitimate – than its reading of literary texts? As Said writes about anthropological discourse,

> Look at the many pages of very brilliantly sophisticated argument ... and you will begin perhaps suddenly to note how someone, an authoritative, explorative, elegant, learned voice, speaks and analyzes, amasses evidence, theorizes, speculates about everything – except itself. Who speaks? For what and to whom?[14]

In the call for a putatively 'purer' approach to African literature via its own anthropology, what is neglected is that this anthropology itself must necessarily also be the object of Western reading; and as such, it is necessarily inflected by Western commitments and agendas. Wherever the point of encounter with the West is mapped – whether with African literature directly, or with African literature as approached through African anthropology – that encounter is always mediated, relational, fraught by the conjugation of two cultures. 'There is no vantage *outside* the actuality of relationships between cultures', asserted Said:

> between unequal imperial and nonimperial powers, between different Others, a vantage that might allow one the epistemological privilege of somehow judging, evaluating, and interpreting free of the encumbering interests, emotions, and engagements of the ongoing relationships themselves.[15]

In fact, some years after calling for an anthropological approach, Miller himself recognised that anthropology had 'consistently proved to be part of both the problem and the solution in approaching African literature'.[16]

A second difficulty in construing the African Other as, effectively, *utterly* other, was that it betrayed a fetishistic care for an implicitly fragile, easily disfigured text-object. Such protectiveness entails ideological dangers, for the very energy invested in defending the African text from cultural appropriation by Western readers backfires; it implies a text too feeble and infirm to resist the disfiguring imperialist aggressions of the Western gaze. Fetishising the African text is implicitly to construe its otherness as weakness, fragility. 'Subjugat[ing] the African text to our [own] theories',[17] in becoming the prevailing danger to be avoided, assumes perhaps too readily that the African text is 'subjugable', or, somehow, culturally fragile, available to appropriation.

Yet a third, unsavoury implication compromised the epistemological cast of concerns over reading the African text. The imperative to know the Other African text as authentically as possible, however well-intentioned, nonetheless smacks of co-optation; the very eagerness to avoid all disfiguration by imperialist Western theory can too easily miscarry as an unfortunate imperialist intention. Such epistemological ambitions, or aggressions, raised the uneasy question of whether colonial imperialism had simply reshaped itself more insidiously as epistemological imperialism. Said boldly identified this uneasy connection when he called anthropology 'the heedless appropriation and translation of the world by a process that for all its protestations of relativism, its displays of epistemological care and technical expertise, cannot easily be distinguished from the process of empire'.[18] In this context, we might notice that Miller's original call for the reading of francophone African texts via a 'literary anthropology' cited, among other works, Camara Laye's *L'enfant noir*.[19] This 1953 novel, rich and resonant in its depiction of indigenous beliefs, customs and rituals, indeed would seem to lend itself readily to anthropological analyses. But as Miller himself has pointed out, it has also been criticised as ignoring, in favour of an idealised West African childhood, the grim political realities of French colonisation.[20] Any critical choice to promote this text as part of a call for 'anthropological' readings thus becomes somewhat suspect. Such selectiveness betrays perhaps too eager a hope of construing an idealised, 'uncontaminated', essentialised Africa, and risks becoming merely another variation of idealising Western projections upon an African Other.

More recently, though, this epistemological monopoly has been displaced by a move towards the recognition of more worldly factors. The very fact that francophone African texts have been written in French, the language of the colonial oppressor, establishes a mediated, culturally and historically hybrid context that renders zealous epistemological ambitions to know the Other somewhat moot. The postcolonial African text emerges within a complex, conflicted, politically fraught climate; as Christopher Miller points out, the very form of the novel itself, in fact, along with the French language, 'arrives at the end of a gun barrel'.[21] Deeply inflected by political issues of power and resistance, francophone African texts implicitly call for attention to the power relations that inhabit any epistemological enquiry.

Accordingly, I would like to complete and emblematise this move on a more local and specific level, uncovering the fraught underpinnings of what has been read as 'knowledge' in *Une vie de boy*. For Toundi's transgression, as mentioned above, has tended to be construed as epistemological. Toundi 'sees', in the novel's prevailing trope, that white superiority is a vicious charade, and dies for his knowledge. 'The narrative develops', suggests Miller, 'as a battle of the glance between colonizer and colonized; Toundi, the houseboy, dares to look back.'[22] 'Toundi has seen', argues Arthur Flannigan, 'still, this alone would not and does not seem to constitute his sin … His sin is that he has seen and that he knows.'[23] Such an equation of the gaze and knowledge is also argued by Maxwell Okolie, who studies the exchanges between Toundi's 'gaze-that-knows' and the white gaze that perceives itself 'to be known'. Okolie develops a remark of Sartre's in 'Orphée noir', the essay with which Sartre introduced Léopold Senghor's anthology of 'négritude' poetry: '[v]oici des hommes noirs debout qui nous regardent et je vous souhaite de ressentir comme moi le saisissement d'être vus. Car le blanc a joui trois mille ans du privilège de voir sans qu'on le voie' ['Here are men upright, who look at us, and I would like you to feel as I do, the seizure of being seen. For the white man has enjoyed the privilege of seeing without being seen for three thousand years'].[24] It is this 'seizure of being seen', argues Okolie, that the whites cannot tolerate, and that brings about Toundi's destruction.[25]

And yet, the novel seems to suggest the inadequacy of these seeing-as-knowledge readings as early as its preface. Published in 1953 and set in French Cameroon, *Une vie de boy* depicts the racial and political tumult of the late colonial context; it appeared on the eve of internal autonomy in 1958, and ultimately of independence in 1960. The novel's role as political manifesto is confirmed in the preface introducing the narrative we are about to read as the diary, scribbled in two schoolboy notebooks, of Toundi, a young houseboy. Toundi himself, persecuted and tortured by his white masters, had managed to flee to Equatorial Guinea, only to die there of his white-inflicted wounds. In a gruesome line, the frame narrator details the horror of Toundi's death, emphasising that the putrefaction of his broken body forces his burial immediately: 'Il était une charogne avant d'être un cadaver' ['He was carrion before being a cadaver'] (p. 14). We thus open Toundi's diary in the wake of his violent death – whose acrid putrefaction permeates the narrative and gives it the bite of political manifesto. The framing of Toundi's story by his gruesome destruction would thus seem to render the 'knowledge' readings too pallid, too abstractly cerebral as full accounts of this novel's bitter energy. Opening with the grisly death scene of the narrator himself, his story seems to exhort us not merely to outrage over his individual fate. It also calls upon us to recognise that Toundi's own deadly transgression ('knowledge') was not the sole cause of his destruction; instead, we are called upon to see Toundi's destruction as symptomatic of deeper, more vicious issues and conflicts of racial oppression.[26]

What has made the 'knowledge' readings so persuasive, however, despite their failure to account for the violence that characterises the narrative, is – in part – that they are fostered by Toundi's own discourse itself. His own rhetoric exploits the gaze as trope for an epistemological complex involving notions of insight, knowledge, the apprehension of truth – a knowledge leading to evaluation, judgement. Toundi writes, for example, that what goes on under the corrugated-iron roofs of the white sector is known in the smallest detail within the native sector's mud huts; and he illustrates this fact rhetorically, using the trope of vision as knowledge, by saying that these white dwellings are figuratively 'mis à nus' ['stripped naked'] by the native gaze. Further contributing to this understanding of Toundi's gaze as knowledge is the warning that Toundi receives to flee while there is yet time; it is a native woman, Kalisia, who explains that for the whites, Toundi is a sort of sorcerer's eye, an eye that sees and that knows (p. 152). And Toundi's knowing gaze is perceived by the whites as judgement; as Kalisia points out to him, 'malgré eux, ils se sentent jugés par toi' ['in spite of themselves, they feel judged by you'] (pp. 152–3). To see is to know, to know is to judge, and the white world cannot tolerate the judgemental gaze of a Black; so runs Kalisia's own reading – anticipating that of most critics – of Toundi's transgression. In Okolie's claim, 'his masters see in him this "mirror of conscience" reflecting their vices and weaknesses'.[27]

Yet, we might ask, why should Toundi-as-'mirror-of-conscience' be so menacing for the whites? To note the function of Toundi's gaze as judgement is only to begin to account for its political valence as intolerable threat for the white colonists. Some nuance is afforded by Bjornson's suggestion that the 'Europeans want to regard the "boy" as a "thing that obeys," but his potential for unmasking their pretentions makes them fear that he is actually a "person who sees."'[28] But it is not merely that Toundi sees as a person – rather than a thing – that becomes so intolerable for the white colonists; it is that he does so *as a man*. Reading the gaze merely as trope for knowledge fails to account for the role of gender manipulation that provides its incisive political power.[29] For gender-dismantling strategies implicitly at work within the gaze are exploited both by the white colonists as tactics of repression, and by the Blacks as strategies of resistance. As one of its power-wielding tactics, the control of gender is manipulated by the implicitly virilised white occupying regime as refusal of manhood; the native is simply denied sexual differentiation and maturity by a white gaze that refuses to see him or her as other than 'un enfant ou un couillon' ['a child or an imbecile'] (p. 81). The native gaze, however, counters such repression by stripping the white colonists of manliness, effectively feminising the myth of virile, white power. Not only discerning the truths of the whites – as in the gaze-as-knowledge trope – the native gaze actively dismantles virile white power by carrying out a particularly *gendered* resistance project. It is in such a dismantling context that Toundi's rhetorical line about the whites being known, or 'stripped naked' by the native gaze, needs to be read less rhetorically. The gaze must be released from its diminished function as mere trope, for it is more than figuratively that the native gaze 'strips' the myth of white virility.

Symptomatic of white refusal to respect gender difference among Blacks is, for example, a white colonist's effort to hide his liaison with a native mistress. He passes her off instead as his 'cook-boy' and forces her to ride with Toundi in the back of the pick-up truck, refusing her the status and privilege of a woman.[30] As the sulky mistress, Sophie, points out, her 'derrière' is just as 'fragile' as the white women's (p. 60). In another example of white refusal of native gender difference, the white Commander's wife has no compunction in obliging the native 'washman' to launder her panties and sanitary materials, 'comme s'il n'était pas un homme' ['as though he were not a man'] (p. 123). This refusal of the natives' sexual maturity is apparent in the white colonists' treatment of them as either children or 'fools'; at a European gathering to welcome the Commander's wife to Dangan, each vies with the next in recounting 'sa petite histoire personnelle avec un indigène pour conclure que le nègre n'est qu'un enfant ou un couillon' ['his own little anecdote about a native to conclude that the Black is only a child or a fool'] (p. 81). The cook warns Toundi that the whites perceive the natives as only specific, defined functions in their service. 'Moi, je suis le cuisinier' ['Me, I'm the cook'] says the cook, 'le Blanc ne me voit que grâce à son estomac' ['the white man only sees me thanks to his belly'] (p. 132). Such refusal to grant sexual differentiation is so thorough that the Commander, Toundi's own master, fails to recognise Toundi in a crowd; as Toundi realises, '[p]our les Blancs, tous les Nègres ont la même gueule' ['for the whites, all Blacks look alike'] (p. 44).

The native gaze, however, counters this particular tactic of repression by debunking white virility. Analysing Toundi's depiction of the whites, Eileen Julien points to Toundi's representation of white bodies as flattened, decontextualised, 'stripped of depth and humanity'; the whites become 'so many marionettes whose corporeality, gestures and crude emotions – vanity, jealousy, carnality – are exposed'.[31] Yet such debunking occurs not only through a flattening, but a 'feminising' of white virility. Father Gilbert, called by the natives 'cet homme-femme blanc' ['this white man-woman'] (p. 17), wears what for them appears to be a woman's dress (p. 16). Toundi discovers with astonishment that the Commander is uncircumcised: a particular sign of immaturity and lack of sexual definition in the eyes of the young African, for whom ceremonial circumcision during adolescence represents the conferral of manhood (p. 45).[32] Such 'unmanliness' is thus gendered as feminine, as Toundi's reaction suggests in comparing the uncircumcised commander to frocked priests – 'Alors, me disais-je, il est comme le père Gilbert! comme le père Vandermayer!' ['So, I said to myself, he's like Father Gilbert! Like Father Vandermayer!'] (p. 45) – and, disillusioned, Toundi wonders why he had initially trembled before the Commander.[33] Reducing virile white masculinity to effeminacy becomes a silent, political act of resistance on the part of what the whites perceive to be an unsexed colonised object. Toundi's transgression, in stripping with his gaze and thus feminising his white masters, is to usurp the virile position of bearer of the gaze.[34] Acknowledged implicitly and resentfully by the whites to be neither a 'child' nor a 'fool', but a man, Toundi fatefully transgresses the colonial code. A hint of the danger posed by Toundi's manliness occurs on an inspection tour made by the Commander and the agricultural engineer, accompanied by their two 'houseboys': Toundi and Sophie, still the engineer's unacknowledged mistress. When Toundi and Sophie are lodged for the night in the same hut, the engineer's jealous threats betray his awareness of Toundi's virility.[35] Later, this virility provides the reason for Toundi's arrest; once Sophie has disappeared with the engineer's cashbox, Toundi is accused of knowing her whereabouts on the grounds that he was her lover. With this accusation, Toundi is seized by a 'terrible', as he puts it, desire to laugh, and we sense his suppressed scorn as he explains, 'Ce n'est pas mon genre de femme' ['she's not my type'] (p. 162). In spite of himself, Toundi effectively out-virilises – with this implicitly condescending claim for a superior taste in women – Sophie's white lover.

Toundi is increasingly, though unwittingly, viewed as a man – hence, as threatening – by his white masters. When the Commander's wife asks him to sweep up glass fragments in her bedroom, Toundi involuntarily discovers her adulterous lover's condoms under the bed, and is mystified by her rage. A white woman will not pardon this discovery, the cook explains to Toundi: 'C'est plus grave que si tu avais regardé sous sa robe' ['it's more serious than if you had looked under her dress'] (p.135). With its suggestion of a more sexually invasive gaze, this is a particularly interesting analogy. For looking under a woman's dress is not merely voyeuristic; it is the voyeuristic gaze become active sexual aggression. In suggesting that Toundi's involuntary discovery is worse than a deliberate, sexually aggressive gesture, the cook confirms that Toundi, with this unwittingly virile, invasive action heavily coded as masculine, has transgressed his assigned, ungendered role as sexless black domestic servant: either a 'child' or a 'fool' in the eyes of the white colonists.

Confirming Toundi's emerging status as a man is the ironic conferral of manhood when Madame mockingly starts calling him 'Monsieur Toundi' (pp. 119–20). Ironically, of course, Toundi himself remains more naive than the threateningly, manly persona he acquires in the eyes of the whites; for, to the great amusement of cook, washman and guard, Toundi does not recognise the condoms as such, nor immediately perceive their function. Yet, in a parallel irony, his nascent manhood would seem to date from the moment he is able to exploit, by pastiching them, white perceptions of the 'boy' persona as simpleton. Toundi is incapable of such ironic distance until he has been disillusioned by both the Commander and his wife. But at that point, startled into a cry by a banana peel underfoot, Toundi parries the Commander's query with 'Oui, mon commandant, c'est pour saluer votre arrivée' ['Yes, Commander, it's to salute your arrival'], accompanying this claim with his 'sourire le plus naïf' ['most naive smile'] (p.105). Later, Toundi – responding to Madame's impatient question as to where he's been – enacts another caricature of repressive white perceptions of the 'boy'. Telling her he's been in the sunshine, Toundi then turns upon her his 'sourire le plus idiot' ['most foolish smile'] (p. 110). Manhood, for Toundi, might be dated from the ironic moment at which he attempts to disguise this fledgling virility by miming the naive foolishness characterising white images of the houseboy.[36] And indeed, Madame's reaction – 'Tu te fiches de moi?' ['Are you making fun of me?'] (p. 110) – demonstrates her awareness that Toundi is more sophisticated – indeed more 'manly' – than the colonist-constructed, caricatured vision of the houseboy that he mimes.

Toundi's gaze, the reader realises, is able to feminise white male virility; but Toundi is unable to take the next step and relinquish the feminine ideal travestied by the Commander's beautiful but unscrupulous wife. It is as though the very 'manliness' or virility of the gaze with which Toundi dismantles masculine white power betrays him when turned upon a white woman; because he looks upon the white *woman* as a heterosexual man, Toundi's virility becomes not a source of strength, but of weakness. For Toundi, enamoured of Madame's beauty, had expressed his rapture with such lyrical flights as 'Mon bonheur n'a pas de jour, mon bonheur n'a pas de nuit … Je le chanterai dans ma flûte, je le chanterai au bord des marigots, mais aucune parole ne saura le traduire. J'ai serré la main de ma reine. J'ai senti que je vivais' ['My happiness knows no end, not measured by the day, not measured by the night … I will sing it with my flute, I will sing it beside the lagoons, but no words shall capture it. I have held the hand of queen. I have felt alive'] (p. 74).[37] Symptomatic of Toundi's reluctance to face fallen white femininity might be his refusal to hear out Mekongo's description of an encounter with a white European prostitute; Toundi walks away, as though unable to bear this account of a white woman selling her sexual services (p. 93). Afterwards, Toundi seems to need confirmation that Madame's beauty is exceptional. When Baklu, in response to Toundi's anxious question, tells him that Madame is like all the other white women of Dangan, Toundi pursues the matter insistently: 'Mais elle est la plus belle?' ['But she's the most beautiful?'] (p. 94). Also symptomatic of Toundi's resistance to the defilement of white femininity is his bout of physical weakness – breaking into a sweat and sudden, dizzy numbness – upon first realising that Madame has spent the night with her illicit lover (p. 96). Toundi cannot, it seems, bring himself to relinquish the ideal of revered white womanhood, as testified further by his ultimate, curious silence over Madame's behaviour; confronted with her infidelity and cruelty, he repeatedly fails to pronounce any sort of judgement. Even as he is beaten by the white chief of police, Toundi, struggling to grit his teeth and distract himself with positive thoughts, thinks first of Kalisia, then of Madame. His power to resist is defeated by his inability to take the final step: to certify, through any sort of explicit acknowledgement, the fallen truth of white femininity.[38]

The gender-dismantling project of resistance undertaken – and failed – by Toundi will be completed, but it will take a native woman to do so. Issues of gender, resistance and spectation at work in the novel culminate in a scene played out, appropriately enough in the narrative's racially and politically tense context, between two women, a Black and a white.[39] The extent to which colonial oppression and colonised resistance obtained even among its most historically marginalised members, women, is dramatised in this scene, generally overlooked by critics. The commander's wife embodies the inherent violence of the colonial dynamic, as Dehon emphasises, in suggesting that Madame's initially hypocritical behaviour becomes verbal violence, evolving into physical abuse. 'En fait, toujours présente, la violence rend le système d'autant plus insupportable qu'elle reste imprévisible dans ses manifestations et qu'elle frappe sans discernement' ['In fact, always present, violence renders the system all the more intolerable in that it remains unpredictable in its manifestations and random in its targets'].[40]

But further issues reach culmination in this scene, as well. For both the Commander's wife and Kalisia have been construed as hyperfeminine, each a choice object of hetero-normative male desire; Madame turns all heads in the marketplace, while Kalisia is 'un morceau de chef' ['fit for a king']. And each exploits her ultrafeminine status; just as the promiscuous Madame charms and seduces her serial lovers, Kalisia drifts from one man to the next, Black and white, leaving heartbreak in her wake. Each – coloniser and colonised, white and Black, mistress and servant – cannily manipulates to advantage her hyperfemininity.

In a brief but searing encounter suggestive of French painter Jean-Léon Gérôme's nineteenth-century works depicting Roman slave markets, Madame evaluates the native Kalisia as a potential housemaid. In this episode, the novel's object of gaze, the Commander's beautiful wife – 'une femme parmi les femmes!' ['a woman among women!'] (p. 84), 'une femme blanche parmi les femmes blanches' ['a white woman among white women'] (p. 89), who turns all heads in the marketplace with her 'to-be-looked-at-ness'[41] – mimes the role of Gérôme's male slave-buyers in such paintings as 'A Roman Slave Market' (1884) and 'Slave Market in Rome' (1884) as she coldly inspects Kalisia. Madame's colonising gaze seeks in this corporeal object confirmation of its capacity to tend her own, Madame's, needs and desires.[42] We recall that in Colette's closing balcony scene, Philippe sought to read the index of his own virility, his own mark upon Vinca, in narcissistic projection. Instead, Madame's coolly evaluative gaze in Oyono's scene is one of narcissistic appropriation, as the political appropriation subjecting Cameroon's citizens to France is replicated corporeally through Madame's appropriation of Kalisia's body and labour.

Again, however, the native gaze – this time, Kalisia's, rather than Toundi's – counters such appropriation by carrying out an equally cool, muscled, and thus masculinised, dismantling of gendered ideals. In this scenario of display and exploitation, Madame, intent on her own evaluation, is not prepared for Kalisia to look back. Indeed, apparently 'entièrement absente' ['entirely absent'], seemingly lost in a profound and indifferent calm, Kalisia appears to turn an unseeing gaze upon Madame; '[e]lle regardait Madame sans intérêt, avec cette expression atone de brebis qui rumine' ['she looked at Madame without interest, with the lifeless expression of an ewe chewing its cud'] (p. 142). Still appearing to be 'complètement ailleurs', however, Kalisia turns her unseeing eyes towards her relative, the cook, yet 'au passage accorda un petit coup d'oeil à Madame qui redevint toute rouge' ['in passing, threw a small glance at Madame who again turned red'] (p. 142). Having unerringly discerned Madame's defining trait – her nymphomania – Kalisia observes to Toundi that a white woman with eyes like Madame's undoubtedly cannot get along without a man for more than two weeks; and goes on to speculate that Madame has a lover. Kalisia thus effortlessly collapses Madame's idealised femininity, in ironic contrast to Toundi's naive, lyrical hymn of praise to Madame upon meeting her. Refracted back and forth in this scene are fragments of gendered violence as each hyperfeminised woman avails herself of a gendered-as-virile assessment of the other, reacting in specular ways to the other's evaluation. The implicit masculinity of Kalisia's cool assessment of Madame is signalled in the strangely cross-dressed suit jacket over her native 'pagne' ['long loin-cloth'] (p.137) – as though she had specifically clothed her hyperfemininity in the vestments of masculinity for this scene of evaluative spectation. Kalisia's glance denudes a venerated feminine ideal, stripping Madame's goddess aura to expose her nymphomania; basking in the limelight of every man's gaze, Madame is scrutinised now by a furtive glance no longer admiring, but shrewdly diagnostic. Suggesting the distinction Norman Bryson elaborates between the aloof, serene gaze, and the furtive, covert glance, Kalisia would seem to employ both in discomfiting Madame. Analysing the difference in French between *regard* ['gaze'] and *coup d'oeil* ['glance'], Bryson writes of an aristocratic taint to *regard*, whereas *coup d'oeil* suggests the plebs: 'as though *regard* belonged to the protocols of the court and were formally reversible, the *regard* of the self becoming visible to the *regard* of others, of the Other; while *coup d'oeil* is vision off-duty and retired from visibility'. The glance is thus 'a sideways look whose attention is always elsewhere', carrying 'unofficial, *sub rosa* messages of hostility' and 'rebellion'.[43] Whereas the gaze would seem to capture Kalisia's unseeing look of profound indifference, '[a]gainst the Gaze', summarises Bryson, 'the Glance proposes desire, proposes the body'.[44] Kalisia's shrewd, dismantling glance at Madame operates at such a covert level of somatic hostility and rebellion.

Furthermore, Kalisia's glance just as unerringly discerns the truth of Toundi's own desire for Madame, as might be inferred in Toundi's indignation when Kalisia presumes that Toundi himself is Madame's illicit lover. Indeed, we have been prepared for Kalisia's startlingly lucid vision by the cook's remark, 'elle connaît les Blancs mieux que nous tous' ['she knows the whites better than any of us'] (p. 138). For Kalisia, he tells us, has made something of a specialty out of devastating the hearts and minds of white men she has charmed: 'Le Blanc pleura, remua ciel et terre pour la retrouver' ['The white man cried, moved heaven and earth to find her'] writes Toundi in his journal, quoting the cook. 'On craignit pour sa raison et le commandant de là-bas le fit rapatrier' ['They feared for his sanity and the commander in charge over there had him sent back to France'] (p. 138). Kalisia's numerous conquests code her as virile, feminising her abandoned, broken-hearted white lovers in a significant gender reversal – and preparing us for the peculiarly covert, yet nonetheless penetrating, virile glance with which she completes the gender-dismantling undertaken by Toundi.

Such power is particularly interesting, given Kalisia's position in the novel as a Black woman, one of the most invisible positions within colonial discourse: invisibility that may partly be due to the fact that 'the black woman has no institutionalized other', as Mary Ann Doane points out. Understanding the position of 'other' as, invariably, a devalued, inferior position, one might subscribe to Doane's claim that the white man has two 'others': white women and Blacks as a race. For the Black man, Black women are 'others'. 'But there is no other,' claims Doane, 'of the black woman'.[45]

Yet again, Kalisia's glance must be understood as more than just knowing. Realising herself to be caught as object of that glance, Madame suddenly blushes furiously, and breaks into a sweat (p. 142); as she completes her circular inspection of Kalisia, she again feels Kalisia's glance, and blushes anew. These physical marks upon Madame represent an important reversal in the colonial dynamic, for the marked body was the colonised – not the coloniser's – body: 'often an engraved body, a bloodied form'.[46] The scenes of Toundi's whipping depict such a somatisation of colonial domination; Toundi's violent, putrid death, his utter bodily decay at the hands of the whites, emblematise Boehmer's claim that the colonised body's 'mutilation represents one of the more extreme forms of colonial marking and subjection'.[47] Yet in the scene between Kalisia and Madame, the colonial hierarchy is reversed; it is Madame's body that, through her blushes and sweats, is marked, subjected to and objectified by the Black gaze.[48] Accustomed to admiration – to bathing in adulatory limelight – Madame is not prepared for a cold, expert evaluation and diagnosis of her own pathology. Here Madame as privileged spectator, assessing Kalisia as a corporeal display whose sole purpose is to serve Madame's needs and whims, is herself displaced; Madame is dislocated from her chosen position as consumer by a different look, a look that is suddenly no longer admiring, but coolly evaluative – even disfiguring, I argue, in the marks it produces on Madame's body. In this dense scene of spectation, Kalisia has effectively stolen Madame's limelight and turned it covertly back on her as surreptitious yet harsh, diagnostic glare. Kalisia is thus able to take the step that Toundi cannot; betrayed by his own desire, Toundi is politically paralysed. While his gaze successfully feminises his white male employer, the Commander, Toundi is unable to take the final step and renounce his unacknowledged feelings for Madame. Instead, a native woman, Kalisia, instantly and effortlessly diagnoses the white goddess's pathology – and in so doing, defiles her body, exteriorising the moral putrefaction standing in symmetry to the physical decay that will ultimately consume Toundi's.

In this way, whereas white virility is debunked and feminised by Toundi's transgressive gaze, it is a woman's gaze that completes the disempowering project by dismantling idealised white femininity. The native gaze does not merely see truth, as critics have generally been content to argue. It actively dismantles the power and authority of its colonial oppressor through a pattern of gender deconstruction in which white virility is feminised, while exalted, 'divine' white womanhood is cheapened. The ungendered object that is the African in the eyes of white colonisers not only 'sees' transgressively but works to 'unman' and 'unwoman' in an implicitly political act of resistance. Culminating in a scene enacted between two women, such a politics of the gaze culminate in the glance with which a native woman strips the last vestige of the superiority myth from its now not-only-feminised, but cheapened and vilified object, the colonial oppressor.

Attempting to harness the gendered implications inhabiting spectation, I have tried to probe issues of sexuality, race and power at work within what has tended to be read primarily – and antiseptically – as a trope for knowledge. I have argued instead for the gaze in *Une vie de boy* as an aggressive manipulation of gender to political purposes. Such a move might formerly have appeared the ill-advised defacing of an indigenous African text, provoking accusations of disfiguration by applying critical instruments used to analyse the film culture of a post-industrialised, media-saturated West. As Miller originally wrote of Western approaches to African texts, we need to approach the use of 'theory' cautiously. 'When we have pinpointed the relation between metaphor and metonymy in an African text,' he asked sceptically, 'have we learned anything new, or have we domesticated the text to our own cognitive system, subjugated it to our "theories"?'[49] Such epistemological worries have been displaced, however, and Miller subsequently defends his own study of gender issues in African texts with the open admission, 'they are construed here in a way that comes from my own American academic environment'.[50] Critical perspectives originating in the West need no longer worry about the danger of disfiguring an African text presumed to be somehow weaker, subject to domestication and subjugation. What matters, instead, is that these critical discussions somewhat, somehow – however tentatively, however incompletely – work towards illuminating the complexity and force of an African work, even as these approaches acknowledge their own limits in this hall-of-mirrors play of cultural codes.

In the next chapter, we turn from display as displacement through gendered dismantling dynamics in the fraught political context of French colonial Cameroon, to display as displacement in self-occulting strategies in André Gide's early (1909) novel, *La Porte étroite* ['The Strait Gate']. Moving from Oyono's tense colonial setting back to Gide's France, Part I closes with an intimate drama in which Protestant ascetic Alissa increasingly absents herself from the pompous and controlling narration of the man she loves. Manipulated, I argue, by Jérôme's very narration into focusing on his relationship with Alissa, critics have neglected the theatrics of an even more extreme, more 'visible' absence: that of Alissa's younger, vibrant sister, who – also in love with Jérôme – abdicates to vanish into an absurd marriage. Juliette's spectacular self-effacement might be read, however, precisely as a different sort of embodied hypervisibility: a different sort of self-display as displacement, legible through interpretive lenses provided by melodrama and pantomime.

Chapter Three
Disappearance as Display: Beyond the Strait Gate in Gide

Turning from the previous chapter's displays and their displacements in the political context of Oyono's colonial narrative, we find embodied display perversely directed inward, displacing and effacing the self in André Gide's 1909 novel, *La Porte étroite* ['The Strait Gate'].[1] As her self-imposed asceticism crushes her love and desire for Jérôme, Alissa increasingly absents herself from Jérôme's pompous and controlling narration, leaving only the written traces of her letters and ultimately her journal: a fanatical self-effacement analysed here in a context of mourning, with its links to mania.[2] Yet critical studies of this novel, manipulated by Jérôme's narration into focusing on the Jérôme-Alissa relationship, have neglected the theatrics of an even more extreme, more 'visible' absence: that of Alissa's younger, vibrant sister, Juliette. Cued by Alissa's journal, however, we have learned to read self-effacement as display – thus preparing us, I argue, to be more attentive to Juliette's disappearance. For, also in love with Jérôme, Juliette cedes to older sister Alissa's interests, and vanishes into an absurd marriage. Juliette's spectacular self-effacement might be read, however, precisely as another sort of hypervisibility: a different yet effective sort of self-display, as Juliette's highly embodied return in the novel's closing scene confirms. In this cataclysmic scene, Juliette converses obliquely with Jérôme about undying love before collapsing onto a chair, her face obscured by dusk. However, the entrance of a servant bearing a lamp in the text's final line implicitly calls upon us, I argue, to recognise the illumination – both literal and figurative – of her mute, enduring love for Jérôme, now fully revealed in the splash of light on her prostrate form. Such display renders visible for us the spectacle of Juliette's self-effacement or displacement from the text, analysed through theories of melodrama and pantomime that argue for the rich power of expression unleashed by muteness and gesture.

The Failure of *Logos*

In Gide's novel, two characters posit an authentic, originary signifying discourse, a pure *logos*.[3] But Jérôme and Alissa read this *logos* too purely, too literally; the Biblical charge to be among the few to enter by the 'strait gate'[4] becomes what Apter calls a 'perversely literalised application of Scriptural teachings'.[5] Ironically, this literal, naive reading, so excessive in its pathological purity and rigour, is enacted throughout the novel as a series of displaced sites of meaning – of authenticity, origin and purity. And this slippage, generated by excessiveness and extreme, is in turn expressed theatrically, becoming increasingly self-reflexive and specular. Such a succession of theatrical scenarios implies that there is always an 'Other' scene, yet another stage of specular and paralytic self-scrutiny. And the unfolding of these scenarios brings about the destruction of the two too-literal readers, Jérôme and Alissa.

Most readings of the novel tend to focus on this destruction, viewing it as the final displacement, the final self-reflexive stage of the specularity that cripples the narrator, Jérôme, and his beloved, Alissa. Readers generally focus beyond Jérôme as narrator in favour of the object of his narration, Alissa; and they conclude with Alissa's death and Jérôme's lasting numbness. Despairing of being sufficiently virtuous, Alissa increasingly absents herself from the narrative's action, ostensibly to allow Jérôme to pursue the virtuous path undistracted. She leaves only the written traces of her letters and ultimately, of her journal: each, however, is heavily edited by Jérôme. To read Alissa authentically is thus to learn to read beyond the deceptive *logos* of Jérôme's text, with its implied claim to authority: to read instead between its lines, for its absences and silences.

And yet, I would argue, learning to read Alissa between the lines of Jérôme's presentation of her letters and journal ultimately teaches us to read even further. Beyond Alissa's own absence, we come to a greater absence. Learning to read beyond *logos*, beyond the word as presence – learning to read instead for absence – is to learn to read the extreme absence of Alissa's sister, Juliette.[6] And Juliette's text is not a text of words, but a text of the body, a somatic text; beyond the strait gate of *logos* as the Word, lies a more transparent form of *logos*, the word as body, the word made flesh. This, it turns out, is the most spectacular discourse in the novel, the one neither Jérôme nor Alissa is able to read. For, as a corporeal, somatic text, it is scorned by such intellectual readers-of-words as Jérôme and Alissa. Yet this most theatrical text of all, that of Juliette, is also the fullest, most unequivocal, most decisive signifying discourse in the novel; but it is a discourse overlooked and lost, displaced and eclipsed by the narrative's intellectual and ascetic imperatives.

Such displacement might be approached by noting the fundamental ambiguity of the novel's place in Gide's oeuvre, and the question – posed by Kevin Newmark, among others – of whether it should be read as autobiography or as fiction.[7] Noting that it is an early 'récit', Newmark nonetheless claims for it a technical mastery more characteristic of Gide's later work. Concluding with the novel's 'eccentric place' in Gide's oeuvre – an eccentricity we might, for the purposes of this discussion, understand as theatrical, situated in the space between life and art, autobiography and fiction[8] – Newmark nonetheless reads Jérôme's own eccentric writing as the failure of 'any kind of narrative transfiguration, or retrospective recapitulation of an individual's lived experience'.[9]

But to read *La porte étroite* as failure, however, is to repeat Alissa and Jérôme's mistake – to buy into their own naive and too-literal exegesis by reading strictly for *logos* as the Word. Instead, there may be strategies at work in this spectacular scrambling of life and art, that, rather than sinking into artistic failure, cue us to read in new ways. For this reason, dismissing Jérôme's narration as 'failure'– as a flat, unreflective enumeration of events – is to miss the artful manipulation carried out by that narration. Himself susceptible to the lure of *logos* – of an authentic, unmediated speech – Jérôme as narrator strives to present his story as such a discourse; he claims simplicity, limpidity and immediacy for his narration, recounting his narrative with 'aucune invention' ['no artfulness'] (p. 495). Yet, after telling us that he is transcribing all that could illuminate the events he describes (p. 548) – inviting us to wonder just what he may be leaving out as '*un*illuminating' – he eventually admits that he is not including all of Alissa's letters to him (p. 551). Ultimately, the extreme narcissism of Jérôme's narration is confirmed when he cries while re-reading the copy of a letter that he himself wrote Alissa (p. 560). We are surprised to learn that he had saved a copy of his letter, and that he does not scruple to describe his emotion upon re-reading it. Jérôme seems so eager to guide and shape the reader's response in this way that, by the time we come upon his renewed claim to transcribe Alissa's remarks 'sans y apporter après coup art ni logique' ['subsequently adding neither art nor logic'] (p. 570), we have learned to mistrust such assertions.

Such gaps, silences and manipulative hints in a narration claiming for itself the transparency of *logos* increasingly invite our suspicion. 'Professions of truth, sincerity and contrition,' suggests Emily Apter, 'typical of the *récit's* first-person narrators, automatically alert the reader to traces of duplicity, unreliability or outright mendacity.' Apter proposes that 'what is dissimulated or not articulated plays a more significant role in the text's interpretation than what is actually reported'.[10] Increasingly suspicious of Jérôme as a self-interested impresario, we begin to seek a less manipulated, less orchestrated Alissa. We might turn to what appears at first to be the most spectacular gap or withdrawal of the text: Alissa's renunciation, and what Apter calls 'one of the most protracted and frustrating accounts of sexual denial to be found in the history of literature', 'a paradigm of textual penitence'. As Apter reads Alissa's journal, it consists of 'desperate appeals to the "Seigneur" to aid her in the arduous task of salvation and deliverance from her persistent feminine longing for *jouissance*'. For Apter, then, the journal represents Alissa's 'last written testament', a full expression of the truth of her anguish.[11]

Similarly, Marty claims for Alissa's journal a present-to-itself truth, which he opposes to what he considers Jérôme's impotent, faulty, deficient recollection. Privileging Alissa's journal for its ongoing record of the present, Marty argues that it contains 'comme un dépositaire tyrannique, la vérité du récit' ['like a tyrannical guardian, the truth of the story']; the journal thus restores what escapes Jérôme's memory.[12] But, we wonder, in reading Alissa's journal as an ultimate expression of truth, might we not be replicating an earlier misreading? The mistake of buying into Jérôme's discourse might appear here to be repeated in displaced form; we might too readily be turning to another unreliable, manipulative discourse – Alissa's own – as the authentic *logos* we eventually learned to mistrust from Jérôme.

For what such readings of the journal-as-truth neglect is precisely the spectacularity of this denial and its penitence. Indeed, Alissa's dramatic role might be read in her very name, the Greek name for Dido – who, deserted by Aeneas in his eagerness to found Rome, kills herself out of love and grief. Alissa is therefore, we realise, destined to destroy herself for love, like Dido; her name alone imposes a harsh script. Similarly, Jérôme's name is inscribed by the Biblical Saint Jérôme, the scholar, often represented as a hermit hunched over his books. Indeed, Gide's Jérôme speaks rapturously to Alissa of his studies (p. 526), and even makes explicit his monkish similarity to his Biblical namesake when he praises the monastic atmosphere of the Ecole Normale (p. 526).[13] Overshadowed by their ancient classical and Biblical roles, Alissa and Jérôme are condemned to play out the destinies borne in their names. Aware of these prescribed roles, we need to understand as highly orchestrated and deliberate the gaps, absences and withdrawals that surround Alissa. In Gide's narrative, display becomes precisely what is *not* written or explicitly conveyed to the reader – that is, what is withdrawn or silenced.

Further scrutiny of Alissa's journal undermines Marty's claim that it contains 'the truth of the story', 'an unshakeable presence-to-itself'. For this infallible presence-to-itself is not a plenitude; rather, as its very rhetorical formulation suggests, it is specular, a presence addressed '*to* itself': an artifice in which Alissa dramatises this intimate form – and, furthermore, watches herself do so. For Alissa's unyielding self-scrutiny has been much cited by critics, culminating in Robert Greene's claim that 'her relentless view of her every thought, word, deed and especially diary entry, her fanatic contemplative's conscientiousness, her scrupulosity, will destroy her'.[14] Alissa carries on a performance not only for Jérôme, but for herself, as she inexorably measures and assesses her every move. 'Combien cette analyse de ma tristesse est dangereuse! Déjà, je m'attache à ce cahier. La coquetterie, que je croyais vaincue, reprendrait-elle ici ses droits?' ['How dangerous is this analysis of my sadness! I'm already attached to this notebook. Might the coquetry I thought defeated be reclaiming me here?'] (p. 583). As Alissa finally admits, 'Je ne l'avais jamais écrit que pour lui' ['I had never written this journal for any reason but him'] (p. 594). We must guard against reading Alissa's journal too literally as a presence-to-itself *logos*, since even this intimate text is a performance for Jérôme's benefit.[15]

Having opened up the theatricality of Alissa's journal, we might look further at critical claims for 'the essentially theatrical quality' of Alissa and Jérôme's relationship.[16] Suggesting that the two 'perform' for each other's benefit throughout the narrative, Albert Sonnenfeld goes on to point out the narrative's extensive use of the verb 'feindre' ['to feint'] in what he calls 'lovers' games'. Citing Alissa's journal as her most daring 'performance', an example of Alissa's manipulation and self-representation, Sonnenfeld concludes that it is an 'un-Christian act of posthumous revenge'.[17] While this is undoubtedly so, such a conclusion neglects the further implications of the novel's extreme theatricality – for, having taught us to read in Alissa's journal the theatricality of absence, the narrative trains us to be attentive to yet further performances by the absent. While the journal may indeed be Alissa's most daring performance, as Sonnenfeld claims, it is not the *text*'s most daring performance.

In exploring such questions of the text's performativity, we might review the ways in which the reader is coached to recognise it as such, beginning with the spectacle of Alissa's disappearance. We begin to wonder whether Alissa's self-effacement might not be an elaborate charade to challenge Jérôme's devotion: to test it against her fear that she is too old for him, and that his love for her will fade as she fades. Asserting as much, her letter of renunciation to him brings Jérôme running with proclamations of undying love – which Alissa readily accepts, as though only too eager to believe them (p. 526).[18] Perhaps Alissa initiates a renunciatory role to test Jérôme, only to fall victim to her own theatrics, trapped in her own theatre of self-effacement and negation: a blank screen behind which she disappears, inviting Jérôme to communicate with her, as Marty puts it, 'par abstention; le silence sera signe!' ['by abstention; silence itself will be meaningful!'].[19] Any truth about Alissa becomes increasingly inaccessible, masked behind an inscrutable façade.[20]

Such progressive vanishing might be read in the context of *aphanisis*, from the Greek word for disappearance or to make disappear. Originally used by Ernest Jones to suggest a woman's fear of losing sexual desire, the notion of *aphanisis* was taken up again by Lacan to define a certain fading of the subject – a disappearance that is itself constitutive of the subject. For Lacan, the subject *is* this 'aphanisis' or fading: 'c'est dans cette aliénation, dans cette division fondamentale, que s'institue la dialectique du sujet' ['it's in this alienation, in this fundamental division, that the dialectics of the subject are instituted'].[21] The subject is condemned, as Lacan puts it, to appear only within this division: 'S'il apparaît d'un côté comme sens, produit par le signifiant, de l'autre il apparaît comme *aphanisis*' ['if it appears on one side as meaning, produced by the signifier, on the other, it appears as *aphanisis*']. Explaining this split or division, Lacan argues that if we attend to the signifier, to meaning, we lose that most intimate and defining feature of subjectivity, unconscious desire; that is, where there is meaning – coherence, *logos* – there is only the distorted trace of a departed subjectivity.[22] In this way, implies Lacan, all human interaction is necessarily theatrical; as he claims, 'c'est par l'intermédiaire des masques que le masculin, le féminin, se rencontrent de la façon la plus aiguë, la plus brûlante' ['it's through the mediation of masks that the masculine and the feminine encounter each other in the most acute, the most burning way'].[23] Indeed, Jérôme himself suspects that Alissa plays with meaning; while he sees it on its most literal level as a means of communication, Alissa makes a game of discourse and signification. Referring to the profusion of quotations, readings and opinions that Alissa seems to manipulate to disguise her own thoughts, even Jérôme wonders significantly whether their relationship itself might not be a game for her (p. 530).[24]

In a poignant paradox, then, the very profusion of quotations in both Alissa's and Jérôme's discourses, rather than creating intimacy, only works as a masquerade, a pitiful pastiche of the vanishing or *aphanisis* of subjectivity behind it.[25] And the poignancy increases as

Alissa progressively refuses herself even the paltry pleasures of this game. Alissa's veneration of Jérôme as well as her own relentless self-effacement might be read in her resolution, expressed in a letter to her aunt, not to write to Jérôme at such length as she had in the past, so as not to bother him in his studies. Yet she goes on to suggest the risk of such a decision, anticipating that her aunt might think that she compensates for fewer letters to him by speaking about him all the more. A substitute gratification for the original game that represents communication for Alissa is thus envisaged, yet immediately refused, foreclosed: 'de peur de continuer, j'arrête vite ma lettre' ['for fear of continuing, I'll end my letter quickly'] (p. 543). In this way, Alissa's 'direct' letter-writing discourse with Jérôme is not only itself cut short, but its substitution – speaking of Jérôme to her aunt – is also silenced, leaving only the blank space of unwritten lines in a letter abruptly broken off. Progressively, all such forms of substitute gratification that mediate her connection to Jérôme will be refused by Alissa's unyielding asceticism.

And yet, curiously, Alissa's very renunciation of Jérôme provides a final – inviolate and inviolable – substitute for him as her spectacular self-effacement culminates in what Marty calls her sacrifice (restoring the etymology of 'to render sacred'). Explaining that renouncing a flesh-and-blood Jérôme allows her to cling to an ideal of him, Marty argues that such a sacrifice provides 'le maintien d'une présence à l'autre (sa répétition) par delà la corruption du temps, du Monde, des mensonges' ['the sustaining of one presence to another (its repetition) beyond the corruption of time, of the World, of lies']. Moreover, beyond maintaining 'l'idéalité d'une présence' ['the ideality of a presence'], suggests Marty, such a sacrifice assures Alissa's 'maîtrise absolue' ['absolute mastery'].[26]

Yet, as she herself painfully realises, Alissa's sacrifice is not really so successful. She praises the idea of difficult duties, such as sacrifice, that build virtue; when Jérôme pays particular attention to her loutish brother Robert in Paris, Alissa writes to her aunt that Jérôme has probably learned that the greater the burden assumed, the more uplifting it is for the soul. But Alissa herself immediately ironises her own claim as 'des réflexions bien sublimes! Ne souris pas trop de ta grande nièce' ['sublime reflections indeed! Don't laugh too much at your pompous niece'] (p. 542). Despite her self-deprecating irony, Alissa's effort to engage the sacred by believing in its power is tragically authentic and consuming. She aspires to a saintliness consonant with Clifford Geertz's definition of the sacred as not only entailing obligation and devotion, but 'intellectual assent' and 'emotional commitment'.[27] As Peter Brooks summarises, 'a true sacred is evident, persuasive, and compelling'.[28] Yet Geertz's powerfully coercive 'ought'[29] fails somehow to obtain for Alissa: a failure that lands her in the realm of melodrama, where, since sacred forces 'achieve no sacred status as wholly other, they appear, rather, to abide within nature and, particularly, within nature's creature, man'.[30] Accordingly, Alissa will die alone, without faith, the walls of her cell-like room 'atrocement nus' ['horribly naked'] (p. 595).

We come, then, to an understanding of Alissa as tragically failing in her chosen role of saintly renunciation: a failure that recalls Rostand character Cyrano de Bergerac's self-assessment: 'J'aurai tout manqué, même ma mort' ['I will have botched everything, even my own death'].[31] Murdered by cowardly thugs, Cyrano dies in a manner he feels unworthy of the heroic role he had chosen and assumed for himself. Elsewhere, the psychic pathos of such non-coincidence with one's own role is expressed somewhat differently by Mannoni, who discerns a sort of anxious desperation behind such histrionic efforts. What is certain about the lover's dramatisation of his love, for instance – argues Mannoni – is that the lover isn't certain of his feelings; the dramatisation of jealousy betrays a fear of not being jealous enough. In such situations, concludes Mannoni, the subject 'est l'acteur de son propre personnage, il met sa propre valeur narcissique dans son rôle, et il se pose devant son spectateur comme devant son propre reflet' ['is the actor of his own character, he invests narcissistically in his rôle, and he poses before his spectator as before his own reflection'].[32] Such display, such caricaturised excess of feeling, pitifully reveals a fear of the inadequacy of one's own emotion. We might read Alissa's fanatical faith in the 'strait gate' of virtue as the index of a fear that her own virtue is lacking.

We might here explore further the failure of Alissa's own chosen role, her failure in this sacrifice. Perhaps it has to do not only with her lucidity, but also with the pathology, even the perversion, of her sacrifice. For while Alissa may have renounced Jérôme on one level, it is only to maintain him – as Marty suggests in his notion of sacrifice – on another, that of an ideal. And Freud argues precisely for the abnormality, the hysteria or obsessiveness of such a sacrifice. Although a patient may have given up a relation to reality, claims Freud, 'he has by no means broken off his erotic relations to people and things. He still retains them in fantasy' (XIV: 74). Alissa, it would seem, progressively insists on greater and greater distance from Jérôme *so as to* substitute, in place of the real Jérôme, an imaginary Jérôme from her memory: a sacrifice that edges into the pathological. Jérôme himself seems aware of this substitution when he tells Juliette, in the novel's closing scene, of his (unyieldingly narcissistic) resolution to remain faithful not so much to the memory of Alissa, as to her image of him (p. 597).

Having opened up the pathology of Alissa's wilful sacrifice of Jérôme, we are positioned to read further into its behaviours and emblems – to understand them as pathological mourning. As we saw above, Marty uses repetition to argue for the success of Alissa's sacrifice. But we might add further focus to the dynamic of repetition by considering it in the context of mourning, attentive to what psychoanalyst Pierre Fédida calls 'l'étrange seduction imaginaire exercée par la répétition de l'absent' ['the strange imaginary seduction wrought by the repetition of the absent'].[33] In pathological mourning, there is fascination with 'une répétition imaginaire à laquelle l'absent donne pouvoir' ['an imaginary repetition to which the absent one lends power'].[34] In this context, Alissa's amethyst cross, given to her by Jérôme in memory of his mother, becomes a relic not so much of Jérôme's mother as of Jérôme himself. Such a relic represents a compromise between knowledge and desire, allowing one to acknowledge loss, yet somehow also to cling to the lost object. Distinguished from the talisman and fetish, in Fédida's argument, the relic affirms both knowledge of the loss, yet also belief that something remains.[35] Nevertheless, Fédida later links the relic to the fetish in that each implies, for the believer, protection against one's *own* death.[36] And indeed, a moment comes when Alissa expresses a wish to return her cross to Jérôme during their last meeting, as though implicitly renouncing her own protection against death (p. 592); she dies in Paris scarcely two weeks later.

Pursuing Marty's suggestion that sacrifice is a rite of perpetual 'répétition', we realise the potential theatricality of the rite of mourning. Reading mourning not only as the Freudian effort to cope with absence, loss, and the effort to decathect, Fédida argues that we might understand it as a heightened, narcissistic, presence-to-oneself in which the bereaved is flooded by memories; such powerful reminders of one's own existence 'approfondissent la subjectivité' ['deepen subjectivity']. In this process of profound re-discovery of the self, argues Fédida, 'le deuil est l'événement – pour ainsi dire: transcendental – de la subjectivité' ['mourning is the transcendental – so to speak – event of subjectivity'].[37] Could Alissa's extreme sacrifice entailing the 'death' of Jérôme be understood, then, as producing a narcissistic, even ecstatic recovery of self for her? Alissa's mourning of Jérôme as the result of such a sacrifice would seem to become, in Fédida's terms, 'la fascination de soi dans la mort de l'autre' ['the fascination of oneself in the death of the other'].[38]

And such fascination focused on oneself and one's past leads to a possible connection between joy – 'le jeu, la fête, la *joie*' ['play, celebration, *joy*'][39] – and mourning, a connection we recognise in the manic joy that occasionally overtakes Alissa. She writes to Jérôme of being 'tout ivre de soleil et de joie' ['drunk with joy and sunshine'] (p. 549): a joy that intensifies as her journal nears its end: 'Joie, joie, joie, pleurs de joie … Au-dessus de la joie humaine et par delà toute douleur, oui, je pressens cette joie radieuse' ['Joy, joy, joy, tears of joy … Above human joy and beyond all pain, yes, I sense this radiant joy'] (p. 595). In her last journal entry, breaking the pose of writing for herself alone and confirming the journal's implicit performance by addressing Jérôme directly, Alissa announces, 'je voudrais t'enseigner la joie parfaite' ['I would like to teach you perfect joy'] (p. 595).

While Fédida did not further pursue a possible link between mourning and joy, Freud, writing in 1915 – only six years after the publication of *La porte étroite* – suggested a connection that might lend further nuance to the spectacle of Alissa's sacrifice of Jérôme. For Freud, articulating the swings of what we now understand as manic-depressive disorder, melancholia's most remarkable trait is its tendency to become mania's pathological joy; he theorised that after the work of melancholy has been completed, the extraordinary energy that had been poured into melancholia is released, making mania possible. Freud further established a link between mania and release from self-condemnation, on the one hand, and melancholy and self-deprecation on the other. The manic person 'in a mood of triumph and self-satisfaction, disturbed by no self-criticism, can enjoy the abolition of his inhibitions, his feelings of consideration for others, and his self-reproaches'.[40] In melancholia, on the other hand, misery results – theorised Freud – from a painful conflict 'in which the ideal, in an excess of sensitiveness, relentlessly exhibits its condemnation of the ego in delusions of inferiority and in self-deprecation'.[41] Such violent swings between self-condemnation and the intense joy of its release articulate a dynamic that helps render visible the spectacle of Alissa's withdrawal from the narrative.

For further energies within this dynamic, we might turn to Melanie Klein's claim for links among mania, idealisation and repression.[42] Klein argues for the importance of idealisation in mania, and similarly, for the importance of denial; she further connects these energies to ambivalence, asserting that omnipotence, denial and idealisation allow the early ego to ward off internal threats, yet also to combat 'a slavish and perilous dependence upon its loved objects'.[43] The powerful dual energy of ambivalence would then mark the site of a fierce inner struggle, a conflict that helps us understand Eric Marty's argument for Alissa's confusing double discourse. As Marty points out, on the one hand, Alissa claims to Jérôme that she has always already been lost to him; on the other, she pours out her passion for him in her journal. Such discourses, argues Marty, obliterate Jérôme himself, dwarfed by Alissa's titanic inner struggle over him; yet they simultaneously elevate him to a level of importance he cannot imagine.[44] Klein's model linking extremes of idealisation and denial help render legible narrative energies swirling around Jérôme.

Pursuing such energies, we might note Klein's emphasis on the importance of triumph – with its links to contempt and omnipotence – in mania. She understands the early ego as eager to triumph over the parents, when the weak, helpless child imagines itself strong and powerful; but such fantasised triumph, argues Klein, can produce crippling guilt.[45] Looking further at Alissa's past, we might identify a 'bad' mother-object: the scandalous, unfaithful mother provoking Alissa's own feelings of rage, helplessness, humiliation and ensuing guilt. Alissa's distress over her mother is apparent in her supplication to Jérôme, after the two overhear the mother laughing with her lover, 'ne raconte à personne … mon pauvre papa ne sait rien' ['not a word to anyone … my poor father knows nothing'] (p. 504). The 'hypomanic' person, continues Klein, tends towards 'exaggerated valuations: over-admiration (idealization) or contempt (devaluation)'.[46] Such temperaments, suggests Klein, 'have been unable in early childhood to establish their internal "good" objects and to feel secure in their inner world'.[47] Understanding Jérôme as a sacred object, sacrificed in order to maintain him in an unaltered state, would seem consonant with Alissa's manic hypervaluation of him. Such idealisation, moreover, could well be the consequence of Alissa's own guilt and shame over her mother's flagrant infidelity and ultimate elopement with a young officer.

Understanding Alissa's sacrifice of Jérôme as pathological would have further implications for one of the gestures that comprise that sacrifice. Suggesting that Alissa's sacrifice of Jérôme is symbolised by her removal of her amethyst cross, Newmark argues that this removal repeats Christ's gesture of renunciation; he points to Christ's own semiotic reversal, his choice of death, or absence, as eternal life and the recuperation of a greater presence. Emphasising the similar semiotic uncertainty and instability of Alissa's removing her cross, Newmark asks, 'how are we to know whether she has sacrificed only Jérôme, or whether she has inadvertently cut the entire text off from any security regarding a consistent interpretation of its signs?' What ground remains, Newmark continues, for assessing meaning in the novel?[48]

The difficulty here is that, in pointing to the semiotic havoc wrought by Alissa's manipulation of her amethyst cross, Newmark reads the cross as an authentic sacred symbol — and therefore, understood to ground an unquestioned, compelling order. Such sacred symbols derive their power from the conviction that they 'identify fact with value at the most fundamental level'.[49] In reading Alissa's cross as bearing a fundamental semiotic valence, Newmark neglects the crucial difference between an authentic sacred symbol

– such as Christ's cross, in Christian theology – and its perverted
version, a relic – such as Alissa's. In the context of Alissa's
pathological mourning and sacrifice of Jérôme, however, her
amethyst cross must be understood as a relic, virtually a fetish, a
fallen cross. We may need to refocus our attention, to reconsider
the terms in which we have been reading the novel. Perhaps we
have been reading with the wrong cross in mind, the wrong
guarantor of signification; it is time now to turn to a different one.

Juliette's Cross

Since words-as-presence – or *logos* – in this novel have proved so
unreliable, so theatrically slippery, we might turn to a language
operating without words – that is, beyond *logos*. We might therefore
turn to 'Juliette's surprising self-immolation'(Newmark), to what
remains as a residue of mystery in the novel. For Juliette has
remained puzzling, in her refusal of Alissa's sacrifice and her
disappearance into marriage and Provence. She has been read
dismissively as object, 'unwitting victim', 'piece of machinery', by,
for instance, Newmark:

> What Juliette never comes fully to understand is the fact that
> she has been chosen for this role of messenger for the sake
> of convenience, in a wholly arbitrary manner, merely because
> she is at hand, as it were.[50]

But how do we know just what Juliette does or does not
understand? She has virtually no voice in the novel. Jérôme listens
to her so little that, in retrospect, he wonders, 'sont-ce là
précisément ces paroles?' ['are those precisely her words?'] (p. 519).
News of Juliette is mediated through her letters to Alissa,
themselves mediated through Jérôme's journal; Juliette becomes an
endlessly mediated trace, overlaid by veil upon veil of other
discourses. The one person who tries to bring Juliette into visibility
– Jérôme's friend and fellow student, Abel – is compromised by his
own vulgarity. To be sure, Abel perceives and scolds Jérôme's
indifference to Juliette: 'Alissa et toi, vous êtes stupéfiants d'égoïsme.

Vous voilà tout confits dans votre amour, et vous n'avez pas un regard pour l'éclosion admirable de cette intelligence, de cette âme!' ['You and Alissa! Your egotism is stupefying. Here you are steeped in your own love, and you don't even notice the admirable blossoming of this intelligence, of this soul!'] (p. 528). Guided by Jérôme's position, however, we are unable to take Abel seriously, and therefore, like Jérôme, we scorn his keener vision than our own. If Alissa allures through her very absence, Juliette is the character eclipsed by Alissa's theatrical withdrawal, and by Jérôme's narcissistic, excessive presence. Even before her own disappearance from the action, Juliette becomes a phantom presence, a virtually invisible mediator between Jérôme and Alissa. In turn, however, Juliette herself is increasingly mediated by Alissa, who communicates details about her sister to Jérôme – who then transmits them to us: 'Les nouvelles qu'Alissa me donnait de sa soeur devenaient cependant meilleures. Son mariage devait se célébrer en juillet' ['The news Alissa was giving me of her sister was improving. Her wedding was to take place in July'] (p. 545). In a letter from Alissa following Juliette's marriage, we learn that Juliette has written enthusiastically of her wedding trip to Bayonne, Biarritz, Fontarabie and Burgos (p. 546). Later, Alissa writes to Jérôme, 'les nouvelles de Nîmes sont si bonnes qu'il me paraît que Dieu me permet de m'abandonner à la joie' ['the news from Nîmes is so good that it seems to me that God is allowing me to give myself over to joy'] (p. 548). Juliette's ruse would appear to be succeeding; the charade of her happiness is convincing to a sister with much at stake – much to gain – precisely from that happiness. Visiting her sister, Alissa confesses that Juliette's joyful letters had made her fear that Juliette 'ne me jouât la comédie du bonheur et qu'elle-même ne s'y laissât prendre' ['was playing a happy rôle for my sake, and that she herself was beginning to believe it'] (p. 552). But Alissa – allowing herself, reluctantly, to be persuaded that Juliette's happiness is genuine – writes in her journal of her disappointment, even bitterness, at Juliette's easy contentment: 'Ce bonheur que j'ai tant souhaité, jusqu'à offrir de lui sacrifier mon bonheur, je souffre de le voir obtenu sans peine' ['This happiness that I so longed for, to the point of offering her the sacrifice my own happiness, I suffer to see it so easily obtained'] (p. 582).

Critical misreadings of Juliette are in some part due to allowing ourselves, as readers, to be guided by Alissa and Jérôme's dismissiveness, by their scorn of Juliette as a too-corporeal being. She has a direct, open beauty (p. 502); and Jérôme's very description of it suggests his misreading of Juliette as an 'exterior' being (p. 502), a misreading that Alissa will also embrace. For Jérôme and Alissa, Juliette's vivacious beauty seems all too superficial, too promiscuously available to view. She represents action, as Jérôme indicates in saying that he talked to Alissa but played with Juliette (p. 502).

But we need to look further into Jérôme and Alissa's disdain for Juliette's vivacity – marked by a corporeality implicitly scandalous, because suggestive of Alissa's and Juliette's mother Lucile. Tellingly, Lucile's theatrics and histrionic 'crises' are condemned in the novel, written off by her sister-in-law as 'de la comédie' ['theatrics'] (p. 501). Lucile is heavily marked as Other, in Jérôme's narration: Creole, scandalously *décolletée*, indifferent to family life when she isn't laughing with a young officer, with whom she eventually elopes. She remains a deep wound and humiliation for both Jérôme and Alissa. Jérôme, listening to the pastor's sermon after his aunt Lucile has fled with her lover, imagines the adulterous pair laughing together: 'l'idée même du rire, de la joie, se faisait blessante, outrageuse, devenait comme l'odieuse exaggeration du péché' ['the idea itself of laughter, of joy, became hurtful, outrageous, became a sort of odious exaggeration of sin'] (p. 505). Juliette's own very vivacity consequently becomes implicitly shocking, scandalous to Jérôme and Alissa, stamped with interdiction; disdain for Lucile's laughter, affectations and 'comédie', compounded by her humiliating betrayal of the family, colour Alissa's and Jérôme's view of a different sort of corporeal theatre, Juliette's.

There is yet a further reason, moreover, for Alissa's and Jérôme's scorn for Juliette's animation. A second negative variation – this one more annoying than threatening – of Lucile's vivacity characterises Tante Félicie, with her perpetually meaningless, excessive, futile agitation (p. 515). Juliette's father defends his sister, suggesting that what has now become silly activity devoid of purpose originally took the form of an 'élan charmant, prime-saut, abandon à l'instant et grâce' ['a charming energy, impulsiveness, an abandon to the moment, grace'] (p. 515); he goes on to specify that in her youth, Félicie was a great deal like Juliette (p. 515). Nonetheless, annoyed by Félicie's useless agitation, Jérôme and Alissa establish an implicit and masculinised hierarchy, 'estimant surtout les facultés contemplatives' ['admiring most highly the contemplative faculties'] (p. 515) – and implicitly scorning Juliette's heavily embodied, feminised vivacity. Marked as excessively corporeal through traits linking her to her sexualised mother and pointlessly active aunt, Juliette is implicitly dismissed by the cerebral Jérôme and Alissa.

We now understand why Juliette's somatic text is misread into invisibility by Jérôme and Alissa, too wrapped up in their own performances to read Juliette's corporeal theatre. In a key scene, Jérôme notices Juliette's animation, without, however, being able to decipher it. Alissa has written to Jérôme renouncing marriage with him; and, though Jérôme does not know it, Alissa intends her own renunciation to pave the way for him to marry Juliette. When Juliette asks whether Jérôme has received Alissa's abdicating letter, she speaks loudly, seems extremely agitated and blushes furiously as she herself reads it; Jérôme even thinks he hears anger in her voice (p. 524). At dinner that evening, Jérôme notices Juliette's wild, almost harsh expression (p. 532). In the subsequent scene in which Juliette tells Jérôme that Alissa wants her, Juliette, to marry him, Jérôme is struck by the extreme of Juliette's expression: 'Elle avait le visage en feu; le froncement de ses sourcils donnait à son regard une expression dure et douloureuse; ses yeux luisaient comme si elle eût eu la fièvre; sa voix même semblait rêche et crispée. Une sorte de fureur l'exaltait' ['Her face was afire; the wrinkling of her eyebrows gave her gaze a hard and unhappy expression; her eyes glistened as though she had had a fever; her voice itself seemed harsh and tense. A sort of fury exalted her'] (pp. 535–6). Yet Jérôme is unable to interpret these embodied symptoms of Juliette's love for him.

Jérôme and Alissa are not the only readers of Juliette to have essentially dismissed her, however; critics have ignored her as well. 'The novel,' writes Reid, 'in its growing obsession with the subjectivity of unmarried Alissa, slowly and relentlessly suppresses all female characters but one.'[51] Further occulting of Juliette in favour of a critical obsession with Alissa is apparent when Reid argues that the substitution of Alissa's writing for her withering body 'reaches its grim conclusion in her death and the subsequent transmission of her diary to Jerome'.[52] One might propose, however, that the grim conclusion of this sequence actually occurs some years later; the substitution of Alissa's writing for her withering body culminates, instead, when her (somatic) writing itself is eclipsed by the ultimate substitute form: the text of Juliette's unread body in the novel's final scene between Juliette and Jérôme – to which we will return.

Even when Juliette is accorded some critical attention, it is only in the form of a misreading; for critics have tended to read her as embodying an insouciant happiness and sensuality that eludes Alissa. 'Renouncing Jérôme,' writes Thomas Cordle, 'leads [Juliette] out of the puritan world of self-denial and into one that is still pagan enough to accept pleasure and joy without reserve or remorse.' Cordle goes so far as to claim that 'the picture of Juliette's happiness is more than a device to stir up uncertainty in Alissa', arguing that 'Juliette represents the way out of the morass of sexual repression, narcissistic uncertainty, and puritanical restraint'.[53] For Doris Kadish, 'Juliette, not Alissa, is the person with whom all of the positive features of nature in the novel are associated, features such as warmth and sunlight or free and open spaces'.[54] Pithily summing up this reading of Juliette is Sonnenfeld's 'embodiment of love, fecundity and July'.[55] Such readings, however, replicate the mistaken reading espoused by Alissa and Jérôme, the face-value reading unable to recognise what lies beneath Juliette's charade of 'love, fecundity and July'.

In an effort to correct such critical views of Juliette, we might turn to the moment that she disappears from the narrative's action – not to return until the final scene of the novel. When Jérôme discovers that Alissa wants Juliette to marry him, his exclamation – 'Mais c'est de la folie! ['But that's madness!'] (p. 536) – prompts an opaque reply from Juliette, and the next thing we know, she is suddenly engaged to the preposterous Edouard. Yet, immediately following the announcement of her engagement, she faints with a sudden cry. 'Ses cheveux défaits semblent tirer en arrière sa face affreusement pâlie. Il parassait, aux sursauts de son corps, que ce n'était point là un évanouissement ordinaire' ['Her undone hair seemed to pull at her horribly pale face. It seemed, by the starts and shaking of her body, that this was no ordinary fainting'] (p. 539). Juliette is gathered up by her aunt and by Edouard ('the suitor', as Jérôme calls him), each supporting a shoulder. With Alissa lifting and kissing her sister's feet and Abel supporting Juliette's head, covering with kisses 'this abandoned hair that he gathered' (p. 540), we as readers are witnessing a virtual 'Descent from the Cross' scenario.[56] In this somatic text, we read an ultimate *logos*, the textual word made flesh in Juliette's crucifixion. If Alissa's amethyst cross, as I have suggested, has been the wrong sacred symbol, Juliette's corporeal cross carries a compellingly authentic, mutely expressive, semiotic weight.

This climactic moment, indeed the last moment in which we see Juliette directly until the final pages of the novel, would appear to engage a new signifying order. Alissa and Jérôme are each paralysed, trapped within crippling futility and sterility, by their own narcissism; Jérôme self-absorbed, Alissa absorbed in watching herself watch Jérôme. Juliette, however, breaks free of this sterility, into a different signifying order: one no longer of difference, deferral and specularity. Rather, Juliette's is an order of plenitude: a mode of unadulterated expression, a discourse that explodes restraint. In the instant in which Juliette – an animated, highly-coloured corporeal being, marked as a female creature of action and of the body – enacts a 'descent from the Cross' scenario, her corporeal expressiveness veers into a new signifying mode. This mode, I would like to argue, is the melodramatic – a mode in which desire 'cries aloud its language in identification with full states of being'.[57]

Confirming this association of Juliette and the melodramatic is the corporeal connection. For the melodramatic mode is not primarily a discursive one; rather, words are felt to be somehow inadequate to expression, as other, more transparent means of expression are urgently sought.[58] Gesture is engaged as expression calls upon every possible resource. Moreover, Brooks points out, melodramas tend – particularly at the end of scenes and acts – to evoke 'tableaux' in which the composition of characters, attitudes and gestures, arranged and frozen for an instant, provides a visual declaration of emotions.[59] We might read Juliette's own theatrical 'descent from the cross' as an example of such melodramatic arresting and composition.[60] It seems here that speech, become somehow inadequate, is discarded and narrative arrested in favour of a fixed and visual depiction. Juliette's fainting might be read as a moment of despair, a final, desperate recourse to inarticulate cry and gesture. It betrays 'a kind of fault or gap in the code, the space that marks its inadequacies to convey a full freight of emotional meaning. In the silence of this gap, the language of presence and immediacy, the primal language, is born anew'.[61] As such, it is connected to the 'ineffability' of what it expresses.[62] The melodramatic is a mode of excess: what Brooks calls 'the postulation of a signified in excess of the possibilities of the signifier'.[63]

So theatrical and extreme a 'tableau' is virtually Juliette's last opportunity for direct expression before she is entirely eclipsed, relegated to occasional traces in Alissa's letters to Jérôme – before that is, she is relegated to perhaps the most melodramatic genre of all, the discourse of muteness. For if melodrama 'suggests the dream world in its enactments, in its thrust to break through repression and censorship, in its unleashing of the language of desire, its fulfilment of integral psychic needs,' argues Brooks, 'the text of muteness in particular suggests expression of needs, desires, states, occulted imperatives below the level of consciousness'.[64] If Alissa and Jérôme are the privileged characters endowed with *logos*, Juliette incarnates a mute, bodily desire – perhaps the more pathetically, perversely expressed in the multitudinous children she bears the wrong man, Edouard – a desire occulted and displaced by the abstract cerebrality and renunciation that stifles the novel.

Understanding the despair of Juliette's fainting, its melodramatic rupture of signifying surfaces, alerts us to the danger of misreading Juliette – for further signs betray the heavy artifice, the staging, of Juliette's putative happiness. Juliette's own reaction upon meeting her future husband is eloquent: 'une espèce de Don Quichotte bon enfant, sans culture, très laid, très vulgaire, assez ridicule et devant qui la tante ne pouvait garder son sérieux' ['a sort of good-natured Don Quixote, uncultured, very ugly, very vulgar, somewhat ridiculous and before whom my aunt couldn't keep her composure'] is her assessment of Edouard. Juliette is indignant at

Jérôme's query as to such a man's chances of marrying her: 'Voyons, Jérôme! Tu plaisantes! Un négotiant! … Si tu l'avais vu, tu ne m'aurais pas posé la question' ['Come now, Jérôme! You're joking! A tradesman! … If you had seen him, you would not have asked such a question'] (p. 524). The absurdity of Juliette's engagement to Edouard is expressed in Alissa's stricken reaction; she cries to Jérôme, 'mais cela ne se peut pas. Mais elle ne l'aime pas! Mais elle me l'a dit ce matin même' [but it can't be. She doesn't love him! But she told me so this very morning!] (p. 539).

Juliette nevertheless disappears into apparent happiness, to return only at the end of Jérôme's narration – where we have a final opportunity to read her somewhat more directly. Showing Jérôme into a small room off her own bedroom, Juliette explains that she takes 'refuge' here, for in this, the most serene room of the house, 'Je m'y sens presque à l'abri de la vie' ['I feel almost sheltered from life'] (p. 597): a subtle indication that her putative happiness in fact obliges her to seek a haven.[65] Juliette's many pregnancies have not been without their burdens; she had great difficulty recovering from the most recent one in particular (p. 596). And, according to Jérôme, she seems to prefer this last little daughter, named after Alissa, to all her other children: an indication that her voluminous motherhood – again – may not have left her as radiantly happy as Alissa herself, along with others, may choose to believe.

Such misreading is precisely the mistaken reading espoused by Alissa and Jérôme, the face-value reading unable to recognise the theatrical props and script of Juliette's extreme sacrifice. For it is, of course, not incidental that Juliette's 'descent from the Cross' occurs at Christmas, the anniversary of Christ's birth. Juliette's cross, rather than Alissa's, would seem to be an ultimate guarantor of signification. Juliette would seem to be the sacrificed Christ, sacrificed on the cross of Jérôme and Alissa's cerebral pursuit of *logos*, the word as presence. But if Juliette has been read as what *is* sacrificed in the novel, she has not been recognised as the character who succeeds in *making* the supreme sacrifice. Whereas Alissa's sacrifice of Jérôme fails, as we have seen, Juliette's sacrifice of Jérôme succeeds: a sacrifice so complete that Alissa never recognises it as such. Such a level of sacrifice is one that Alissa cannot achieve, and we recall her searing expression of doubt over her own sacrifice of

Jérôme: 'ce sacrifice était-il réellement consommé dans mon coeur? Je suis comme humiliée que Dieu ne l'exige plus de moi. N'en étais-je donc point capable?' ['was this sacrifice truly accomplished in my heart? I feel humiliated that God was no longer requiring it of me. Was I not capable of it?'] (p. 582).

Moreover, readings that trivialise Juliette fail to account for the indisputable weight born by her return in the novel's closing scene: a scene that obliges us, at last, to recognise her sacrifice. For the fact that she reappears at the end of the novel is significant, as though to remind those readers who may have forgotten her to look again, more closely, at Juliette, 'whose unrequited love for [Jérôme] seems to have survived undiminished'.[66] We need to pursue further, however, the implications of this undying love. Without this scene, we might have been persuaded, as Alissa was, that Juliette's maternal and conjugal happiness was authentic. Yet Juliette's portentous, searing, ultimate question to Jérôme leaves no doubt as to her continued love for him: 'Alors tu crois qu'on peut garder si longtemps dans son coeur un amour sans espoir? … Et que la vie peut souffler dessus chaque jour sans l'éteindre?' ['So do you believe one can keep a hopeless love for such a long time in one's heart? … And that life can blow upon it every day without extinguishing it?'] (p. 597). The two are ostensibly discussing Jérôme's failure to love any woman other than Alissa. Yet again, Juliette's mute, somatic behaviour conveys a more searing truth, for she falls limply into a chair, covers her face with her hands and appears in the dusky obscurity to be weeping. We again recognise the somatic, melodramatic mode of pantomime as 'an important device toward the representation of conditions, concepts, forces held to be beyond the possibilities of rational apprehension and literal statement'.[67]

Reading this closing scene according to his Baudelairian intertextual model, Sonnenfeld argues that the answer to Juliette's poignant question is not Jérôme's 'yes', but rather, the novel's final image of a servant entering with a lamp: an image that, as Sonnenfeld points out, echoes Baudelaire's line, 'Ah! que le monde est grand à la clarté des lampes!' ['Ah! how large is the world, by lamplight!].'[68] While this final image is indeed 'beautiful and perplexing', as Sonnenfeld suggests, Kadish goes further to complete the link of light with Juliette as she notes the contrast between the darkness and the lamp, suggesting that 'Jérôme's remembrance of Alissa and the past [is] associated with night and obscurity … whereas Juliette's commitment to life is associated with light'.[69] But this particular light is not the radiant natural luminosity of sunny Provence; instead, such lamplight can be only a pallid, fallen imitation of Provençal sunlight. Lamplight is thus particularly appropriate as an emblem of 'sunny' Juliette's sacrifice: the wan pallor of married life with the wrong man. Moreover, in this specific scene, with Juliette's face obscured by dusk, the lamp illumines – both literally and figuratively – her mute, enduring love for Jérôme, now fully revealed in the splash of light upon her collapsed body in the chair. For the lamp can only reveal Juliette's face, implicitly confirming the tears that Jérôme was not sure, until that moment of illumination, he saw (p. 597). Cued by the melodrama of Juliette's mute 'descent from the Cross' collapse during the Christmas of her preposterous engagement to a man she didn't love, we recognise its somatic traces now, years later, as Juliette's strength twice deserts her; 'se laissant tomber dans un fauteuil' ['allowing herself to fall into an armchair'] (p. 597), she arises and takes a few steps, only to 'retomber comme sans force sur une chaise voisine' ['fall as though without strength upon a nearby chair'] (p. 598). Knowing of Gide's admiration for Caravaggio,[70] we think of the analogous collapse of that painter's 'Penitent Magdalene' upon a chair, with Juliette's own sensuous vivacity – both scorned and feared by Jérôme and Alissa – emblematised in her 'sinful' female body. Another 'repentant Madeleine', Georges de La Tour's 'Madeleine à la veilleuse'– a painting Gide considered 'si remarquable' ['so remarkable'] in his journal entry of 11 April 1948[71] – helps us imagine *La porte étroite*'s closing scene, with its splash of illuminating lamplight. Juliette's question to Jérôme about whether one can harbour an enduring love 'sans espoir' ['without hope'] seems captured in this *vanitas* painting, illuminating – with a single candle – a futility expressed by the skull La Tour's Madeleine holds in her lap.

We recall that Alissa's theatricality is dictated by a classical, tragic role, that of mythology's Dido. But we might now recall that Shakespeare's Juliet also dies for love. Given that Gide greatly admired Shakespeare[72] and did much – through his translations of

Anthony and Cleopatra and *Hamlet* – to foster appreciation for Shakespeare in France, Juliette's name cannot have been chosen at random. Moreover, Shakespeare figures explicitly in *La porte étroite*, quoted in one of Alissa's letters (p. 564); additionally, comparing Shakespeare to Racine, Gide decides that 'Shakespeare, sans doute, est plus humain' ['Shakespeare is probably more human'].[73] Could it be, then, that – overshadowed as she is by the weighty antiquity of mythic Alissa-Dido – Juliette's less stately, more human, Shakespearean role is nonetheless the ultimate theatre of renunciation? Alissa becomes the victim of her own pride, demanding for herself too extreme and exalted a role, and dies. Juliette's, however, is the secret, unwritten, untold truth of a theatre of renunciation. She lives in Provençal sunshine amidst emblems of fertility and happiness – yet she bears within herself, inscribed by her name, the Shakespearean Juliet's *Liebestod*. In her marriage and all its progeny with the wrong man, Gide's Juliette thus lives out a protracted variation of her Shakespearean predecessor's 'love-death'.

Any reading of Juliette as, in the words of one critic, 'the embodiment of love, fecundity and July',[74] dismisses her as readily as did Jérôme and Alissa. Such a reading fails to understand her – and to do her justice – as a more significant, more profound, sort of embodiment. She is the embodiment of the sacrifice that eluded Alissa; she is the most authentic *logos* in the novel, a somatic text in which words are made flesh. It is she, not Alissa, who has carried out the truly sacred act; Juliette thus deserves recognition as the one who *is*, ultimately, able to enter through the strait gate. Yet it is only in passing beyond a different strait gate, beyond that of *logos* as the word, that we ourselves learn to read Juliette's sacrifice. Excluded from the word – that is, from Alissa's journal and Jérôme's narrative – she nonetheless accedes to expression via the word as flesh. It is only once we learn to read the theatrical display of her self-displacing absence that Juliette's somatic text becomes legible.

Concluding with Juliette's heavily embodied display of disappearance prepares us to turn from the somatic displays and displacements of Part I to the wider, more abstract narrative practices of display and displacement in Part II. Here, we will study such dynamics in a 1927 novel by François Mauriac; a 1965 detective narrative by Sébastien Japrisot; and Marguerite Duras's

1984 autofiction, *L'Amant* (including its 1991 rewrite). Following upon Juliette's self-eclipsing, self-displacing display in *La porte étroite*, we will begin Part II by tracing the narration's effort to isolate, through display – thereby displacing – the threat posed by Thérèse Desqueyroux in Mauriac's eponymous novel.

Part II
Narrating Display, Narrating Displacement

Chapter Four
Framing Monstrosity in Mauriac's *Thérèse Desqueyroux*: 'Buried Hearts' and 'Filthy Bodies'

Expanding our exploration from somatic displays as displacement in Part I to narrative practices of display as displacement in Part II, we begin with François Mauriac's novel, *Thérèse Desqueyroux*[1] – where a narrating voice engages visual strategies to construe and display the eponymous heroine as monstrous. Despite the dismissal of Thérèse's case on the novel's opening page, the narrating voice presents her – 'frames' her, both literally and figuratively, as I will argue – as nonetheless monstrously criminal. Through a pattern of enforced display, largely accomplished through framing practices, Thérèse is isolated and 'monstrified' in various ways throughout the text. Although her meditation during the long journey back to the husband that she attempted to poison produces an obscure compassion in the reader – who comes to understand just why Thérèse was led to her crime – the narration itself works to block such sympathy. Thérèse is repeatedly construed as monstrous not only through an explicit lexicon, but, more subtly, a narration that manipulates representation and visibility to isolate her – appearing only to confirm Thérèse's monstrosity, whereas such a practice actively imposes it upon her. The 'limelight' thus forced upon Thérèse is indeed stolen, illicit: an unfounded imposition of visibility designed to indict her in the reader's mind. Indeed, such a link between hypervisibility and monstrosity inhabits the very etymology of the word 'monster', originally thought to come from the Latin 'monstrare': to show, to display, conveying notions of an unwelcome limelight, the construction of a 'monstrous' glare or visibility. More recently, however, suggests Huet, the word is thought to derive from 'monere', 'to warn'[2] – which carries its own implied visibility; for a warning involves a designation, an identifying and isolating of danger; to 'see' the glare of danger is to be warned.

Thinking about Mauriac's narrative, we realise that both meanings – on the one hand, showing or displaying; on the other hand, warning – are apt here as the narration works to construct Thérèse's monstrosity. Such a repressive narrating practice appears to cue the tenor of critical discourse, which only replicates the construction of Thérèse as monster. Although monsters are granted the privilege of having narratives, according to one of the novel's two prefatory, frame texts – one that implies that monsters have narratives because evil is interesting, whereas virtue is boring – Mauriac's narrator ultimately dispossesses Thérèse of her own narrative, through various practices involving display.

As the narrative opens following the dismissal of her case, Thérèse travels home to the husband she tried, on some obscure level, to poison.[3] During the long, nocturnal journey, she searches for an explanatory narrative to present to Bernard: an account of just why, exactly – however blindly, however obscurely – she tried to find out whether an earlier ailment had indeed been due to an accidental overdose of his medication. Yet Thérèse is ultimately made to reject her own narrative; to believe that there is no explanation, other than that she is 'monstrous'.[4] The reader, however, in following this confessional meditation comprising half the novel (yet recounted by the distancing third-person narrator), comes to find Thérèse's crime conceivable, understandable, perhaps almost forgivable – and comes to feel empathy and compassion for her. Yet, although Thérèse's case has been thrown out of court on the novel's opening page, a more insidious trial is only beginning. A narrative practice that judges Thérèse as monstrous – coercing Thérèse herself into embracing such a judgement and thereby shaping critical response against herself – invites our suspicions.

Just what repressive dynamic might be at work here between a masculinist narrating voice and a female heroine? For Thérèse's very materiality as cumbersome, out-of-place female body is emphasised on the novel's opening page; she descends the courthouse steps between her father and lawyer, who confer as though she were not there, inconvenienced by 'ce corps de femme' ['this woman's body'] they attempt to elbow aside (p. 20). This bothersome female corporeality, materially intervening to trouble a dialogue between men, points emblematically to the threat Thérèse represents for them. At once framed by the men's bodies on either side, yet pushed, manipulated, displaced by them in their effort to rid themselves of the troublesome barrier she poses, Thérèse incarnates – here on the courthouse steps – the threat that her own story becomes within the narrative, and which the narration works to contain and neutralise.[5] Increasingly construed as monstrous, she is – along with her story – isolated in a lime-lit glare, a hypervisibility that safely pinpoints and distances her. She stands out in disfigured images: hideous in a wedding dress that only emphasises an inhuman pallor (p. 37); an unrecognisable 'créature' ['creature'] while reading her sister-in-law Anne's letters describing her own, Anne's, discovery of the sexual passion that has eluded Thérèse (p. 41). Such obvious 'monstrification', however, is only the most apparent of the narration's strategies to pre-empt any possibility of humanising such a beast.

Hoping for Bernard's forgiveness, Thérèse – during the long journey home following the dismissal of her case – imagines him assuring her, 'Je comprends maintenant; lève-toi; sois pardonnée' ['I understand now; arise; be forgiven'] (p. 27). Yet she realises her folly upon seeing Bernard, a crude, uncomprehending caricature of the dull husband, inadvertently fostering the reader's empathy for Thérèse; not only does Bernard have no interest in hearing her confession, he essentially refuses to let her speak at all. Crueller still, however, Thérèse herself is made to believe that the arduous reconstruction effort occupying her journey home is ultimately 'une histoire trop bien construite [qui] demeurait sans lien avec la réalité' ['a story too well-constructed, without connection to reality'] (p. 82). Such rejection of her own confessional narrative is accompanied by an implicit capitulation, as she is made to embrace her community's reading of her crime in accepting that 'ils avaient raison de la considérer comme un monstre' ['they were right to consider her a monster'] (p. 82). In this cruel and culminating moment, Thérèse dismisses her own explanatory effort to come to terms with what led her to attempt to poison Bernard – embracing, instead, the 'monstrous' image of herself promoted by the narrating voice.[6]

Through what devices is Thérèse construed as monster for the reader, making monstrosity the only explanation for her crime? As we will see, the narrating voice sabotages Thérèse's confession. Not only is she relentlessly framed in ways that isolate and distance her, emphasising her otherness, she is made to reject her own account of what happened. No sooner is Thérèse granted a story, on the rather distasteful condition of being monstrous, than she is made to believe that it had no connection with what really happened. Following the narrator's lead, certain critics choose to emphasise 'Thérèse's inability to judge correctly and to narrate accurately', claiming that 'the long, carefully worked story does not hold together at all'.[7] As Joubert puts it, '[l]e texte donne à entendre que Thérèse se sait monstre' ['the text leads one to understand that Thérèse knows herself to be a monster'].[8]

The construction of Thérèse as monster begins as early as two frame texts that precede the narrative proper. We are reminded that the frame's function, in Derrida's Kant-inspired argument, has been understood as 'non pas de se détacher mais de disparaître, de s'enfoncer, de s'effacer, de se fonder au moment où il déploie sa plus grande énergie' ['not to detach itself but to disappear, to sink, to efface itself, to melt at the moment it deploys its greatest energy'][9] – and we will see the extent to which such disappearing, self-effacing 'grande énergie' is nonetheless surreptitiously at work in Mauriac's novel. The reader opens to an epigraph by Baudelaire, followed by an unsigned statement in an authorial voice, with both frame texts stressing Thérèse's monstrosity. The Baudelaire epigraph – an apostrophe to God, asking 'O Créateur! peut-il exister des monstres aux yeux de Celui-là seul qui sait pourquoi ils existent, comment ils se sont faits, et comment ils auraient pu ne pas se faire' ['O Creator! Can there exist monsters in the eyes of the One who alone knows why they exist, how they were created, and how they might not have been made'][10] – implies that only God understands 'monsters', having created them himself. For him alone, then, they are not monstrous; he alone, implies Baudelaire's epigraph, controls the infinitely divine and forgiving narrative that can 'de-monstrify' them: the sort of narrative that Thérèse herself fails to provide, hints Mauriac's novel, in her own confession.

In the second framing text – this one unattributed – an authorial-sounding voice proclaims Thérèse's monstrosity even more decisively, in pronouncing her 'plus odieuse encore' ['even more odious'] than all the author's other heroes. Women like Thérèse are compared to caged beasts: 'Que de fois, à travers les barreaux vivants d'une famille, t'ai-je vue tourner en rond, à pas de louve' ['How many times, behind the living bars of a family, have I seen you circling with she-wolf steps']. This authorial voice claims that virtue does not have a history, a narrative; on the other hand, pronounces the voice, 'je connais celle des coeurs enfouis et tout mêlés à un corps de boue' ['I know the one [story] of buried hearts joined to filthy bodies']. 'Buried hearts' and 'filthy bodies' *do* have narratives, by implication; unlike the dullness and insipidity of virtue, they have stories that merit telling. We realise that Thérèse is allowed a story *because* she is monstrous, hence interesting – for 'les "coeurs sur la main" n'ont pas d'histoire' ['the "hearts-on-their-sleeve" don't have stories']; virtuous, altruistic women are not worthy of narrative.

In the wake of such harsh, 'framing' judgements, Thérèse's story is shaped by further control and repression through various forms of display, recurring within the narrative as reactions to the threat posed by what in Thérèse is understood as 'female autonomy'.[11] Such threatening, subversive, feminine energy is traced to another 'monster', Thérèse's grandmother, whose own transgressive story is suppressed. Any trace – any portrait, any photograph – has been effaced, and Julie Bellade is known only for having departed one day (p. 21). Thérèse explicitly links herself to such a monstrous ancestry, imagining that, similarly, she might be obliterated from family history – that her own daughter, Marie, might not be allowed to 'retrouver dans un album la figure de celle qui l'a mise au monde' ['find in an album the face of she who had given birth to her'] (p. 21). Such an explicit lineage of maternal transgression (for the scandalous Julie Bellade is identified as Thérèse's *maternal* grandmother) is implicitly at work within the construction of Thérèse's monstrosity; '[s]ince the monstrous mother', argues Huet, 'erases the image of the real father, the monster can be seen as the most illegitimate of offspring'.[12] Monstrous offspring of a monstrous mother, Thérèse, in marrying Bernard, is – hints the narrating voice – seeking a refuge from her own monstrosity: 'elle voulait être rassurée contre elle ne savait quel péril' ['she wanted to be reassured against she knew not what peril'], an idea repeated as 'elle se sauvait' ['she was fleeing'] (p. 35).

Looking further at the ways in which Thérèse is construed as monstrous, we might notice transgressions coded as cross-gendered – confirming Cohen's argument that the monster's function is 'to call horrid attention to the borders that cannot, *must* not, be crossed'.[13] Masculine interests set Thérèse apart from other women of her class, designating her as different, other, aberrant – in tastes that run to passionate discussions of property evaluation, of land use and management, tenant farming, pine resin, turpentine (p. 35). Indeed, of a bourgeois, landed family, Thérèse is not indifferent to the prospect of uniting Bernard's property with her own. She smokes excessively – 'comme un sapeur' ['like a fireman'], an act seen as so artificial, so unnatural for a woman, as to be a pose (p. 34). She is not particularly maternal towards her daughter, Marie, provoking rumours that she is not overcome (or 'smothered', as the text puts it) by motherly feelings (p. 69). Her renowned intelligence is threatening for a husband, who must, according to social codes, be more educated than his wife (p. 31). With spiteful scorn, Bernard's housekeeper, Balionte, calls her 'cette garce' ['that bitch'] in an insult whose etymology from the word 'garçon' ['boy'] confirms the particularly cross-gendered cast of Thérèse's monstrosity (p. 90).

Yet such threats to gendered normativity are accompanied by assertions of the strange attraction that Thérèse exerts, a fascinating charm: 'on ne se demande pas si elle est jolie ou laide, on subit son charme' ['one doesn't ask whether she's pretty or ugly, one succumbs to her charm'] (p. 27). 'On ne peut pas prétendre qu'elle soit jolie, mais elle est le charme même' ['One can't claim that she's pretty, but she's charm itself'] (p. 105). Both transgressive and fascinating, the deep ambivalence that Thérèse provokes in others incarnates a monstrosity that, in Cohen's definition, 'lurks somewhere in that ambiguous, primal space between fear and attraction'.[14] Such ambiguity, suggests Cohen, with its mix of interdiction and fascination, 'can evoke potent escapist fantasies; the linking of monstrosity with the forbidden makes the monster all the more appealing as a temporary egress from constraint'.[15] Breaking all the oppressive codes of her landed bourgeois culture, Thérèse scandalises, yet also, through such monstrous behaviour, demonstrates the fragility and permeability of these codes, their availability to transgression; she thus becomes all the more dangerous as an implicit invitation to such 'egress from constraint', rendering her isolation and containment all the more urgent.

Framed by the text as perhaps most threatening, most dreadful of all, however, is Thérèse's refusal and scorn for normative male sexuality. Mauriac's evocation of her grim honeymoon with Bernard has been called 'one of his most famous' pages; unfortunately, however, it has given rise to a perception of Thérèse as 'frigid'.[16] The memory of her wedding night provokes only Thérèse's aversion, expressed in her pithy and decisive assessment: 'ce fut horrible' ['it was horrible'] – which the narrating voice proceeds to explain, offering a sombre and arresting image of Thérèse's discovery of passion: 'comme devant un paysage enseveli sous la pluie, nous nous représentons ce qu'il eût été dans le soleil, ainsi Thérèse découvrait la volupté' ['just as, before a countryside enshrouded under rain, we imagine what it might have been in sunshine, thus Thérèse made the discovery of voluptuousness'] (p. 38). Such a dismal initiation to conjugal sexuality is emphasised in Claude Miller's 2012 film by setting the wedding trip in an elegant yet oppressive Germany. As Thérèse looks out from a stifling and ponderous bedroom upon sheets of rain, it is – in an appropriate and ironic departure from the text – Bernard himself who suggests to her that one must imagine the landscape under sunshine (p. 38). For Thérèse, imagining sexual pleasure with such a husband is equally impossible.

This apparently sympathetic image of Thérèse's sexual despair, however, will be used against her by a narrating practice that seeks to isolate and label her as monstrous. In the midst of his own carnal rapture, Bernard often suddenly notices Thérèse 'comme sur une plage … rejetée, les dents serrées, froide' ['as though discarded upon a beach, teeth clenched, chilled'] (p. 39). During her wedding trip,

Thérèse melancholically anticipates married life with Bernard, 'comme une déportée qui s'ennuie dans un cachot provisoire est curieuse de connaître l'île où doit se consumer ce qui lui reste de sa vie' ['in the way that someone deported, languishing in a provisional prison, is curious about the island where what remains to her of life shall be spent'] (p. 39). Such perceptions, contributing to the construction of an 'unnatural', 'monstrous' Thérèse, must be recognised as cruelly male-centric. For any reader could be expected to sympathise with Thérèse's revulsion at Bernard's pig-like wallowing in his own pleasure, 'comme ces jeunes porcs charmants qu'il est drôle de regarder à travers la grille, lorsqu'ils reniflent de bonheur dans une auge' ['like the charming young pigs one is amused to observe through the fence, when they snort with happiness in a trough']. The narrative deepens this image by providing Thérèse's reaction: '"c'était moi, l'auge", songe Thérèse' ['"I was the trough", thinks Thérèse'] (p. 38). Yet, despite this depiction of Bernard as thoughtlessly wrapped up in his own gratification, some readers imply that Thérèse's aversion is really not so hard to understand, after all; it is simply sexual frigidity, defined by '[l]e refus violent, absolu, de la sexualité' ['the absolute and violent refusal of sexuality'] characterised by '[l]a défiance, la peur ou la haine de la sexualité' ['defiance, fear or hatred of sexuality'],[17] by her putative 'powerful repugnance for sexuality'.[18] 'One would be foolish,' suggests Edward Gallagher, in implicit summary of such a position, 'to try to explain away her aversion to conjugal sex as simply a reaction to the brutish insensitivity of her cloddish husband Bernard'.[19] What is not clear, however, is why the 'brutish insensitivity of her cloddish husband' is viewed as an insufficient explanation for Thérèse's 'aversion to conjugal sex'. Moreover, Gallagher subsequently admits that Bernard is 'a sexual sadist with Thérèse'; nonetheless, it seems, curiously, that 'brutish insensitivity', 'cloddish[ness]' and 'sexual sadis[m]' are not considered sufficient justification for Thérèse's 'aversion' to her husband.

An alternative explanation for what has been seen as Thérèse's 'frigidity' with Bernard might be an unacknowledged homoerotic attraction to her friend, Bernard's sister, Anne: a possibility that leads Diana Festa-McCormick to view Thérèse's repulsion of Bernard as the result of 'a jilted lover' pining for her beloved (Anne).[20] Similarly,

Timothy Williams explains Thérèse's resistance to sexual relations with Bernard as a consequence of her changed relationship with Anne.[21] In Williams's claim, Thérèse's dread 'equates the sexual act to a fundamental change in her relationship with her friend and rival'[22] for, as Mauriac's narrator puts it, the virginal Anne 'demeurait sur la rive ou attendent les êtres intacts' ['remained on the shore where intact beings wait'] (p. 37). Anne's dreams, like her virginity, are unscathed, provoking Thérèse's possible, bitter envy. Ultimately, however, Thérèse's repugnance seems too specifically justified by Bernard's brutish egotism to render credible such claims for its source in a disappointed relationship with Anne.

Yet such blanket, dismissive judgements become more sweeping in Garfitt's claim that Thérèse 'will be incapable of forming satisfying relationships'.[23] Joubert goes further in explicitly linking Thérèse's sexual alienation from Bernard to abnormality, even pathology and, by implication, monstrosity: 'Sans doute la question se pose-t-elle de l'entière normalité de la jeune femme … Si l'accord avec le réel est le premier signe de l'équilibre de la personnalité, Thérèse est-elle capable d'une pleine entente avec la réalité qui l'entoure?' ['The question might be posed of the young woman's complete normality … if consonance with reality is the first sign of a well-balanced personality, is Thérèse capable of full accord with the reality surrounding her?'].[24] Dismissing a homoerotic explanation, Joubert suggests that the tenderness of the girls' friendship is summarised by Thérèse's memory of it as an 'informe et chaste bonheur' ['vague and chaste happiness']. In Joubert's argument − which claims that all allusions to any ambiguous attachment to Anne have been removed from the final manuscript − homoeroticism would not suffice to explain Thérèse's physical aversion to her husband;[25] but with such dismissal of a homoerotic explanation, implies Joubert, no narrative other than monstrosity remains to account for Thérèse's repugnance towards Bernard.

In contrast to these readers, however, others acquire a powerful and empathetic sense of Thérèse's emotional desert and sexual despair. We feel the cruel blow, the bitter stab to the heart, as a honeymooning Thérèse reads the impassioned letters of her new sister-in-law, Anne, describing her own, Anne's, rapture at the very approach of physical intimacy with Jean Azévédo:

Chérie, quel est donc ce bonheur que tu possèdes aujourd'hui et que je ne connais pas encore, pour que la seule approche en soit un tel délice? … je sens le bonheur en moi, pareil à quelque chose que je pourrais toucher. Je me dis qu'il existe pourtant une joie au-delà de cette joie.

[My dear, what is this happiness that is yours today and that I don't yet know, such that its approach alone is so delicious? … I feel happiness within me, like something I could touch. I tell myself that there are nonetheless joys beyond this joy.] (p. 41)

Cruellest of all for Thérèse, perhaps, is Anne's assumption that Thérèse herself is enjoying the sexual fulfilment whose timid 'approach' Anne finds so exalting. Reading Anne's letter, this 'cantique des cantiques, cette longue plainte heureuse' ['this song of songs, this long and happy lament'] (p. 40), some readers might sympathise with Thérèse's violent reaction from within her bitter and barren honeymoon: sticking the picture of Anne's beloved, Jean, with a pin before flushing it down the toilet (p. 42). Far from questioning Thérèse's sanity, many readers will understand what prompts this act in Thérèse's effort to relieve her despair, loneliness, frustration and envy; as her story unfolds, such readers increasingly empathise with the very human panic and desperation leading to a gesture that seems less 'insane' than anguished, but pitifully ineffective.[26] A more dramatic and spectacular gesture of destruction occurs in Claude Miller's cinematic interpretation of the scene, however, where, rather than sticking a pin into it, Thérèse burns the photo of Jean Azévédo on her hotel-room dresser – in a blaze that alludes, as we will see, to the text's conflagration topos. Consonant with the text's own framing practices, Miller's film scene frames Thérèse in various ways: first, from within a round mirror resting on the dresser, then moving on to her reflection in the dresser's upright mirror. This sequence would seem to concentrate, isolate and display the violence of her act – which concludes in Thérèse's studying her own mirrored reflection in suspended, spectral immobility, yet again 'framed' and distanced by a display practice that safely sequesters, so as to emphasise, her 'monstrosity'.

Similarly, the text's narrating voice has no compassion for Thérèse's plight. As though to block any potential empathy, even the third-person narration of her own meditation on what led to her attempt to poison Bernard is regularly punctuated with reminders of Thérèse's monstrosity. The tranquillity of her engagement to Bernard, for instance, is cast as 'le demi-sommeil, l'engourdissement de ce reptile dans son sein' ['the somnolence, the drowsiness of this reptile in her breast'] (p. 36). Struck by Thérèse's pallor on her wedding day, the assembled guests blame her ugly, even 'affreuse' ['awful'] appearance, on her white gown, or on the day's heat. Other voices, however, are not so generous; the anonymous narrator, for example, claims pointedly, 'ils ne reconnurent pas son vrai visage' ['they didn't recognise her true face'] (p. 37) and likens Thérèse, alone at Argelouse during Bernard's hospitalisation and increasingly aware of mounting suspicion, to a 'bête tâpie qui entend se rapprocher la meute' ['a hidden beast who hears the crowd approaching'] (p. 73). Her husband (who, admittedly, might be forgiven for such a position) later judges her 'un monstre sans doute' ['a monster, probably'] (p. 81). Minutes before her interrupted suicide attempt, Thérèse kneels in front of her daughter's cradle, having read that those in despair occasionally take their children into death with them. Again, the narrating voice presses its point, indicating that Thérèse, as a monster, understands such monstrous acts: 'Parce qu'elle est un monstre, Thérèse sent profondément que cela est possible' ['Because she's a monster, Thérèse feels profoundly that such an act is possible'] (p. 84). As Thérèse pours chloroform into a glass of water (which would have killed her, had she not been interrupted), the narrator intones a request that God lovingly welcome 'ce monstre, sa créature' ['this monster, his creature'] (p. 85). Perhaps most cruel of all, Thérèse herself is made to admit to the monstrous power within her: 'Je n'ai jamais su vers quoi tendait cette puissance forcenée en moi et hors de moi: ce qu'elle détruisait sur sa route, j'en étais moi-même terrifiée' ['I have never known to what end this powerful force within me and beyond me tended: what it destroyed in its path; I was myself terrified by it'] (p. 26).

Ultimately, it is the insidious use of framing mechanisms – the prefatory texts being only the most visible example in a collection that includes Thérèse's distancing and isolation by the narration – that accomplishes Thérèse's displacement in setting her apart, designating her as other. The implicit purpose of such framing practices, argues Mary Ann Caws, is apparent in the ways in which such mechanisms work to isolate their subjects: '[t]he framed passage, by definition, stands out against the average one, or deep within it.' That is, suggests Caws, frames serve to separate, to isolate and set apart, rendering their contents other, different. '[W]e perceive, in the high picture so highly bordered, a peculiar delay and a singular arrest … The framed passage is, for everything that is ordinary, dispersed, and unorganized, the other.'[27]

Such 'othering' mechanisms manipulated by the narration prompt the reader to judge Thérèse with the same pompous dispatch and conviction as Bernard. She is often positioned, for example, within framing doorways and windows, even within human elbows – as we saw on the narrative's opening page when Thérèse, surrounded by her father and lawyer, emerged from within the framed doorway of the courthouse (p. 20). In the scene following Thérèse's return to Bernard after the dismissal of her court case, a scene in which his boorishness demonstrates how greatly Thérèse herself had overestimated him, she approaches and opens a window, a gesture that invites the reader to imagine her framed against it. Bernard, triumphant, looks at her: 'comme il la domine ce soir!' ['how he dominates her tonight!'] (p. 79), as though the window frame effectively isolates, contains and neutralises Thérèse, encouraging Bernard's feelings of domination and mastery. Attending church services with Bernard and his parents as an effort to mount a united, harmonious front in the public eye, Thérèse is carefully 'cernée' ['enclosed'] on all sides, with the crowd behind, Bernard to her right, Mme de la Trave to her left (p. 85). Such framing again serves effectively to localise and control the threat Thérèse incarnates, even as it would appear to confirm and display the danger she represents. For the frame, as Meyer Shapiro argues, is part of the observer's space; since it does not belong to the world depicted within the frame, but belongs to the space of the viewer, it emphasises the distance between the spectator and the depicted as 'a finding and focussing device placed between the observer and the image'.[28] In Mauriac's narrative, these relationships become particularly antagonistic. A frame, as Shapiro suggests, is not only complicitly allied with the viewer (in this case, the narrating voice); it actively opposes the framed contents, imposing not only distance between narrating voice and monstrous character in the case of Mauriac's narrative, but potential hostility on the part of the viewer.[29]

Indeed, the hostility of these framing practices is particularly apparent in the narration's manipulation of carceral images, such as cages. We have seen that, as early as the preface, the unidentified authorial voice describes women like Thérèse within 'les barreaux vivants d'une famille' ['the living bars of a family'] (p. 17): a caged-beast image within a frame of iron bars. With her wedding, indicates the narrator, Thérèse 'se casait' ['closed herself into position'] (p. 35); 'elle s'incrustait dans un bloc familial' ['she rooted herself within a family group'] (p. 35). However, the 'bloc familial' soon becomes a 'cage aux barreaux, cage tapissée d'oreilles et d'yeux' ['a cage with bars, one lined with ears and eyes'] (p. 44). The caged-beast metaphor for Thérèse recurs in an allusion to 'brancards' – or constraining wooden arms between which an animal is harnessed to pull a cart – as Bernard, his mother and their lawyer refer to their plan to 'release' Thérèse in Paris: 'il fallait que Thérèse sortît des brancards' ['Thérèse had to emerge from constraint'] (p. 99). Through such a cage topos, the framing mechanism becomes insidiously carceral, evoking entrapment and, implicitly, containment of the savage, monstrous beast.

Furthering the carceral thematic is a network of tunnel images; as Thérèse confesses in stream-of-consciousness fragments, 'je crus pénétrer dans un tunnel indéfini – crainte de l'asphyxie' ['I felt myself to be entering an endless tunnel – the fear of asphyxiation'] (p. 63). Leading up to the poisoning attempt and exhausted by caring for an ailing Bernard, Aunt Clara and her own child, '[Thérèse] traversait, seule, un tunnel, vertigineusement; elle en était au plus obscur; il fallait, sans réfléchir, comme une brute, sortir de ces ténèbres, de cette fumée, atteindre l'air libre, vite! vite!' ['[Thérèse] was traversing a tunnel, alone, vertiginously; she was at the darkest point; it was urgently necessary to get out of this darkness, this smoke, without thinking, like a brute, to reach the free air, quickly! Quickly!'] (p. 73). Such fear of asphyxiation implies the monstrosity of the 'brute' caught within the tunnel's cage. In this way, through a topos of carceral images – cages, tunnels, harnesses, 'the living bars of a family' – Thérèse is framed and isolated within the narrative: contained and confined as monstrous, dangerous energy, poised to explode.

Indeed, images of conflagration increasingly mark Thérèse's experience of her own 'madwoman in the attic' victimisation after Bernard confines her to her room. She dreams of rising one night and leaving the house to enter the forest's thick undergrowth, throwing her cigarette until an enormous smoky cloud covered the dawn sky (p. 70). The obscure beginnings of her project to poison Bernard coincide with the great fire at Mano, when 'le parfum de la résine brûlé imprégnait ce jour torride et le soleil était comme sali' ['the scent of burned resin filled the torrid day and the sun seemed dirtied'] (p. 71) in an emblem of Thérèse's clouded, exhausted lucidity. Continuing the conflagration thematic, she asks Bernard to burn all pictures of her (p. 77). In anticipating Bernard's return to their home with Anne and her fiancé, Thérèse struggles at the end of her imprisonment to come back to life, to eat, to walk – as though returning to a countryside devastated by a fire that she herself had caused. '[E]t comme elle fût revenue dans une lande incendiée par elle, qu'elle eût foulé cette cendre, qu'elle se fût promenée à travers les pins brûlés et noirs, elle essaierait aussi de parler, de sourire au milieu de cette famille – de sa famille' ['And as though she had returned to a countryside she had burned, had walked upon its ashes, had strolled through the burned, blackened pines, she would try to talk to smile, amidst this family – her family'] (p. 94).

As Mauriac was well aware, such a constellation of monstrosity and incineration framing Thérèse is shared by her literary ancestor, Racine's Phèdre – whose tragic lucidity holds her love for stepson Hippolyte to be monstrous. In the long tirade confessing her love to him, Phèdre asks that he '[d]élivre l'univers d'un monstre qui t'irrite' ['deliver the universe of a monstrous irritation'] (line 701), of a 'monstre affreux' ['an atrocious monster'] whose appalling, incendiary love ignites the tragedy. Afflicted by her 'folle ardeur' ['mad passion'], Phèdre burns with a 'feu fatal' ['fateful flame'] (line 680), 'un feu qu'il vous faudrait éteindre' ['a flame you must extinguish'] as her maidservant and confidante Oenone tries to insist (line 754); yet Phèdre's 'ardeurs insensés' ['senseless ardour'] (line 765), her 'flamme adultère' ['adulterous flame'] (line 841); 'feu mal étouffé dans [s]on cœur' ['unextinguished flame in her heart'] (line 1194), 'la fureur de [s]es feux' ['the furore of her flames'] (line 1228) are such that, she laments in self-loathing horror, 'mon époux est vivant et moi je brûle encore!' ['my husband lives and yet I still burn!'] (line 1266). Beyond the play's explicit allusions to her monstrosity and the flames of her destructive passion, framing practices that isolate and 'monstrify' Phèdre are apparent in stage productions. In one example, the closing death scene stages Phèdre expiring while standing upright against a backdrop of tall, narrow window frames looking onto the sea.[30] The décor of these repeating, elongated frames aligned across the stage only seems further to dwarf and isolate the lonely, dying body, rendering it other, alien, monstrous. Analysing the relationship between a body and the space around it, Shapiro claims that such a space is perceived as 'belonging to the body and contributing to its qualities. For the aesthetic eye the body, and indeed any object, seems to incorporate the empty space around it as a field of existence'.[31] In this way, a body alone in space – like Thérèse's, in the text's carceral scenes – absorbs the loneliness and solitude of its surroundings, thus assuring its isolation.

Thérèse's 'framing' continues with enforced confinement to her room on Bernard's orders, once the community has been led to believe her slightly 'neurasthénique' ['neurasthenic'] (p. 79). This imprisonment, marked by Thérèse's feverish reveries, indifference to food and increasing detachment from reality – 'elle crut avoir dit merci; en vérité, aucun son n'était sorti de ses lèvres' ['she believed herself to have said thank you; in fact, no sound emerged from her lips'] (p. 92) – evokes the sequestration of another 'madwoman in the attic', *Jane Eyre*'s Bertha Mason.[32] Such an association may perhaps be deliberately sought by filmmaker Claude Miller's staging of Thérèse's confinement in what is clearly an attic room, dominated by the protruding walls that frame a recessed dormer window. Setting the camera directly opposite this sole window, the film shows Thérèse walking towards its light in dark silhouette. Severely framed by a distance that dwarfs her between the alcove's projecting walls, Thérèse is further set off by a wardrobe mirror that reflects the scene, creating an effect of repeating frames. Her darkened figure within the harsh frames created by the alcove's protruding side walls effectively isolates and dehumanises Thérèse, contributing to the effect of monstrosity and madness. A long shot resting on the stained, cracked and peeling alcove walls appears to point to Thérèse's own physical deterioration and growing madness within such confines.

Miller's film effectively manipulates framing shots in other ways. When both the ailing Bernard and daughter Marie are removed from proximity to Thérèse, Miller positions the camera on the other side of the car about to bear Marie away from her 'monstrous' mother. From this position, looking through both window frames from the opposite side of the car, the spectator observes Thérèse emerge from the house to bring the departing child a stuffed toy. Enclosing Thérèse within the car's two window frames, made by perspective to appear concentric, the shot's manipulation of the mechanics of display effectively isolates and distances her.

Such isolation is also emphasised in the film's interpretation of Thérèse's meditative return to Argelouse following the final courthouse scene in which her case is dismissed. Miller has Thérèse study her reflected image framed in a car window as she briefly imagines a sympathetic and forgiving Bernard. Appearing quickly to realise the folly of such an illusion, she smacks her gloved hand against her reflection in a gesture of angry despair: a scene that perhaps too briefly and ambiguously implies the rejection of her own narrative, a rejection detailed by the text. For in the novel itself, as we have seen, this meditative journey back to Argelouse is the setting for Thérèse's effort to construct an explanatory narrative of her own in a searching confession before she is ultimately made to reject her account as 'sans lien avec la réalité' ['without connection to reality'] (p. 82). The film dramatises Thérèse's angry and frustrated dismissal of her own confession as the scene culminates in her angry blow to her own framed reflection, a specular and framed scene that would seem to encourage, through its hostility and rage, a 'monstrous' reading; yet so human a reaction instead encourages the viewer's empathy at Thérèse's self-rejecting outburst.

Such 'monstrous' framing of Thérèse culminates in the scene of Bernard's return, after a month's absence, accompanied by his mother, sister Anne, and Anne's fiancé – who claims he wishes to call on Thérèse, as his future sister-in-law. But, as Bernard suspects, the fiancé really wants to assess the authenticity of Bernard and Thérèse's marriage – and thereby, the respectability of his intended's family – following the hushed-up poisoning attempt and trial. The group has arrived, Thérèse has been summoned, and all await her in the salon as – pitiful, emaciated, feverish – Thérèse slowly descends the stairs. 'Comme elle descend lentement l'escalier! Ils sont tous debout, tournés vers la porte que Thérèse ouvre enfin' ['How slowly she descends the stairs! They're all on their feet, turned towards the door that Thérèse finally opens'] (p. 95). The scene's impact is further underscored – indeed, further framed – by the foreshadowing of its future effect on Bernard, who was to remember, many years later, the approach 'de ce corps détruit, de cette petite figure blanche et fardée' ['of this destroyed body, of this little white and made-up face'] (p. 95). We are thus cued to imagine the impact of Thérèse's apparition as she emerges, a grotesque wraith framed in the doorway, with all eyes upon her. Emphasising the doorframe, the Miller film underscores the distance, literal and figurative, between Thérèse and her husband's family by opening the scene with a shot showing Thérèse from behind, framed in the doorway, the family distantly visible and aligned in an opposing phalanx in the room beyond. The camera then jumps to frame Thérèse anew within the doorway – this time, however, positioned in front of her, and replicating the family's viewpoint as the group watches for her to appear; these symmetrical paired shots each imprison her within the doorway, producing an effect of immobilised alterity. The second shot, moreover, reveals Thérèse's grotesquely made-up face, shocking the viewer with its corpse-like pallor. Although the text explicitly emphasises the pitiful aspect of the spectacle when the family reacts with 'étonnement et pitié' ['astonishment and pity'], Miller's film scene exposes the monstrous effect created by the narrative's framing mechanism. Ostensibly inviting compassion ('pitié'), both narrative and film act insidiously to isolate Thérèse, marking her as different, other – not so much pitiful as monstrous.

Thérèse will be given a last opportunity to make a confession, however, when Bernard, having accompanied her to Paris, is about

to leave her to her new life. In a curious moment of openness and
vulnerability for Bernard, he asks Thérèse directly, for the first time:
'Je voudrais savoir … C'était parce que vous me détestiez? Parce
que je vous faisais horreur?' ['I would like to know … was it because
you detested me? Because I appalled you?] (p. 101). Such a return
to a confessional mode, brings with it – this time – a more
auspicious, more hospitable setting, prompted by the open, honest
question Bernard is finally able to ask. Here is an invitation for
Thérèse to admit the simple truth; yes, Bernard himself was the
monster, albeit innocently and uncomprehendingly. Yet again,
however, Thérèse is made to renounce her own effort to understand
her crime. She explains to Bernard, 'Si vous saviez à quelle torture
je me suis soumise pour voir clair … Mais toutes les raisons que
j'aurais pu vous donner, comprenez-vous, à peine les eussé-je
énoncées, elles m'auraient paru menteuses' ['If you knew what
torture I have endured to understand … But all the reasons I might
have given you, don't you see, scarcely would I have pronounced
them than they would have seemed false'] (p. 102). Thérèse is
unaware of just why these reasons she might have given Bernard
'would have seemed false'; as the reader now realises, however, their
'falseness' has little to do with these reasons themselves, nor with
Thérèse. Rather, such falseness lies within the repressive climate of
reception her reasons might find, emblematised by the caricature
of a crude, boorish, uncomprehending husband; Thérèse's reasons
thus sound false to her because she is explaining them to
uncomprehending ears. The narrator would have us conclude that
there is simply no coherent explanation for Thérèse's crime; that, as
a 'créature odieuse', a 'monstre', she is fatefully condemned to do
evil.[33] However, through the confession Thérèse herself ultimately
rejects as 'sans lien avec la réalité', the attentive reader, increasingly
sceptical of the harsh narrating voice, comes to understand Thérèse's
crime – and therefore, I argue, to empathise.[34] Confronted with a
second self-rejection by Thérèse at the end of the novel, when –
yet again – she refuses her own explanation for her crime, the reader
feels only sympathy and compassion for such a 'criminal'.

Our compassion increases with Thérèse's realisation that what
attracted her most was not the land itself with its pines, consonant
with the bourgeois masculinist value of acreage. Rather, it was 'les

êtres de sang et de chair' ['beings of flesh and blood']: 'Le gémissement des pins d'Argelouse, la nuit, n'était émouvant que parce qu'on l'eût dit humain' ['The groaning of pines at Argelouse, at night, was only moving because one might have thought it human'] (p. 106). After her lonely childhood, what Thérèse most craved was not land and bourgeois ownership, which Bernard provided, but true companionship, which he couldn't offer. Thérèse's rejection of her own confession would seem to exemplify Freeman's notion of 'internalized oppression, one of the principal strategies through which patriarchy reproduces itself' and through which 'women learn to do to themselves and other women what society has done to them'.[35] Ultimately, Mauriac's novel explores the brutal power of patriarchal social codes through the 'monstrification' of Thérèse, while nonetheless arousing compassion and empathy for her on the reader's part. In dynamic tension throughout the novel, these two opposing constructions of Thérèse culminate, as detailed above, in the scene of her stairway descent and doorway-framing before the hostile gaze of her husband's family; both pitied as victim – not only by her readers, but even by Bernard and relatives – yet framed as monstrous, Thérèse acquires a complexity and stature worthy of her literary ancestor, Racine's Phèdre.

However, as we close the novel, the back cover of Grasset's paperback editions carries out a final injustice in the construction of Thérèse; as though, both victim and monster, she had acquired too much complexity by the narrative's close, the synopsis on Grasset's back cover would seem implicitly to eliminate her altogether.[36] The novel's title, of course, emphasises that this is Thérèse's narrative; and, as we saw above, the preface suggests that only monsters have stories, because virtue is boring. Yet the paperback cover robs Thérèse not only of her own explanatory account, but even of her story itself; for the back cover presents the narrative as *Bernard*'s, not Thérèse's. In this brief summary, most active verbs take Bernard as their subject.

> Pour éviter le scandale et protéger les intérêts de leur fille, Bernard Desqueyroux, que sa femme Thérèse a tenté d'empoisonner, dépose de telle sorte qu'elle bénéficie d'un

non-lieu. Enfermée dans la chambre, Thérèse tombe dans une prostration si complète que son mari, effrayé, ne sait plus quelle décision prendre. Doit-il lui rendre sa liberté?

[To avoid scandal and protect their daughter's interest, Bernard Desqueyroux, whom his wife attempted to poison, succeeds in having her case dismissed. Sequestered in her room, Thérèse falls into a prostration so complete that her husband, frightened, no longer knows what to decide. Should he free Thérèse?]

Such a summary presents the central interest of the novel as a decision to be taken by Bernard, as a dilemma of *his*: the issue of whether he should, or should not, free Thérèse from her marriage to him. Having concluded the narrative with the conviction that Thérèse is not really so monstrous, after all, we feel an obscure compassion for her; but as we close the novel, our final impression of Thérèse's story is that it is ultimately not even her own. As we have seen, the narrative opens with Thérèse 'framed' as monstrous, yet, at least, granted a narrative of her own on the basis of such monstrosity; for we recall that the novel's second, anonymous frame text – a text following the Baudelaire epigraph – implies that whereas virtue is too dull to be worthy of recounting, monstrosity merits a narrative. Yet Thérèse is repeatedly made to deny her own story, with the synopsis on the back cover bringing the final blow in stripping her of her story altogether; it has become Bernard's, not Thérèse's.[37]

In the next chapter, dynamics of display and displacement produce a different outcome. Rather than the successful occulting of a threatening, ambiguously gendered energy through narrative tactics of enforced, isolating display, these dynamics will work to opposite effect. In Sébastien Japrisot's detective novel *Piège pour Cendrillon* ['Trap for Cinderella'], the masculinist genre on display is surreptitiously displaced by a covert feminine between-the-lines scenario of what one character scornfully calls 'une histoire de filles' ['girl stuff']. The very scaffolding of the detective genre – as displayed in this novel – depends upon residual, normatively masculinist, Cartesian values involving binary either/or logic:

unambiguous solutions, such as definitive identity, reached through 'macho' values modelled on the hunt's dynamics of pursuit and capture in the virile detective's relentless tracking of the truth. *Piège pour Cendrillon*, however, manipulates such display precisely to construct a trap not only for its 'Cinderellas' (the three main female characters), as the title announces, but also for its readers. As we saw in Chapter One with Colette's novel *Le blé en herbe*, it is precisely through manipulation of feminine display that such masculinist generic norms are not only displaced, but dismantled.

Chapter Five
'Girl Stuff':
Genre, Masquerade and
Displacement in Japrisot's
Piège pour Cendrillon

In contrast to the confident masculinist narration displaying and displacing Thérèse herself in Mauriac's novel, Sébastien Japrisot's 1965 detective fiction, *Piège pour Cendrillon* features a reversal of this dynamic; here, a gendered-as-masculine script, its virile quest for answers bathed in limelight, is itself surreptitiously displaced by covert feminine energies.[1] A brilliant example of the detective genre, the novel involves an inheritance, murder, mistaken identities and amnesia. As it induces us to search for answers to its enigmas, Japrisot's narrative thus privileges rationality, analysis, logic: elements of an intellectual quest. Indeed, the novel's claim to these elements is flamboyant; it proudly displays the features that make it, in Shoshana Felman's claim, likely to be the most 'literarily remarkable' detective novel written in French, seducing readers into casting it precisely as an example of that genre.[2] Yet the novel is also a love story, and a homoerotic love story, at that: an improbable fairy tale that unfolds insidiously, surreptitiously, from within the very detective enterprise itself of intellection and rationality. In this way, what Uri Eisenzweig considers a decentred, marginal genre – that of detective fiction – is itself, in turn, displaced, decentred, by a narrative that ultimately fractures generic definitions.[3] The ultimate 'trap' of the novel – the 'piège' announced as early as its very title – is thus to read it precisely according to its own overt and persuasive claims: as a detective novel. It seduces us through the very theatricality with which it displays the codes and plays the role of a detective fiction – yet all the while, I argue, engaging in a surreptitious takeover that ultimately displaces the very genre it appears so brilliantly to illuminate and exemplify. For genres, as Jameson defines them, 'are essentially literary *institutions*, or social contracts between writer and a specific public whose function is to specify the proper use of a particular cultural artefact'. Jameson goes on to specify the fragility of this contractual situation, a fragility that generates an anxious need to programme and receive the right response: '[n]o small part of the art of writing, indeed, is absorbed by this (impossible) attempt to devise a foolproof mechanism for the automatic exclusion of undesirable response to a given literary utterance'.[4] Yet, in a genre-bending discourse, *Piège's* trap is precisely to *appear* to programme – masterfully – 'the automatic exclusion of undesirable response', even as it subtly encourages and validates this 'undesirable response': an oxymoronic accomplishment that ultimately dissolves the very possibility of generic definition and boundaries. Articulating this 'undesirable' readerly response, with its ethic of transgression and co-optation, is the project of this chapter. It is the insistence, the persistence, of the undesirable – the undesirable genre, the undesirable past, the undesirable identity, the undesirable hysterical behaviour – that will repeatedly surface in *Piège pour Cendrillon* as the return of the repressed: the persistence of an interdicted desire. The persistence of the desiring, or wish-fulfilment genre – the fairy tale – within the rational, analytic detective genre yields a complex genre-defying text that succeeds, simultaneously, in both offering and refusing conformity to two contradictory genres. Such 'hysterical' combining of opposing genres beyond generic borders and definition ultimately dismantles the masculinist script of intellection, displacing it in favour of a 'feminised' genre: the love story. Although Japrisot's detective narrative, lavishly displayed, concludes – in conformity with its genre – with an ostensibly satisfactory solution, the alert reader realises that this solution has also been discreetly and efficiently displaced – whereas other readers, however, less aware of such undermining, come away with the satisfaction of closure. In this way, the limelight bathing the detective genre's display of its features is surreptitiously stolen by the text's covert love story – so craftily, so intricately, however, that many readers close the book on what may appear to be the triumphant conclusion of the (insidiously displaced) detective quest.

Having survived the fire that killed her friend, Japrisot's amnesiac heroine has been so disfigured as to be physically unidentifiable. She herself is forced to wonder, along with the novel's readers, who she is – that is, which of the two friends – 'Mi' (Michèle) or 'Do' (Domenica) – died and which survived. Furthermore, as the survivor and her readers eventually discover, the deadly fire was not an accident, but a murder attempt: one girl's effort to kill the other, her friend. The mystery of the survivor's identity is thus further compounded by other questions. Whichever of the two girls the amnesiac survivor turns out to be, is she the murderer, or the victim who survived the murder attempt? And why would one friend have plotted to kill the other, to begin with?

As a peerless specimen of the detective genre, *Piège pour Cendrillon* cues us to believe that perfect knowledge of the crime – the unambiguous solution – is to be found. It is out there and available, if we are only clever enough to solve the mystery with the account – the narrative – that perfectly matches the crime. Formulating this implication as the 'superposition parfaite de l'interprétation sur l'action' ['perfect superposition of interpretation upon action'], Tzvetan Todorov describes the 'coïncidence', or match, of narrative explanation upon event in which '[l]'enquête disparaît devant le crime dévoilé' ['the inquest disappears before the crime unveiled']. Todorov points to the character George Burton, prolific detective-novel writer in Michel Butor's *L'emploi du temps* (translated into English as '*Passing Time*'), who compares the interpretive, explanatory account to a second murder.[5] The first deadly crime, committed by the assassin, is merely the occasion for the second, in which the assassin himself or herself, suggests Butor's character, 'est la victime du meurtrier pur et impunissable, du détective' ['is the victim of the pure and unpunishable murderer, the detective'].[6] That is, just as the assassin has murdered, so the second, intellectual killer – the detective – in turn 'murders' the assassin in laying bare the crime. To accomplish this second murder, the detective's account must correspond perfectly to events of the crime itself – must perfectly match the action, just as Cinderella's prince must find the exact foot, and fit, for the mysterious, abandoned glass slipper. Yet, the Cinderella reference in Japrisot's title invites us to note that even as it claims to be a detective novel, the narrative also engages the genre of the fairy tale: a curious partnership indeed, for the two genres appear to be mutually exclusive. Whereas the detective genre privileges analysis, reason, logic and history – its effort being to reconstruct the truth of an occulted past – the fairy tale privileges the fantastic and fanciful, dream and wish-fulfilment: all that is often precisely opposed to the truth. Moreover, in further contrast to the detective narrative's effort to elucidate a mysterious past – implicitly working back towards an unknown source or origin – the fairy tale works ahead, towards an outcome (typically, a happily-ever-after ending) generally long known in advance by its audience. We become increasingly aware, therefore, that against the analytic quest for truth and identity in Japrisot's narrative, runs a countervailing energy, animated by a kind of fairy-tale desire.

To begin to trace the work of this countervailing desire within *Piège*, we might wonder about the implications for the survivor of the mystery's solution. Regardless of her biological identity, if it turns out that she indeed murdered her friend, will she *want* to accept such knowledge? Wouldn't anyone prefer instead to deny such a truth, in favour of a more acceptable, more complimentary and flattering, more wish-fulfilling role? Indeed, the survivor's amnesia is ultimately diagnosed as deliberate, elective: a frantic refusal to remember (p. 163). The analytic quest is thus blocked by a desiring energy, and a desperate one; as the heroine herself realises, '[l]'amnésie était une fuite. Si je ne me rappelais pas, c'est que pour rien au monde, pauvre petit ange, je n'aurais supporté de me rappeler' ['the amnesia was an escape. If I didn't remember, it's that I couldn't have stood remembering, poor little angel, not for anything in the world'] (p. 155).

As we begin to trace this tension between detective narrative and love story, between the search for truth and the resistance to truth – a resistance expressed as the desire for wish-fulfilment – we realise that the 'trap' in the title is our first hint that appearances may be deceptive: that the 'truth' of this detective novel may lie within the far older genre of the fairy tale. It may thus somehow involve what is culturally coded as feminine, becoming what a male character calls derisively, 'une histoire de filles', or 'a girl story' (perhaps more colloquially, and more effectively registering scorn, 'girl stuff') (p. 186): a 'story' that turns out to be a love story, running counter to the imperatives of the detective quest. Indeed, the character's scornful 'girl stuff' accusation captures the 'undesirable' readerly response identified by Jameson in his analysis of genre;[7] implicit to the detective genre is that no 'girl stuff' like love stories should contaminate its pure, intellectual, macho valences. Yet we begin to discern the possible work within the narrative of 'girl stuff', or a love story – a fairy-tale narrative – when the surviving amnesiac surprises a glance from Jeanne – a slightly older, governess figure – and realises, 'qu'elle m'aimait de toutes ses forces' ['that she loved me with all her strength'] (p. 90). When Jeanne, also involved in the murder plot, is queried as to whether her motive was the fortune that stood to be gained, she hints at this love in her reply: 'non, non, je n'en pouvais plus, je me moquais bien de l'argent, tais-toi, je t'en supplie' ['no, no, I couldn't bear it any longer, I could have cared less about the money, be quiet, I beg you'] (p. 211). The survivor indeed ultimately understands that the fortune itself was not the real reason for the crime, but a convenient pretext, a smokescreen, for a crime of passion. For although Jeanne's love for Mi – the real motive – was returned by Mi, it was as 'complete' adoration (pp. 120–1) for the woman serving as surrogate mother, big sister, mentor and governess to Mi, rather than as object of erotic desire. Yet, when Mi laments to Do that 'Jeanne était perdue pour elle à jamais' ['Jeanne was lost to her forever'] (p. 140), or, when, having had a bit to drink, Mi talks of Jeanne (p. 146), we understand that the relationship had become problematic, though we do not know why. Ultimately, we discover the reason when Jeanne claims that 'il ne s'est rien passé, rien, une bêtise, un baiser, rien, un baiser, mais elle n'a pas compris, elle n'a pas compris' ['nothing happened, nothing, a silliness, a kiss, nothing, a kiss, but she didn't understand, she didn't understand'] (p. 211). Jeanne's unwelcome kiss – following which, laments Jeanne, Mi couldn't stand being near her (p. 211) – changes the relationship between herself and Mi in ways that Jeanne ultimately cannot bear: 'je n'en pouvais plus' ['I couldn't stand it any longer'] (p. 211). Ironising the trope of the prince's life-giving, transformative kiss in, for instance, the 'Sleeping Beauty' tale, Jeanne's romantic but unrequited kiss in Japrisot's deadly fairy tale becomes the source of the murder plot conceived by a rejected and forlorn Jeanne. Symmetrically, Mi's reasons to appropriate the plot (murdering her friend Do so as to impersonate her) to her own ends are based – as we come to realise – on her enduring but filial love for Jeanne, and not her desire for the fortune. The amnesiac survivor ultimately understands what, if she indeed is Mi, might have led her to plot to kill Do so as to impersonate her: 'pour retrouver je ne sais quelle tendresse perdue, celle de Jeanne' ['to regain I don't know what kind of lost tenderness, Jeanne's']: that is, to recover – from within the utterly different identity of being someone else – some sort of emotional bond and closeness with the woman who had essentially raised her, with the troubled past of Jeanne's unwelcome advances now erased (p. 214). In this way, for Mi – as for Jeanne – the fortune is merely the outward pretext for a crime secretly motivated, instead, by love between women: indeed, 'une histoire de filles', or 'girl stuff'.

Following the account of the deadly fire occurring in the original crime of passion, the love story is renewed by an additional such crime: the survivor's murder of Serge Reppo – who knows that the fire was criminal rather than accidental – to prevent him from denouncing Jeanne. Driving away from this new, second, murder scene, the survivor thinks, 'maintenant, on ne pourra plus inquiéter Jeanne, elle me prendra dans ses bras, elle me bercera jusqu'à ce que je m'endorme, je ne lui demanderai rien que de continuer à m'aimer' ['now, no one can trouble Jeanne any longer, she'll take me in her arms, she'll rock me until I fall asleep, I'll ask nothing of her but to go on loving me'] (p. 209). The survivor's love for Jeanne suffices to establish the probability of such fierce, powerful feelings *before* the deadly fire, adding further weight to the love story. Other indications demonstrate the survivor's love for Jeanne; she decides at one point, 'Je remettrais mon passé, mon présent et mon avenir entre ses mains' ['I'll put my past, my present and my future in her hands'] (p. 92). Later, at Cap Cadet, the survivor tells Jeanne, 'j'aurais voulu, de toutes mes forces, me souvenir et l'aider. Je lui dis que j'aimais bien ma voiture bleu ciel et tout ce qui venait d'elle' ['I would have liked, with all my strength, to remember and to help her. I told her that I liked my sky-blue car and everything that came from her'] (p. 170). Despite her deadly attempt to revenge herself for Mi's unrequited love,

Jeanne still loves the survivor, as we see when she ultimately denounces herself in order to protect the girl; the survivor is presented as Mi in order to ensure that Jeanne, as Mi's governess, be viewed as the most culpable. 'Si j'étais Micky, la peine qu'on m'infligerait serait plus légère. Elle était ma gouvernante. Ce serait donc elle la vraie coupable' ['If I were Micky, the punishment inflicted on me would be lighter. She was my governess. She would thus be the truly guilty one'] (p. 213).

Such love between the two women is what begins to trouble any reading of the novel as a detective quest for solutions: a search for answers to the crime and, beyond that, the answer to the mystery of the survivor's identity. For such identity-quest readings draw on the Oedipal myth of self-discovery as the revelation of a criminal past. One problem for these readings, however, is the extreme father/son emphasis in the Oedipus myth, with its marginalisation of the feminine; as Mulvey points out, in the Oedipal paradigm, 'desire for the mother is more significant as a symptom of father/son rivalry'.[8] Yet Japrisot's novel, I am suggesting, invokes – beyond its visible embracing of the masculine detective genre – not myth, or Oedipus's genre, but the 'feminised' genre of the fairy tale – Cinderella's genre – as announced in the Cinderella allusion in its title.

One might notice, it is true, that the fairy tale contains similar elements to those of myth: a certain agelessness, a universality.[9] That is, the fairy tale may contain the same psychic resonance that, for Freud, explained the power of myth; like myth, the fairy tale's universality may provide a sort of template in which we each recognise our own truths. Yet the fairy tale, with certain strongly feminine codes, may offer a feminine alternative to what seems overbearingly masculine in the Oedipus myth. Indeed, the strongly feminine sense sedimented in fairy tales is perhaps the trace of their origins as oral, matriarchal folk tales having undergone subsequent 'patriarchalisation'; as Zipes argues, symbols originally based on matriarchal rites and emphasising maturation and integration were progressively redirected to emphasise wealth and authority.[10] Unlike Bruno Bettelheim, however, Zipes departs from the notion of fairy tales as psychic templates, expressive of universal conditions,[11] in order to emphasise the ideological exploitation of the fairy tale by social interests. Emerging from folk culture, shaped by desire, emblematic of peasant aspirations and wishful beliefs, the fairy tale is appropriated to become a legislative social tool, having much to do with power and oppression. Such appropriation or 're-codification' of the tales towards powerfully repressive ends is particularly apparent in the context of French courtly society and its imperative of 'civilité', or politeness. With his seventeenth-century collection of fairy tales, Charles Perrault, in particular, engineers what Zipes calls the 'literary "bourgeoisification" of the oral folk tale'.[12] The desire coded in the folk tale, while originally understood as fantasy, as wish-fulfilment, eventually becomes the index of ideological manipulation and struggle; such desire becomes prescriptive, coercive − as Zipes puts it, 'internalized, potent, explosive'.[13]

To retrace such cultural, social and moral manipulation in the case of the Cinderella tale, we might turn to Zipes's claim for Perrault's 'hostility toward the pagan folk tradition and fear of women'. Citing the strongly matriarchal tradition within which the various oral Cinderella tales emerged, Zipes contrasts Perrault's passive character with a rebellious, active, folk Cinderella, availing herself of her wits to reach her goal: not marriage with the prince, but recognition. For this folk Cinderella, suggests Zipes, her wedding becomes 'symbolically an affirmation of her strong independent character'.[14] The Grimm brothers' version of the tale presents just such a dynamic, resourceful heroine, without fairy godmother and coach, and who establishes her own curfew. In this version, the evil stepsisters cut off parts of their own feet to fit the slipper, and are blinded by vengeful doves for their treachery. Cinderella, on the other hand, wins the prince essentially out of loyalty − as Kay Stone argues: '[s]he is rewarded with magic objects because she follows precisely the instructions of her dying mother. She wins the prince at least in part because she is *not* a manchaser, as are her stepsisters.'[15] Perrault, however, in Zipes's claim, evacuates such an interesting heroine, making her submissive and industrious, saved by a fairy godmother and prince 'only because she minds her manners'.[16] Perrault's 'distinctly limited view of women', creates, in Zipes's view, an 'ideal *femme civilisée* [civilised lady] of upper-class society … beautiful, polite, graceful, industrious, properly groomed, and know[ing] how to control herself at all times'[17]: ultimately, argues Zipes, a 'model of passive femininity'.[18]

Perrault's passive Cinderella (in Zipes's reading) echoes through contemporary cultural constructions of Cinderella. Through interviews with women, mothers, children and teachers, Kay Stone convincingly details such a common, popular perception of Cinderella as the prototypically passive fairy-tale heroine. Many of the adult women interviewed by Stone particularly remembered the tale because, theorises Stone, 'Cinderella seems to present the clearest image of our idealized perfect women – beautiful, sweet, patient, submissive, and an excellent housekeeper and wife'.[19] A renowned complaint comes from Simone de Beauvoir, who points to 'Cinderella' as one of the most pervasively influential tales encouraging women to expect to find fortune and happiness in the arms of some Prince Charming, rather than to attempt risk and challenge on their own.[20]

Such readings of Cinderella as typical of beautiful, passive, fairy-tale women who – as Carol de Dobay Rifelj puts it – 'have only to bear their distress until their prince comes and their dreams come true' culminate in Dobay Rifelj's argument for the similar victimisation of women in Perrault and Sade. Noting that both writers portray women as extremely young, 'perfectly beautiful', and notable for their 'gentleness', Dobay Rifelj goes on to trace a common master-plot of feminine victimisation, concluding that 'if the texts of Sade echo those of Perrault, it is partly because an underlying dynamic of victimization associated with Sade is already present in Perrault'.[21]

Yet, turning to Perrault's tale itself, one realises that – contrary to the claims of Zipes and Dobay Rifelj – Cinderella is not quite as passive, dull and victimised as many readers have perceived. Noting that Perrault's Cinderella 'sobs out her inchoate discontent and desire in front of that fairy protector and obtains the needed outfit to go to the ball', Huang Mei further points out that Cinderella herself asks that the slipper be tried on her foot.[22] If Cinderella suffers her misfortunes patiently, it is because she is shrewd enough to realise that, in her stepmother-dominated household, complaining will do her no good.[23] Cinderella participates actively in her own transformation; when the fairy godmother cannot think of how to provide a coachman, it is Cinderella who proposes going to see whether there might be a serviceable rat in the rat trap. When the godmother believes all is in readiness, it is Cinderella who asks whether she is to go to the ball in her rags. One might also distinguish a certain playfulness and humour in Cinderella's choice to sit with her mystified stepsisters at the ball, sharing with them the oranges and lemons that the prince has given her, yet not revealing her identity: a move that might also be read as a calculated display of the prince's attentions, and therefore, a subtle revenge. Cinderella is, moreover, sufficiently crafty as to pretend that she has just awoken when she lets her stepsisters in after the ball.[24] She even toys with them in asking to borrow clothes so as to see the beautiful and mysterious princess herself – suggesting, as Mei remarks, 'a born actress and an experienced schemer [rather] than a submissive heroine'.[25] And Cinderella is not altogether docile and obedient to her godmother the second evening of the ball, when she so enjoys herself that she forgets her curfew.[26] As mentioned above, it is, furthermore, Cinderella who laughingly proposes to try the mysterious lost slipper herself, and who certifies her legitimacy by producing the other slipper from her pocket. As the little moral at the end of Perrault's conte attempts to remind us, 'La bonne grâce est le vrai don des Fées/Sans elle on ne peut rien, avec elle, on peut tout' ['Good grace is the true gift of the Fairies/Without it one can do nothing, with it, one can do everything'].[27] Yet Perrault's Cinderella is, as we see, endowed with other qualities than grace: initiative, shrewdness, irony, humour and the ability to abandon herself to the moment and its pleasures. Indeed, this portrait of Cinderella's temperament and personality is so nuanced, so subtly singular and human, that Perrault's moral about 'bonne grâce' ['good grace'] strikes us as somewhat jarring and discordant at the end. Reading such a tacked-on, stilted little lesson in comportment, we are all the more impressed by how richly Cinderella departs from the passive role it legislates.[28]

Such a clever, assertive Cinderella helps prepare us to appreciate and respect – indeed to identify – the Cinderella intertext at work in Japrisot's novel. Before leaving Perrault's Cinderella to turn to Japrisot's, however, we might note the importance of appearance –

that is, display – in the Perrault tale: display performed in the text through emphasis on sartorial detail. Cinderella's very function in the household is defined sartorially; it is she who irons her sisters' linen, and who carefully pleats their starched, seventeenth-century cuffs.[29] Descriptions of their ensembles for the ball are lavish and precise, as the stepsisters announce plans to wear red velour with English trim, a gold-flowered coat and a diamond tiara. More than twelve corset laces are broken in slenderising efforts.[30] Cinderella's own ball gowns, of gold and silver fabric richly studded with jewels, are sumptuously described. Her arrival at the ball is marked by dazzled silence, yielding quickly to more purposeful scrutiny as the ladies study her hairstyle and clothes, 'pour en avoir dès le lendemain de semblables, pourvu qu'il se trouvât des étoffes assez belles, et des ouvriers assez habiles' ['so as to have similar ones the very next day, provided such beautiful fabrics be found, and sufficiently handy workers'].[31] Such extreme attention to appearance and sartorial display can be written off as trivially 'feminine'. Yet beyond the imitative effort at work here is an intention that will recur in more sinister, deadly form in Japrisot's novel. Just as Perrault's ladies at the ball scrutinise Cinderella's ensemble in order to imitate it, so Do and Mi secretly study each other, in their respective plots to kill the other and take her place in a murderous impersonation. Moreover, Cinderella's utter transformation is such that, as we have seen, her own stepsisters do not recognise her, so extreme is her disguise. Again, disguise will take on more sinister implications in Japrisot's novel, when the survivor, believing that she is Do, finds herself successfully impersonating Mi – and not only to Mi's former lover, but to Mi's own father. Mi is a role – a persona – into which Do must fit, just as Cinderella, in stepping into the slipper, must step into a designated role as the mysterious, beautiful princess. The slipper itself, a sartorial detail, contains an entire role in search of an actress. Perrault's 'Cinderella', as emblematised in the slipper, is a tale about costume, disguise, masquerade; it is a tale about roles, theatricality, display and imposture. This story of theatricality and display is further, more decisively, imposed by the novel's Cinderella referent in that it engages an entire dramatic script, obliging the novel to negotiate this intertext. A 'storied body' – that is, as Peter Brooks would put it, 'a prime agent in narrative plot and meaning'[32] – embodying an entire narrative, Cinderella must, somehow, be negotiated – incorporated, rejected, countered or ventriloquised – in Japrisot's detective narrative.

Yet the insertion of Cinderella's story within a very different genre demands an explanation, an accounting. For Cinderella, with her known-in-advance ending, stands in symmetrical opposition to the cadaver of a murder mystery: the cadaver incarnating a scandalous absence of explanation, a scandalous lack demanding narrative completion. 'The cadaver of the assassinated character,' as Eisenzweig puts it, 'is, in the end, nothing other than the privileged, but definitively amnesiac, narrator of his own story, that's to say, the story of the crime.'[33] Yet if the cadaver cries out for *an* explanatory narrative – which could, for the detective determined to solve the mystery, be any account that 'fits' properly – Cinderella bears within her persona a far more coercive imperative, a *single*, detailed narrative. The detective begins with the ending, the cadaver – and searches back towards the beginning. To establish the narrative that will produce precisely that ending, the detective must evaluate multiple possibilities, multiple solutions, in the quest for the match between ending and story. The Cinderella story, however, is always already known in advance, from beginning to end: from Cinderella's cinders and rags to her happily-ever-after reward. The value or pleasure of the Cinderella tale, therefore, lies elsewhere than in the teleological suspense of the detective novel; it lies in the exercise and satisfaction of wish-fulfilment. This kind of value – pleasure – however, is the dimension that detective readings of *Piège pour Cendrillon* neglect; this is the covert (feminised) script that the detective reading, with the linear teleology of its (masculinised) analytic quest, refuses to acknowledge. For the cerebral detective, what matters is to piece together clues leading to the 'right' solution. But a genre in which the solution is long known in advance, as in the fairy tale, poses a contradiction to the detective's effort; in such utterly other genres, readerly gratification works differently, otherwise. One recalls Litvak's study of 'the ways in which such [theatrical] energies break or complicate that kind of natural-seeming teleology'. He specifically invokes a feminine energy in pointing to a conflict between 'the patriarchal, heterosexualizing pressure of narrative linearity, on the one hand, and the antilinear counterpressure of a feminist or gay spectacle or masquerade, on the other'.[34]

Perhaps the particular 'antilinear', 'feminist' energy embodied by Cinderella is the love story, which traditionally stands antithetically to the detective novel. Quoting the ('particularly dogmatic') detective writer S. S. Van Dine and his twenty rules of the genre, Todorov asserts, 'L'amour n'a pas de place dans le roman policier' ['Love has no place in the detective novel'].[35] In her discussion of *Piège pour Cendrillon*, Shoshana Felman would appear to agree with this claim; she does not engage the love story in *Piège pour Cendrillon* significantly as she argues for the overturning of the analytic, logical, rational imperatives that conduct the detective script.[36] In Felman's claim, '[s]i le savoir du criminel emblématise le savoir inconscient dont le propre est d'*échapper à la détection*, la victoire du détective, en revanche, est la victoire de la conscience' ['if the criminal's knowledge emblematises unconscious knowledge, whose very nature is to seek to escape detection, the detective's victory, on the other hand, is the victory itself of the conscious mind'].[37] Criminal knowledge flees detection; the detective's victory is the victory of knowledge, reason, logic, analysis, over the evasive criminal's countervailing efforts. In collapsing the difference between detective and criminal, argues Felman, Japrisot effectively stages the undoing of reason by the unconscious, which 'la traverse, l'habite de l'intérieur' ['traverses it, lives within it']; the unconscious subverts the conscious mind.[38] Ultimately, reading Japrisot's fiction as a detective novel allows Felman to demonstrate that *Piège pour Cendrillon* overturns all the conventions of the genre. These include conventions based on binary logic: that the detective cannot also be the criminal, that the perpetrator cannot also be the victim, the witness cannot also be the investigator, the solution cannot also be ambiguous.[39] As Felman points out, the novel attacks 'la convention qui ne définit que par leur *opposition* l'un à l'autre, voire par leur *séparation* radicale, les rôles divers et multiples du malfaiteur et de la victime, du témoin et de l'enquêteur' ['the convention that only defines diverse and multiple roles by virtue of their *opposition* one to another, that is, by their radical *separation*, the traditional, mutually exclusive roles of detective, victim and murderer'].[40]

But such a demonstration of the ways in which *Piège pour Cendrillon* subverts the conventions of the (detective) genre has a crucial limitation: it fails to account for the ways in which the novel subverts the convention itself of *genre*. For Japrisot's novel goes further, subverting not only the detective genre, but the very notion of genre itself.[41] In espousing the topos of the detective novel *so as to* overturn it, in collapsing its characters' mutually exclusive roles, Japrisot's text also collapses generic conventions based on opposition and separation, inclusion and exclusion, the desirable and the undesirable readerly responses. And this is carried out through the covert script of its intertext, the Cinderella fairy tale: a story not of analytical effort and intellectual prowess, but of desire: a love story. Thus, while *Piège pour Cendrillon* may indeed be read as the story of an Oedipal search for identity, involving loss of identity and its laborious, painful recovery, this obvious loss is not the only one in the novel. There is also a loss of love; indeed, I argue that the loss of identity works, effectively, as smokescreen – veiling or obscuring the more traumatic, more searing loss, that of love.

Opening in the fairy-tale idiom of 'il était une fois' ['once upon a time'], the narrative depicts Mi crying on her mother's grave.[42] We read of Mi's needy craving for love – 'J'ai besoin, j'ai besoin, j'ai besoin qu'on m'aime' ['I need, I need, I need to be loved'] (p. 10), emphasised in such details as Mi always wanting to hold Do's hand on walks, and saying to Do, 'Si tu me donnes un baiser, si tu me tiens contre toi, je ne le dirai à personne, je me marierai avec toi' ['If you give me a kiss, if you hold me against you, I won't tell anyone, I'll marry you'] (p. 11): a neediness constantly recalled in the novel. Jeanne, for instance, refers to Mi's pronounced need to share her bed with all and sundry (p. 56), 'de se dorloter avant de dormer, à coups de somnifères, de garçons ou de bla-bla-bla, un besoin qui n'était que l'ancienne peur du noir, quand maman quitte la chambre' ['to coddle herself before falling asleep, with doses of sleeping pills, of boys, of chatter, a need that was only the old fear of the dark, when Mummy left the room'] (p. 115). Later in the narrative, the amnesiac heroine's emerging bond with the older Jeanne might be read as the recovery of a rightful heritage of love. Similarly, Perrault's Cinderella, having lost her mother, is dispossessed of a love that is rightfully hers as a devoted, deserving daughter, 'd'une douceur et d'une bonté sans exemple' ['of unparalleled gentleness and goodness'] (p. 171). In this way, the rags-to-riches narrative allegorises Cinderella's recovery of a rightful heritage of love. The dramatic transformations along the surface of the story, from Cinderella's sooty rags to her princess's brocades, obscure the fact that her marriage to an adoring prince[43] is merely her rightful restitution to love; the repossession of a love originally lost with her mother's death.

The importance of love – and its rightful restitution – in the Cinderella story, however, has been neglected: a lapse that evokes another neglected instance of love in a narrative context. The mysterious contents, for example, of the Queen's letter in Poe's story 'The Purloined Letter'[44] are discounted by Jacques Lacan, who claims that it is, instead, the position of the letter as material object either in or not in one's possession – rather than what the letter specifically says – that is determinative. 'Lettre d'amour ou lettre de conspiration, lettre délatrice ou lettre d'instruction, lettre sommatoire ou lettre de détresse, nous n'en pouvons retenir qu'une chose, c'est que la Reine ne saurait la porter à la connaissance de son seigneur et maître' ['Love letter or conspiratorial letter, letter of betrayal or letter of instruction, letter of summons or letter of distress, we can only be sure of one thing, that the Queen cannot bring it to the knowledge of her lord and master'].[45] Rather, as Felman points out, Lacan emphasises the letter's exploitation for purposes of domination.[46] The letter's possible love message (and we duly note that Lacan lists that possibility first) is obscured, hijacked for purposes of power – and a power that derives from knowledge. For whatever the letter says is less important, in Lacan's reading, than the power that would come from *knowing* that it says something that the Queen does not want the King to know. Lacan's reading implicitly suggests that love, in Poe's story, is sacrificed in favour of knowledge.

The quest for knowledge in *Piège pour Cendrillon* obliges the amnesiac heroine to accept the shock and trauma of being other, criminal; to accept Rimbaud's claim that '"I" am another'[47] and with it, the scandal and horror of such knowledge. Felman further reads *Piège pour Cendrillon*'s suspense, its deferral of the solution to the mystery, as 'la suspension de la présence à soi du récit' ['the *suspension* of the narrative's presence-to-itself]: the state of not knowing, of losing one's mastery, losing self-possession.[48] For the detective, of course, such loss is experienced as traumatic. Referring to such loss of mastery in the case of Poe's detective, Dupin, Felman suggests that Dupin 'est sans le savoir *piégé*, précisément, par sa propre victoire, par la lettre énigmatique qu'il croit posséder, alors que c'est elle qui le possède' ['is without knowing it, *trapped*, precisely by his own victory, by the enigmatic letter he believes he possesses, whereas it possesses him'].[49] Indeed, love – as in criminal desire, as in unconscious desire – may be what undoes the operations of knowledge, of the detective's mastery, of reason and analytical thought.

Pushing this insight further, however, we realise that for the lover – as opposed to the detective – such loss of self-possession, with its suspension of self-mastery and obliteration of boundaries, is experienced not as traumatic, but as intoxicating, blissful. 'Jeanne me prendra dans ses bras' ['Jeanne will take me in her arms'] (p. 202), imagines Japrisot's amnesiac heroine. Felman's psychoanalytic model of reading, based on a long labour of detection, cedes before Roland Barthes' model of the reader as lover.[50] Reading becomes not an effort of detection, but an act of love. In the case of Poe's Dupin, what is this 'enigmatic' letter, if not a love letter? For a love letter would most fully model the overtaking of awareness by unconscious desire, the secret inscription of the fairy tale within the detective story, the unwriting of critical analyses by love, the undoing of knowledge by desire; the undoing of Freud by Dora.[51] In Felman's argument, the presence of love is recognised, just as it is implicitly accepted by Lacan as the possible contents of the Queen's letter. But I would argue that love, in both Felman's and Lacan's readings of 'The Purloined Letter', is displaced, disinherited, from its rightful position; each claims that the interest and pertinence of the 'story', whether the detective fiction or the psychoanalytic allegory, is *not* love. Whereas Japrisot's novel appears to recount a quest for fortune, Felman reads it more deeply as a quest for identity, mapping *Piège pour Cendrillon* onto the story of Oedipus. But this quest for identity, masquerading as a quest for riches, is itself the masquerade of a quest for love. The eau de cologne named 'Piège pour Cendrillon' and worn by the sleazy

Serge Reppo designates its wearer as princely, the worthy love-object for any self-identified Cinderella. And the novel's trap is to induce (seduce) the reader into choosing the wrong quest-object: money or identity, whereas these two quest-objects – I maintain – are masquerades for a third, more crucial one: love. What is Japrisot's Cinderella really after? The princely riches of Marraine Midola's fortune? An identity of her own, emblematised in the tiny glass slipper fitting her foot alone, itself inscribed in Japrisot's text as the Florentine slippers sent every year by Marraine Midola to Do (p. 12)? Or, as I am suggesting, her return to a love she deserves?

Following the novel's preface in fairy-tale idiom (which concludes with the Florentine slippers) comes a short chapter entitled 'J'aurai assassiné' ['I will have murdered']. With its future anterior tense, it announces a sort of pre-emptive possession or arrogating of the future: an aggressive co-optation implying an outrageous, disproportionate desire. Such notions of overwhelming, almost monstrous desire – as well as notions of its proper place, and its overflowing of that place – are all engaged with this chapter title. But we recall the opening fantasy, with its fairy-tale idiom, 'Il était une fois, il y a bien longtemps, trois petites filles' ['Once upon a time, a long time ago, there were three little girls'] (p. 9). It is a brief, opening fairy tale that concludes, scarcely three pages later, with a symmetrical allusion to 'ce conte' ['this tale']: 'c'est Do qui invente ce conte, dont elle sait bien, parce qu'elle n'est plus une petite fille, qu'il est faux' ['it's Do who invents this tale, knowing very well, since she's no longer a little girl, that it isn't true'] (p. 11). These claims for the fantasy status of this 'once-upon-a-time' tale – claims with which it closes – confound the subsequent, confessional assertion of the first chapter title, 'J'aurai assassiné' ['I will have murdered']. As we open this chapter in the wake of its grim and deadly title, what can the status of this arrogated future be now? Is this possessive appropriation of the future, like the opening tale, merely a fiction, a fantasy? The conflict between a sort of dark, criminal reality – 'I will have murdered' – and the fairy-tale preface, is thus established at the novel's outset. The status of each is confused all the more by the preface's teasing conclusion, claiming that the tale is 'juste assez vrai' ['just true enough'] to keep Do, inventor of the tale, from sleeping (p. 11). Such an ambiguous formulation –

'just true enough' – adroitly scrambles the boundaries between fairy tale and detective quest, fiction and truth.

This opening, enigmatic tale concludes with the further scrambling of the two contradictory genres when we find that Do receives slippers from Florence each year for Christmas: 'C'est pour cela, peut-être, qu'elle se prend pour Cendrillon' ['It's for that, perhaps, that she takes herself for Cinderella'] (p. 12). Just as Do arrogates for herself a possible criminal future in the mysterious 'I will have murdered' assertion, is she also appropriating the role of princess in a wish-fulfilling fairy tale? Is this co-optation of a Cinderella role perhaps as illegitimate, as illicit, as the murder plot? Finally, given that the novel's title is *Piège pour Cendrillon*, we are perhaps meant to understand that Do's monstrous arrogation of the fairy-tale role is itself the trap mentioned by the title itself. Could Do, 'who invents this tale,' be trapped – victimised – by her own desire? Indeed, a favourite fairy tale, argues psychologist Eric Berne, could coercively provide a lifelong behavioural script, inducing one to devote one's life to 'making it come to pass'.[52]

Piège pour Cendrillon's refusal to choose between fairy tale and detective inquest, of course, is scandalous to the detective genre, which is based upon elucidating, and thus eliminating, ambiguity. Consequently, for the detective inquest, the resolution of the survivor's identity is paramount. Yet, as Felman argues, the novel's ending refuses to decide between the two identities. In the final scene, the unnamed survivor is escorted from the courtroom following her sentencing to ten years of prison as Jeanne's accomplice in the murder. She recognises the name of the eau de Cologne worn by the accompanying policeman as 'Piège pour Cendrillon': 'quelque chose d'attendrissant et de soldatesque, presque aussi infect que l'odeur' ['something poignant and virile, almost as vile as the scent itself'] (p. 220). Knowledge of the cologne's name would suggest that the survivor must be Mi, as Serge Reppo, another wearer of the cologne, divulged its name only to Mi – not to Do, whom he never met. However, argues Felman, 'le nom du parfum sent trop le roman' ['the perfume's name smells too much of the novel, of fiction']. Couldn't this same name, she proposes, be an invented one, concocted after the fact by Do – who, Felman reminds us, has 'invented' this tale?[53] The survivor could be

Mi, or she could be Do: each identity allows for an entirely coherent understanding of the whole. The only coherence that is subverted in this way, argues Felman, is that based on a univocal solution, whereas the text – she maintains – teaches us how to read a solution that remains 'radicalement *dialogique*' ['radically *dialogical*'].[54] The novel's real trap, in Felman's assertion, is to snare any reader who would conclude with a univocal solution: 'une vérité univoque, une certitude, un savoir garanti' ['an univocal truth, a certainty, a guaranteed knowledge'].[55]

But we need to take such a 'radically dialogical' insight further. Although Felman points to the overturning of univocal solutions in favour of a residual ambiguity, she nonetheless argues for the 'radically dialogical' co-existence of *two* solutions to the mystery of the survivor's identity. That is, identity is still discrete; the surviving girl can be either Mi or Do, but she is one *or* the other. Each possibility is available, but each excludes the other. There is, however, a third possibility, a more radical one that we might pursue now: that the survivor ends up being *neither* Mi nor Do, but a third, blended identity. Such a new, composite identity would 'fit' the novel, in the way the glass slipper fits Cinderella, far more appropriately than any dual solution. For one thing, the narration itself is not recounted from two, but from multiple perspectives. Each perspective is seductive, even arrogant, leading us to believe that it is recounting the truth. Some distance into the novel, for instance, we turn a page and a new chapter begins the story over again, in an authoritative narratorial voice given to using the French *passé simple* tense reserved for historic narration: 'Tout commença un après-midi de février' ['Everything began one February afternoon'] (p. 99). Yet what we now take to be, at last, the discourse of historic, objective truth is itself soon revealed to be yet another personal version of events – that is, to be yet another discourse animated by its own desire, its own agenda. For we turn the final page of this chapter only to discover, in the opening line of the next, 'Ma main gantée de blanc lui ferma la bouche' ['My white-gloved hand closed her mouth'] (p. 133) – forcing us to recognise that the authoritative recounting voice we had taken in the previous chapter to provide the definitive, historic reconstruction of events had, instead, been that of a character; the voice was Jeanne's, offering us her own account of events.

A similarly coquettish flirtation with readerly expectations occurs yet later in the novel, when an equally unidentifiable narrating voice opens a chapter with yet another assertive, simple-past tense: 'Le garçon surgit dans le soleil de juin alors que Micky venait de refermer son magazine' ['The boy appeared in the June sunlight just as Micky had closed her magazine'] (p. 175). And once again, the subsequent chapter resituates the authoritative, 'historical', narration we have just completed as yet another desiring discourse, with its own agenda – for this subsequent chapter opens, 'Il me dit qu'il se nomma Serge Reppo' ['He told me his name was Serge Reppo'] (p. 195), indicating that the chapter we have – again – just read as factual, historic record was itself recounted not by an omniscient narrator, but – yet again – by another character involved in the action itself. In this way, the narrative becomes a succession of different discourses, with the narrating voice slipping among different roles and identities – revealing itself belatedly, each time, *not* to be the voice of omniscience, but rather to belong to a particular subject and player in the story only after we have completed that particular chapter. Each chapter becomes a masquerade, clothing itself in the vestments of truth, authority, only to be demasked by the following chapter when a new voice overturns that authority by, itself, masquerading as truth. The 'story' that we, with every chapter, are led to read anew as 'historical' is subtly, repeatedly, unwritten as 'hysterical', in the proliferation of the multiple truth claims, multiple identities and multiple voices that characterise both Japrisot's narrative and the pathology of hysteria.[56]

Such dispersal of identities, such a profusion of voices, overturns the notion of singular subjectivity: a notion, as we have seen, upon which the detective genre generally depends, with its exclusionary logic separating detective, criminal and victim; one cannot be the other. What we might call, however, a 'hysterical' narrating practice, cues us to be open to further traces of a hysterical subtext – such as a movement away from separate Mi and Do identities, towards a floating, new composite or hysterical persona.[57] Once her bandages have come off in the clinic and she has a reconstructed face of her own, the amnesiac heroine realises that she doesn't much care about her fifteen lost years of identity. 'Quand je me regardais dans le miroir, j'étais moi, j'avais des yeux de petit bonze, une vie qui m'attendait dehors, j'étais heureuse, je m'aimais bien. Tant pis pour "l'autre", puisque j'étais celle-là' ['When I looked in the mirror, I was myself, I had the solemn eyes of a little monk, a life waiting for me outside, I was happy, I liked myself. Too bad for "the other one", for I was this one'] (p. 38). Indeed, Jeanne's observations would seem to confirm the emergence of a composite persona in the survivor, who seems no longer to be either Do or Micky. 'Tu ne marches pas comme elle, mais pas comme tu marchais avant non plus' ['You don't walk like her, but you also don't walk the way you used to'] (p. 136). Searching for clues as to her identity, the survivor reviews both possibilities, first that she is Mi, then that she is Do; and, reliving her awakening in the clinic, she decides 'Je suis la troisième. Je n'ai rien fait, rien voulu, je ne veux plus être aucune des deux autres. Je suis moi' ['I am the third one. I haven't done anything, I haven't wanted anything, I don't want to be either of the two others any more. I am me'] (p. 214).[58]

Any solution to the detective problem of identity, even Felman's dual solution (that the survivor can be either Mi or Do) cannot accommodate one troubling fact. And that is the increasing energy of a desire that might be understood as hysterical; for, ultimately, the survivor does not particularly care about the solution to the mystery of her identity; she does not want to be either of the past selves – Mi or Do – she might once have been. Her doctor's fear is indeed realised; having warned the survivor that there was only one 'folie' ['crazy thing'] she could do, which would be to dismiss her old inaccessible memories, thinking 'Des souvenirs, j'ai tout le temps de m'en fabriquer d'autres' ['Oh, memories, I have plenty of time to create new ones'] (p. 38). And it is precisely this 'crazy thing', this hysterical denial, that motivates the survivor's assertion that she doesn't want to be either Mi or Do. Any dual solution emphasises the *otherness* of identity, the part of alienation within the self, as Felman suggests: 'La question "qui suis-je?" se complique, de la sorte, de la question "qui est l'autre?" Combien autre est l'autre? L'autre est-il à l'extérieur ou à l'intérieur du "je"?' ['The question, "who am I?" is complicated by the similar question, "who is the other"? How other is the other? Is the other without or within the "I"?].[59] But Japrisot's novel overturns this question by emphasising the (hysterical) *identity* of 'otherness': the blended, blurred identity construed by hysterical desire, based both upon rejection of past identities – and desire for new, composite identities. The intellectual recuperation and proper distribution of identity that generally defines the detective genre – the correct identification that distributes the roles of murderer, victim, detective, and so on, modelling the psychoanalytic quest for proper recognition and acceptance of one's own identity – is here swept aside, displaced, by the survivor's desire precisely *not* to recover her past, her identity: her desire precisely to reject any such knowledge.

Additional aspects of this hysterical subtext serve to subvert the detective-novel paradigm. For the greatest threat to the detective genre is not the failure of the detective, nor even the ultimate absence of sufficient explanation or solution to the mystery. Rather, the greatest threat is the foolishness of such efforts of detection devoted to an object that essentially ridicules coherence, such as – in Freud's view – the hysteric's discourse: 'full of gaps, inconsistencies, and faulty connections anyway. In fact, such incoherence is one of the primary symptoms of hysteria.'[60] In the hysteric's discourse, argued Freud: 'the connections ... even the ostensible ones – are for the most part incoherent, and the sequence of different events is uncertain. Even during the course of their story patients will repeatedly correct a particular or a date, and then perhaps, after wavering for some time, return to their first version.'[61] Freud, as Evans points out, had his own creative solution for such incoherence, as suggested in his treatment of Dora's story; he viewed women patients as 'exchangeable', argues Evans; 'parts of one story can fill in the gaps of another, and when no parts that fit are available, he will devise some himself'.[62] And yet, Freud himself recognised the improbability of construing a plausible narrative from the hysteric's discourse when he wrote, 'no one, I believe, can have had any true conception of the complexity of the psychological events in a case of hysteria – the juxtaposition of the most dissimilar tendencies, the mutual dependence of contrary ideas, the repressions and displacements, and so on'.[63]

How else might hysterical paradigms be at work in Japrisot's novel? An erratic, impulsive behaviour seems to characterise the heroine. She flies into a rage at the clinic, lifting her plastered arm against the doctor (p. 25). Jeanne's very suggestion that the survivor might be simulating amnesia throws her into a fury: 'Ma main droite partît avant que j'eusse entendu. Je frappai Jeanne au coin de la bouche' ['My right hand flew up before I had even heard her. I hit Jeanne at the corner of her mouth'] (p. 59). Doctors diagnose her past behaviour as hysterical, and accounts of this past now fill the amnesiac survivor with distaste: 'Je n'avais aucune envie de boire, de lever la main sur une domestique maladroite, de danser sur le toit d'une voiture, de tomber dans les bras d'un coureur à pied suédois ou du premier garçon venu qui aurait de beaux yeux et la bouche tendre' ['I had no desire to drink, to lift my hand against a clumsy servant, to dance on a car rooftop, to fall into the arms of a Swedish runner or the first boy to come along with beautiful eyes and tender lips'] (p. 56). What he does know, claims Dr Chaveres, is that the survivor was 'malade *avant* l'accident. Etait-elle exaltée, violente, égocentrique? Avait-elle tendance à s'apitoyer sur elle-même, à larmoyer dans son sommeil, à faire des cauchemars? Lui avez-vous connu des colères soudaines, comme ce jour où elle a levé une main plâtrée sur mon beau-frère?' ['ill *before* the accident. Was she excessive, violent, egocentric? Was she prone to pitying herself, to weeping in her sleep, to having nightmares? Did you know her to fly into rages, like the day she lifted a plastered hand against my brother-in-law?'] (pp. 162–3). Dr Chaveres goes on to explain that beyond these characteristics 'd'une nature hystérique' ['of a hysterical nature'], the girl's amnesia itself is traditionally a stigmatum, or mark, of hysteria (p. 163). And he concludes that the amnesia is 'le refus psychique caractéristique d'une petite qui était déjà malade' ['the psychic refusal characteristic of a child who was *already* ill'] (p. 164). But Jeanne herself, however, engages in the same impulsive, violent behaviour. She speaks threateningly to the survivor in an 'enraged murmur' (p. 59), before actually striking the girl, who finds herself suddenly spread out on the carpet (p. 60). In Serge Reppo's claim, Mi herself felt that Jeanne was 'détraquée' ['unhinged'] (p. 178).

Perhaps the confusion of Mi and Do within the somatic behaviour of the amnesiac survivor is only the most spectacular, the most theatrical of the various blended identities and desires in the novel; for is the Mi/Do relationship one of sisters, or one of lovers? Is Jeanne's relationship with each girl that of a surrogate mother, that of a sister, or that of a lover? The trope of theatricality scrambles such relationships, as Litvak remarks, allowing us 'to denaturalize – to read as a *scene* – the whole encompassing space in which that subjectivity gets constituted: the intricate web of "romantic" bonds and family ties'.[64]

Further questions of acting and simulation disrupt the detective mission of *Piège pour Cendrillon*, the search to parse out truth and falsehood. In Jeanne's accusation, it would be so easy for the amnesiac survivor to 'jouer la comédie!' ['play a role!'] (p. 59), for, like hysteria, amnesia can be simulated, as Jeanne claims (p. 61). Yet increasingly, as the text makes clear, any possibility of voluntary simulation on the part of the survivor is cancelled by the involuntary coercion of *being acted*, rather than acting: by the haunted sense of finding oneself an involuntary puppet with no notion of how to exit the stage, obliged to mime a role dictated now by one mastermind, now by another. Looking at herself in mirrors, the amnesiac survivor talks of her impression of being controlled:

> Plus que le crime que j'avais commis, c'était cette sensation de subir une emprise qui m'angoissait. J'étais un jouet vide, une marionnette dans les mains de trois inconnues. Laquelle tirait les fils le plus durement? La petite employée de banque envieuse, patiente comme une araignée? La princesse morte qui finirait bien un jour par me regarder de nouveau en face dans mon miroir, puisque c'était elle que je voulais devenir? Ou la grande fille aux cheveux dorés qui m'avait guidée vers le meurtre pendant des semaines, sans me voir?

> [More than the crime I had committed, I was troubled by the feeling of being manipulated. I was an empty toy, a puppet in the hands of three strangers. Which one pulled hardest at the strings? The envious little bank employee, patient as a spider? The dead princess who would indeed end up one day looking me in the face in my mirror, since she was the one I wanted to become? Or the tall woman with golden hair who had guided me towards the murder for weeks, without seeing me?] (p. 139)

Such a fragmented, alienated condition, in which the body appears to act independently 'of will and knowledge',[65] lends Japrisot's novel a particularly psychoanalytic cast, for such behaviour involves impulsiveness, coercion. 'Mal motivé[s] aux yeux même du sujet' ['Poorly motivated in the eyes themselves of the subject'], these are behaviours from which the subject himself or herself feels estranged.[66] An example of such involuntary 'acting out' (in which the subject, in Lacan's formulation, is 'spoken' rather than 'speaking') is the moment the amnesiac survivor, in flight from the very effort to derive her own past, involuntarily signs her hotel registration as 'Doloi' – Domenica Loi's signature – in an 'acting out', or unconscious obeying of a coercive script. 'Loin d'être libératoires, de tels agis hystérisent, pour ainsi dire, le retour du refoulé et ils en majorent l'impact hallucinatoire' ['Far from being liberating, such acts hystericise, so to speak, the return of the repressed, and they increase its hallucinatory impact'].[67] These notions of alienation, fragmentation and involuntary 'acting out' suggest certain similarities between the histrionic hysteric and Japrisot's amnesiac heroine, particularly the idea of numbness – an absence of affect – that characterises the act of searching without conviction against a feeling of one's own emptiness.[68] In the absence of a consolidated self, the actor-hysteric becomes a puppet, mouthing feelings that are assumed, contrived. Such an inner absence or alienation is explored by Octave Mannoni as a hysterical phenomenon in which subjects are victimised by the very roles they play without conviction: 'Ils représentent ainsi dramatiquement l'amour, la jalousie, l'honneur outragé, mais aussi le deuil ou la jubilation, parce qu'ils se défendent contre l'insuffisance de ce qu'ils éprouvent' ['they thus dramatically stage love, jealousy, outraged honour, but also grief or jubilation, in an effort to ward off the inadequacy they feel'].[69]

This blurred boundary between authenticity and simulation, characteristic of early attempts to explain the perceived disorder of hysteria, is partly what renders it such a threat to the detective enterprise, whose mission is precisely to bring to light the truth by setting it apart from falsehood. Indeed, a model of the encounter between the detective genre and the love story – the encounter staged in Japrisot's narrative – is to be found in the peculiar subject/object model that structures the study of hysteria, marked by distaste at the prospect of soliciting information from an unreliable source. A certain paradigmatic scorn for hysterical desire might be noticed in the attitude of the earliest figure associated with hysteria, Briquet, whose work was later to catch the attention of Charcot. Briquet is emphatic in his distaste, registered as early as 1859, for the task of treating hysterics:

> Traiter des maladies que tous les auteurs s'accordaient à regarder comme le type de l'instabilité, de l'irrégularité, de la fantaisie, de l'imprévu, comme n'étant gouvernées par aucune loi, par aucune règle, et comme n'étant liées entre elles par aucune théorie sérieuse, était la tâche qui me répugnait le plus. Je me résignais et me mis à l'oeuvre.

> [Treating illnesses that all authors agreed in viewing as the very model of instability of irregularity, of fantasy, of whimsicality, as being governed by no law, and being linked to each other by no serious theory, was the charge I found most repugnant. I resigned myself and got to work.][70]

Charcot, however, criticised Briquet's attitude and the distasteful, pathetic objects it made of hysterics, claiming that Briquet reduced hysteria to a shameful disorder of lubricity;[71] and Charcot set out to redeem hysteria as an authentic pathology. Yet Charcot himself nevertheless regarded hysteria, if not with Briquet's disgust, with suspicion. Haunted throughout his career by the possibility that hysteria might, in the end, be mere simulation, Charcot tried – both condescendingly and desperately – to track, detect and surprise any such ruse.[72] He placed, in one case, a hysteric under the surveillance of other women: 'J'eus soin, en outre, de placer auprès d'elle deux infirmes dévouées, comme elle confinées au lit, et prêtes à tout me révéler si elles découvraient quelque supercherie. J'avais là la meilleure police, celle des femmes; car vous savez que si les femmes font complots entre elles, il est bien rare qu'ils réussissent' ['I was careful, moreover, to place near her two devoted, infirm women, confined – like herself – to their beds, and ready to reveal everything to me if they discovered any hoax. I had there the best surveillance, that of women; for you know that if women plot amongst themselves, it is rare indeed that they succeed'].[73]

And yet, Charcot himself might largely have been responsible for the threat of simulation that so closely haunted his work. As Gasser points out, Charcot's own method favoured the most spectacular cases he studied; his penchant for investigating these exceptional cases as a way of understanding, through them, the more 'ordinary' cases, promoted the most exaggerated examples.[74] Other aspects of the study of hysteria, as conducted by Charcot at the Salpêtrière hospital in Paris, further favoured its 'spectacularisation'. Charcot himself was an accomplished caricaturist. As a catalogue issued in honour of the centenary of the establishment of a Chair in Neurology, first filled by Charcot, claims, 'les aptitudes caricaturales de Charcot lui ont été quelquefois profitables dans son métier de clinicien: l'artiste était inséparable du médecin' ['Charcot's aptitude for caricature was occasionally useful in his profession as a clinician: the artist was inseparable from the doctor'].[75] Charcot's artistic talents were even emphasised by Freud in his obituary for Charcot in 1893:

> He had an artistically gifted temperament – as he said himself, he was a *visuel*, a seer … He himself told us the following about his method of working: he was accustomed to look again and again at things that were incomprehensible to him, to deepen his impression of them day by day, until suddenly understanding of them dawned upon him. Before his mind's eye, order then came into the chaos apparently presented by the constant repetition of the same symptoms.[76]

Charcot also, it seems – in Gasser's claim – sought, in artistic representations of madness, correspondences with his own descriptions of hysterics, consulting his own 1887 work with Paul Richer, *Les démoniaques dans l'art*[77] (an art-historical treatise analysing traces of madness in visual masterpieces through the ages) for analogies with his experience of hysterics.[78] Charcot's public examinations of hysterics during his celebrated 'Tuesday lessons' in an amphitheatre for 500 were renowned for their 'circus atmosphere' and 'theatrical aura'.[79] 'Charcot transformed that sanctum of privacy, the mad mind,' agrees Nina Auerbach, 'into an arena of theatrical display.'[80]

Such 'theatrical display' was carried further by Charcot's followers. A former intern who later became Professor of Anatomy at the Ecole des Beaux Arts, Paul Richer contributed to the spectacularisation of hysteria by publishing in 1879 his drawings of subjects in various hysterical poses.[81] In 1882, Richer was named head of the laboratory of Charcot's Clinique des Maladies Nerveuses ['Clinic for Nervous Illnesses']; in this capacity he collaborated with Albert Londe, a photographer whose darkroom had been established at the Salpêtrière Hospital under Charcot. According to Londe, the patient was photographed on the day of admission to the hospital and thereafter, with the various photographs organised to display the series of 'phénomènes survenus chez un malade en un temps donné' ['phenomena occurring for a patient over a given time'].[82] Pointing to the objectification of hysterical subjects by these recording devices, Evans suggests the control they exerted 'over the untamed, tumultuous fits of hysterics'.[83] Such recording mechanisms contributed, however, not only to the objectification, but to the theatricalisation of hysteria. A final emblem of that theatricality is recounted by Charcot's biographer Guillain, who remembers, as a young intern at the Salpêtrière, seeing certain older women patients originally hospitalised under Charcot. Praising the women's talents as actresses, Guillain notes that they could be bribed into imitating the great hysterical crises of their pasts.[84] Such patients, notes Evans, became 'imitations of themselves'.[85]

In the face of such theatricality, with the danger of simulation and ruse it posed for the (male) doctor, Joseph Babinski – one of Charcot's favourite students – along with another Charcot pupil, Edouard Brissaud, will be led to conclude with the impossibility of assessing, definitively, the hysterical subject's degree of sincerity.[86] Yet a third follower, Anatole Chauffard, will go so far as to claim that the study itself of hysteria created the disorder: 'Ces hystériques si nombreux, si démonstratifs, si typiques, c'est nous, médecins, qui, par nos méthodes imprudents d'examen, en faisions la culture artificielle et intensive' ['These numerous hysterics, so demonstrative, so typical, it is we doctors ourselves, who, with our imprudent methods of examination, have artificially and intensively created their culture'].[87] The Babinski school thus represents an extreme moment of doubt, suspicion and scepticism in the study of hysteria.[88] It emblematises the uncertainty and confusion of the detective quest in the face of a hysterical energy we might increasingly recognise as subverting *Piège pour Cendrillon*'s search for definitive identities. In relation to the text's official quest for answers and solutions, the love story – the hysterical subtext – is merely, as the scornful Serge Reppo puts it in an unconscious reprise of the Babinski group's dismissal, 'une histoire de filles, c'est pas sérieux' ['girl stuff, nothing serious'] (p. 186).

Further associations liken the disdain characterising hysteria's early doctors to that of the detective. Pointing to an assumed equation between women and hysteria, Evans quotes Charcot's assistant Richet, who claimed that mild hysteria was not so much an illness as merely an expression of the 'caractère de la femme' ['female character'], and asserted that hysterics 'sont femmes plus que les autres femmes' ['are more womanly than other women'].[89] Summarising Charcot and his followers' views, Evans notes that such womanliness is associated with the character faults assigned to hysterics: 'impressionable, capricious, malleable, coquettish, seductive, lazy, untruthful, recalcitrant'.[90] One might point here to the scrutiny by an ultra-masculinised (detective) subject of an ultra-feminised (hysterical) object, a gendered divide enforced by Paul Hartenberg's 1910 claim: 'These sensitive beings live by emotion and imagination, while we live by logic and by reason. The cold deductions that guide our scientific mind have nothing in common with the spontaneity of their impulsions. In us, everything is judgment, understanding, abstraction: in them, everything is impression and sentiment.'[91]

As we have seen, the quest for identity in Japrisot's narrative, likened by Felman to Oedipus's search for his father's murderer, is undone by a hysterical narrating practice: a practice that proceeds through tactics of seduction and simulation. Hysteria opposes and undoes the primacy of the Oedipus complex in the Freudian construction of sexuality; hysteria might represent the woman's refusal to comply with the positioning forced upon her by the Oedipus model. Instead, as Maria Ramas argues, hysteria is related to indifferentiation, to the pre-Oedipal: to access to – not interdiction of – the maternal body. In Ramas's view, Freud's analysis of Dora is based on an erroneous understanding of female sexuality and femininity, a patriarchal 'fantasy' marking psychoanalysis as 'profoundly ideological'.[92] Scrutinising Dora's refusal, Ramas argues that her 'hysteria, insofar as it expressed a wish, sought to preserve preoedipal love for the mother/woman and to retain access to the maternal/female body':[93] a wish echoed, in Japrisot's narrative, by the amnesiac survivor's love for the older Jeanne. What the (male) character Serge Reppo derisively calls 'une histoire de filles' ['girl stuff'] is the story of feminine refusal of masculinist paradigms, not only of identity, but of sexuality. The reader in search of unequivocal solutions comes away satisfied, convinced of the text's perfect conformity with the detective genre. Biologically, the survivor is Mi, as demonstrated by the survivor's knowledge of the eau de cologne's brand name, 'Piège pour Cendrillon': a knowledge, implies the text, that Do cannot have, for she never met Serge Reppo, wearer of the cologne. However, on another level – that of the love story – such a univocal solution is essentially displaced. For the detective-reader's solution is an empty one in the face of the survivor's desire to be *neither* Mi or Do; rather, to be a third, different, other, identity – an identity shaped by desire, motivated by love for Jeanne. Whereas a detective solution to the text's identity quest can be identified – one that ultimately appears to 'fit' the narrative, with a 'fit' as perfect as that of Cinderella's slipper – we discover that Japrisot's Cinderella herself no longer desires the fit, the slipper or the prince.

We might speculate that one reason readers of Japrisot's detective novel have so neglected the work of its intertwined love story involves a particular threat posed by this surreptitious narrative for the detective's categories of analysis, intellection, reason, rationality: and that is the threat incarnated by the female double. Returning to Evans's phrase about Charcot's hysterics bribed into becoming 'imitations of themselves', we find ourselves in the realm of specular reflection, mirror images, doubling, the uncanny sense produced by the 'twice-behaved' – in Schechner's term[94] – behaviour of theatricality, the split and repetition of another self. Female doubling, as Naomi Schor has argued in the case of George Sand's

Indiana, subverts canonical, heroic, coded-as-masculine individuation.[95] As opposed to a long literary and artistic tradition of cross-gendered impersonation, the female travesty of women impersonating other women is threatening, Schor argues: 'the exchange of *female* identities, the blurring of difference *within* difference remains a largely marginal and unfamiliar phenomenon.' Pointing to the identities of female characters as 'so unstable as to be in constant danger of an uncanny coalescence', Schor notes that what she calls 'the striking commutativity of Sand's female doubles … causes male desire to misfire'.[96] This notion of feminine doubling, we realise, is particularly threatening for any analytical, rational, interpretive effort to impose causal explanation, confining narrative within Cartesian plausibility. Antithetical to what has been read as a quest for identity in Japrisot's novel is my suggestion that the survivor, at the end of the novel, is both Mi and Do, yet neither – that she rejects the pressure of 'masculinised' either/or individuation of being either one or the other, in favour of a third, new and different persona: 'Je suis la troisième. Je n'ai rien fait, rien voulu, je ne veux plus être aucune des deux autres. Je suis moi' ['I am the third one. I haven't done anything, wanted anything, I no longer wanted to be either of the two others. I am me'] (p. 214). Such a refusal disrupts binary logic, the very foundation of Cartesian structures upon which definitive identity, and thus the definitive resolution of the detective narrative, depend.

In the context of Japrisot's novel, we are now in a position to appreciate the disclosure and disruption of the aesthetic ideology upon which the notion of genres is based – in particular, the aesthetic ideology that defines the detective genre. Cued from the outset to read *Piège* as a detective novel in all its virile, lime-lit display, the reader triumphantly seizes its solution on the final page; yet the alert reader also realises that such a solution – while providing closure – is surreptitiously displaced, its limelight craftily stolen by a another, covert narrative: that of a homoerotic love affair between women. In this way, the co-habitation of contradictory genres at work within the same narrative – with the detective quest on display, while the fairy tale furtively yet steadily steals its limelight – scrambles Cartesian either/or categories while simultaneously respecting the conventions of each, in a cannily 'hysterical' narrating practice.

In this study's final chapter, we move from Japrisot's contradictory yet simultaneous fictional genres to the curiously contradictory yet simultaneous *genders* of Duras's *L'Amant* narratives. An autobiographically inspired account of a French teenager's love affair with a Chinese gentleman in the French Indochina of the 1930s, the narrator's transgressive display might be read – I argue – as a weapon against her mother's madness and obliteration. For the daughter's forbidden yet highly visible affair displays her feminised lover as mother-surrogate, displacing (and replacing) the mother herself – thus neutralising the danger the mother represents.

Chapter Six
Spectacular Scripts: Transgendering the Mad Mother in Duras's Different *Lover(s)*

Following the previous chapter on Japrisot's blending of identities and hysterical blurring as tactics to displace a normative, masculinist detective script, this closing chapter turns to a display narrative generated, instead, by energies that precisely resist such feminine blending. In Marguerite Duras's 1984 novel *L'Amant* ['The Lover'] and its 1991 reprise, *L'Amant de la Chine du Nord* ['The Lover from North China'],[1] it is the threat of engulfment *within* a blended feminine relationship (that binding mother and daughter) that propels the daughter into display. In these two works, the threat of engulfment within the mother's madness motivates the daughter's flight into a transgressive love affair; itself merely symptom, the affair expresses the daughter's resistance to a too-intimate, engulfing menace. Perversions that might be traced back to toxic, exploitive masculinist power have destroyed the mother, as figured in the brother's crippling hold over the family. An implicit weapon against her mother's madness and obliteration, the daughter's forbidden affair is construed by the narrative as scandalously visible display. The threat posed by one spectacle – the danger of absorption within the mother's spectacular madness – produces the daughter's flight into another spectacle: a forbidden liaison. Yet, even as it constructs as glaringly transgressive this cross-cultural, cross-social-class, interracial liaison of a French teenager and an older Chinese lover in the French Indochina of the 1930s, the narrating voice subtly re-positions the lover as feminised mother-surrogate. Transgendered in this way by the narrative, the Chinese lover effectively displaces and replaces the mother herself, thus neutralising the danger that the mother represents.

While the two *Amant* narratives serve as complementary accounts of the daughter's affair with an interdicted Other, the daughter's liaison with a Chinese lover must be read further, more deeply, as the expression of another, different, sort of love. That is, more compelling – more problematic, more intense, more intimate, more consuming – than the daughter's relationship to her Chinese lover is the daughter's troubled bond with her mother. This bond is heavily ambivalent; for the mother, destroyed by the bitterness and poverty of her struggle in the French colony as well as by her helpless love for her brutal son, is an abject figure: 'une lugubre force gothique', as Kristeva puts it.[2] The otherness embodied by the lover – racial, cultural, sexual, linguistic, social – both obscures and mediates another – more decisive, more absolute, more dangerous because more intimate – alterity: the more menacing otherness of the destroyed mother's madness.[3] Whereas Duras's two titles invite us to read her novels as love stories, the narrating daughter herself only belatedly and equivocally recognises such a possibility for her own narrative. It is only at the end of the *Amant* narrative, on the ship taking her back to France from Indochina, that the daughter hears the sudden burst of a Chopin waltz, and weeps: 'elle n'avait pas été sûre tout à coup de ne pas l'avoir aimé d'un amour qu'elle n'avait pas vu' ['she suddenly hadn't been sure not to have loved him with a love she hadn't recognised'] (*L'Amant*, p. 138). Such a formulation – not just doubly, but triply negative (she suddenly had *not* been sure *not* to have loved him with a love she had *not* seen) – betrays through vertiginous grammatical oscillation and ambiguity, the narrator's own abiding uncertainty and confusion over the ultimate meaning of her interdicted affair with a Chinese lover.[4] The project of this chapter is to explore the text's dynamics of display and displacement in an effort to provide a possible answer.

The narrator's mother's behaviour is governed by the destructive son that she loves far more than her other son and daughter, calling him 'mon fils' ['my son'] and the other two, dismissively, 'les plus jeunes' ['the younger ones'] (*L'Amant*, p. 75); she is, moreover, unable to explain such unreasonable love to her daughter (*L'Amant de la Chine du Nord*, p. 26). Unaware of the need to provide bribes, she buys an infertile piece of land from corrupt officials, only to struggle for years, in deranged determination, against persistent flooding by the sea. The mother's reaction to her own destruction as she descends into poverty and debt is increasingly recognised by her daughter as madness. Looking at her mother one day, the daughter tells us, 'dans une sorte d'effacement soudain, de chute, brutalement je ne l'ai plus reconnue du tout' ['in a sort of sudden effacing, a fall, brutally I didn't recognise her at all'] (*L'Amant*, p. 105); suddenly – in a whiff of hallucinatory madness that recurs throughout the text, blending and binding daughter and mother – this stranger with a mildly dazed air no longer seems to be her mother. Significantly, *L'Amant de la Chine du Nord*'s opening, bacchanalian scene is infused by a certain hysteria as the entire house – walls, floor, ceiling – is washed by the children and young houseboys, while the mother dances and plays the piano among the suds (*L'Amant de la Chine du Nord*, p. 13). Elsewhere, she responds to her older son's brutality with what the narrator calls 'un opéra de cris' ['an opera of cries'] (*L'Amant*, p. 75). Increasingly drunk as the rich lover's guest in the family restaurant scene featured in both texts, the mother laughs randomly: 'Elle rit de tout, du vol de l'argent par son fils, de la peur de son fils, de son affolement comme s'il s'agissait là d'une comédie très comique, ['she laughs at everything, at the theft of money by her son, at her own fright, as though it were a very funny comedy'] (*L'Amant de la Chine du Nord*, p. 170). She is 'comme d'habitude, sans bien comprendre, ahurie, comique, toujours' ['as usual, uncomprehending, dazed, comical, always'] (*L'Amant de la Chine du Nord*, p. 223) on the ship travelling back to France. Ultimately, the lover himself will be construed as 'maddened' by his love for the daughter, in the course of the daughter's effort to displace and recast the engulfing threat of the destroyed mother's own madness. In the two *Amant* texts, then, display dynamics are symptomatic of the daughter's attempt to feminise and maternalise her lover as her mother's safely transgendered surrogate.

Against the backdrop of the mother's madness, her daughter, beginning with the pathetic and discordant pastiche of her patched silk dress, man's hat and evening heels on the ferry, engages in a display that would appear to be her own – marking her independence and distance from the mad mother. For such self-staging and styling has been read as the girl's management of her own representation, her own sexuality; '[s]he controls positions in regard to desire: she is no longer the passive object of the gaze … but actively exhibitionist'.[5] Viewing such sexual autonomy with more reserve, however, Leslie Hill suggests that while it provides the daughter with a measure of independence, 'to leave the family in Duras is also to rediscover, in displaced or transformed ways, the powerful but ambivalent bond of desire that has its origin in the promiscuity of family relations'.[6] Yet such displaced desire might be stated more forcefully and precisely; while problematic family bonds indeed propel the daughter's effort to flee family relations, she is unable, contrary to Hill's claim, to 'leave the family'. In particular, she is unable to leave the mother, for she takes the family's damage with her. What is perceived as excessive, transgressive sexuality, is instead, a *screen* excess, a symptom – its underlying cause a different excess, her imbrication within the mother's infectious – in the text's metaphor – madness. Rather than a means of liberation, this spectacular self-display is driven by a powerful and haunting otherness; what appears as a fiercely defiant manipulation of erotic independence is instead, I maintain, the symptom of failed independence from the mother's madness. Significantly, the daughter regularly thinks of her mother in the midst of lovemaking in the lover's bachelor apartment – and bursts into tears (*L'Amant*, p. 123). Her claim for being sheltered 'pour toujours' ['forever'] (*L'Amant*, p. 46) within the lover's black limousine from the damaging mother and family dissolves; for even the limousine, as the extension of the equally fragile and unstable refuge of the lover's apartment, is seen by the daughter as a 'lieu de détresse, naufragé' ['a site of distress, shipwrecked']: a shipwreck engulfed by the mad, maternal sea (*L'Amant de la Chine du Nord*, p. 79).

The daughter's frantic self-display, whose most visible symptom is the affair with the Chinese lover, might thus be read as her effort to reverse another spectacle: that of her mother's mad, destitute destruction. Prompted by the mother's undesirability amidst generalised indifference to her as a mad beggar that no one wants, the daughter scripts herself as an object of desire – forcing her way not only back into visibility, but back into the economy that has destroyed her mother. She reverses the flow of that economy; the mother's disastrous land investments and losses are, in a sense, returned to her through the lover's gifts. Mediated by the Chinese lover, money flows back to the mother from the fortune made, ironically enough – given the mother's catastrophic purchase of sterile property – through land investment: the successful real-estate business operated by the lover's father.[7] Just as the narrative is organised around a photograph that was never taken – not one merely lost or destroyed, but a photo that never existed, an utter, irrecuperable absence – so the visible, spectacular and forbidden relation, that of the daughter and her Chinese lover, is generated by the obliterated, destroyed, mad, 'absent' mother. And just as, back in France, the mother manipulates photos of the absent, scandalous daughter whom relatives now refuse to receive, so the mother also unknowingly manipulates her daughter, with a pathetic yet fearsome power figured explicitly in the case of the narrator's friend, Hélène Lagonelle, 'qui fera finalement ce que sa mère voudra' ['who will ultimately do what her mother wants'] (*L'Amant*, p. 90).

Even as the daughter appears to be crafting her own display, the mother is complicit in the preparation of this spectacle. For it was the mother who bought her daughter the man's pink felt hat, one of several startling, even jarring elements in the curious ensemble worn by the daughter in the narrative's early ferry scene (*L'Amant*, p. 32).[8] The mother's complicity is further apparent when, alone in the lover's room, finding a large envelope, the daughter reflects, 'Avec la mère elles ont fait ça: elles ont pris: l'argent' ['With the mother, they did this: they took: the money'] (*L'Amant de la Chine du Nord*, p. 173). The lover senses this complicity, realising that the daughter wanted his ring only in order to give it to her mother – in an imbrication of child and absent mother figured in the very ring itself, set with a diamond that once belonged to the lover's own dead mother (*L'Amant de la Chine du Nord*, pp. 141–2). In this way, both lover and daughter are haunted by dead or destroyed, maddened mothers, whose children are marked by the ring belonging to these maternal phantoms. From dead Chinese mother to son to French daughter to destroyed French mother, the ring traces a path of troubling phantasmatic maternal presences within the very heart of the love affair.

Returning to the decisive yet absent photograph that – in the narrator's claim – generates her narrative, we see that the mother's complicity in the daughter's display on the ferry is not the only complicating factor of the scene. Adding further complexity is the fact that the scene is presented as a photograph that might have been taken, yet wasn't: an image presented 'sous rature' ['under erasure'][9] as somehow effaced, yet necessarily visible, legible. However, this untaken, non-existent photograph is the image, claims the narrator on the text's opening page, 'qui me plaît de moi-même, celle où je me reconnais, où je m'enchante' ['that pleases me most about myself, in which I recognise myself, that enchants me'] (*L'Amant*, p. 9).[10] Is it *because* the image never existed that the daughter most readily recognises herself in its fantasised forms? This instant of self-recognition becomes a Lacanian, mirror-phase moment of decisive alienation, as such recognition arises from an absence: a photograph never taken, an image never recorded. Such alienation is explicit in *L'Amant de la Chine du Nord* as the daughter looks at herself – wearing the man's felt hat, evening heels and red lipstick – in a passage that tellingly scrambles first and third-person pronouns: 'Elle se regarde elle – elle s'est approchée de son image. Elle s'approche encore. Ne se reconnaît pas bien' ['She looks at herself she [*sic*] – she approached her image. She comes closer. Doesn't easily recognise herself'] (*L'Amant de la Chine du Nord*, p. 84). This absent photograph is described by a discourse that claims to render visible, apparent, what had previously been obscured: 'Ici je parle des périodes cachées de cette même jeunesse, de certains enfouissements que j'avais opéré sur certains faits, sur certains sentiments, sur certains événements' ['Here I'm talking about the hidden periods of this same youth, of certain burials I had made of certain facts, of certain feelings, of certain events'] (*L'Amant*, p. 14). However, even as the daughter claims she is going to reveal what she had hitherto kept hidden – certain truths – she asserts that 'écrire ce n'est rien que publicité' ['writing is nothing but publicity'] in a dismissal of her own narrative as showy, mendacious. Yet she goes further, claiming, within the very narrative of her own story, that there *is* no story of her life, no centre, no trail, no direction (*L'Amant*, pp. 14–15).[11] Again, what is present in writing is asserted to be false; the account narrated is declared to be precisely *not* the true story, which does not exist. What is privileged remains the photo never taken – the absent, the unspoken, the unwritten, the invisible – implicitly exhorting us to search beyond any visible traces, beyond the very discourse we are reading: beyond the spectacle itself of the daughter's scandalous affair with a Chinese lover.

Such distancing and self-alienation is apparent throughout *L'Amant* as the narrator presents herself as 'both subject and object' in Selous's claim, 'not just because she is writing about herself many years ago, but also in the way that she portrays herself always as an object of someone's desire'.[12] Selous points to the book's opening anecdote in which a man tells the daughter, now grown old, that he finds her aged, ravaged face more beautiful than her young face. In representing the narrator's face as object of *another's* desire, the text cues the reader to understand self-recognition in *L'Amant* as always fissured by self-alienation: an important step towards understanding that anything the daughter apparently does *for herself* is shadowed by the alienating presence of the mother. In an eloquent scene in *L'Amant de la Chine du Nord*, the daughter, secretly watching her mother leaving an interview with the head of the daughter's boarding house, thinks of the shame she feels over her mother: 'elle n'était pas allée vers elle, honteuse de sa mère, elle était remontée au dortoir, elle s'était cachée et elle avait pleuré sur cette mère pas sortable dont elle avait honte. Son amour' ['she hadn't gone to her, she had gone back up to the dormitory, she had hidden and she had cried over this unpresentable mother she was ashamed of. Her love'] (*L'Amant de la Chine du Nord*, p. 120). Such shame defines the mother/daughter bond, in an alienation extending to all other bonds, compromising all relationships for the daughter. 'A cause de ce qu'on a fait à notre mère si aimable, si confiante, nous haïssons la vie, nous nous haïssons' ['Because of what was done to our mother, so kind, so trusting, we hate life, we hate each other'] (*L'Amant*, p. 69).

Given such powerful ambivalence in the tangled mother-daughter bond, we begin to sense the daughter's transgressive affair itself as marked – that is, as a symptom or trace of other, more occulted, energies. Now, such 'other' energies and desires are not absent, to be sure, from critical discussion of the novel. Emphasising the notion of an 'erotic transaction', Peter Brooks suggests that in 'experiencing her own desire for Hélène Lagonelle's body, ['the narrator'] can experience her own body as the object of the lover's desire'.[13] Expanding the idea of a 'transaction' among other energies, Leslie Hill argues for the 'mingling of bodies and sexes' in 'a round of desire'.[14] We might go yet further, however, and suggest that what Hill calls an 'indeterminate process of simultaneous fusion and division, identification and detachment'[15] in the bond with Hélène, might usefully figure – as well – the more complex mother/daughter bond, with its problematic confusion of self and other. Such an imbrication of self and other, of sexual and material pleasure, is expressed in the ring offered, as we saw above, by the lover to the daughter: a ring into which we might read, as Hill suggests, 'fusion and division, identification and detachment' as the lover himself realises: 'Alors le Chinois avait su qu'elle avait voulu la bague pour la donner à sa mère autant qu'elle avait voulu sa main sur son corps' ['So the Chinese had known that she had wanted the ring so as to give it to her mother as much as she had wanted his hand on her body'] (*L'Amant de la Chine du Nord*, p. 141). The lover sees what the daughter herself does not: her binding relationship to the mother: 'Elles sont bavardes toutes les deux de la même façon, à l'infini. Infiniment bavardes elles sont. Extasié, le Chinois la regarde, elle, et l'enfant, elle et la ressemblance avec l'enfant' ['They're both chatty in the same way, infinitely. Infinitely chatty they are. In ecstasy, the Chinese man looks at her, the mother, and the child, the mother and her resemblance to her child'] (*L'Amant de la Chine du Nord*, p. 154). In discovering and pursuing her own sexual pleasure, the daughter perhaps attempts to mediate this lack for her mother, who *hasn't* known – in her daughter's assertion – such 'jouissance' ['erotic gratification'] (*L'Amant*, p. 50) and has, moreover, as the mother herself claims, 'perdu le goût de mon plaisir' ['lost the taste of my own pleasure'] (*L'Amant de la Chine du Nord*, p. 202). Similarly, the daughter's aggressive arrogation of visibility might indirectly attempt to restore the effaced, destroyed mother to visibility. The daughter's love affair thus emerges not so much as decisive flight from – but rather as displaced symptom of bondage within – a crippling, specular maternal economy.

Within these displaced symptoms, the lover becomes a transgendered, tender, attentive, 'corrected' mother. As Ellison puts it, 'the mother is replaced/negated by the maternal caring of the lover'[16] as the daughter becomes 'son enfant' ['his child'] (*L'Amant*, p. 122). One might even read a childbirth image in the lover's devotion to 'cette enfant qui va partir, s'éloigner à jamais de lui, de son corps' ['this child who's going to leave, to depart forever from him, from his body'] (*L'Amant de la Chine du Nord*, p. 165). And yet, such 'replacing/negating' of the mother by the lover's caring would appear to fail, falling short before the enveloping, oceanic madness that defines the mother. For even as the lover is transgendered and maternalised by his caring, he is weakened, feminised, by his love for the daughter, herself 'amoureuse des hommes faibles' ['in love with weak men'] (*L'Amant de la Chine du Nord*, p. 36). His love renders the lover impotent, both before the daughter's departure – 'son corps ne voulait plus de celle qui partait' ['his body no longer desired the one who was leaving'] (*L'Amant de la Chine du Nord*, p. 177) – and once he is married to another: 'Il a dû être longtemps à ne pas pouvoir être avec [sa femme], à ne pas arriver à lui donner l'héritier des fortunes' ['He must have spent a long time unable to be with [his wife], unable to give her the heir to the fortunes'] (*L'Amant*, p. 140). Moreover, his love for the daughter has become a madness of its own – 'il l'avait aimée comme un fou à en perdre la vie' ['he had loved her like a madman, beyond life itself'] (*L'Amant de la Chine du Nord*, p. 178). Just as the lover assumes the role of maternal incarnation or mother surrogate, he appears to be contaminated by the mother's own madness: 'il y a dans cet excès une folie qui plaît à l'enfant' ['there is in this excess a madness that pleases the child'] (*L'Amant de la Chine du Nord*, p. 88). Just as the daughter sees her mother as 'une reine … de la folie' ['a queen … of madness'] (*L'Amant de la Chine du Nord*, p. 117), the lover himself is maddened at the thought of separation: 'je deviens fou' ['I'm going mad'] (*L'Amant de la Chine du Nord*, p. 106). His cry of despair on the eve of the daughter's departure for France is not only 'la plainte … d'une femme' ['the lament … of a woman'] (*L'Amant de la Chine du Nord*, p. 195), but a cry that reprises the mother's own blend of madness, death and passion: 'ce cri, terrible, obscène, impudique, illisible, comme la folie, la mort, la passion' ['this cry, terrible, obscene, shameless, illegible, like madness, death, passion'] (*L'Amant de la Chine du Nord*, p. 195). Whereas Françoise Lionnet sees such feminisation of the lover as an example of Duras's 'most clichéd form of "Orientalism"',[17] Panivong Norindr takes the opposite position, arguing instead for *L'Amant*'s subversion of 'sterile masculinity associated with Western clichéd notions of virility'.[18] However, as I am suggesting, beyond such claims for either a stale, 'exoticizing' orientalism, or its opposite – the subversion of Western virility – lies a more urgent, more intimate and troubled, more compelling reason for such feminisation: transgendering the lover as the corrected mother, maddened not by her own destruction, but (in the narration's phantasmatic, rectified version) by love for the daughter. In this way, the narrative's 'maternalisation' of the lover, down to his very madness, provides the daughter with a safely remedied mother.

Such feminisation of the lover, effectively displacing and thus neutralising the mother, would barricade the daughter against the threat of engulfment within the mother's crazed destruction. Whereas the trope of permeable, blended spaces has been read in the *Amant* texts as joyous, liberating and utopian, such flows – I maintain – ultimately become dystopian haemorrhages in which identities are destructively intertwined.[19] The possibility of a joyful Dionysian expenditure of self is too compromised by the destructive dispossession of the self in the daughter's bond with – and bondage to – her mad mother.[20] Understanding the centrality of this bond, Kristeva reads it on the model of the numerous feminine 'reduplications' in Duras's oeuvre, in which female characters slip towards identification and replacement, one with another. For Kristeva's reading of *L'Amant*, such imbrication is prompted by the traumatic fantasy of inevitable abandonment or separation from the mother. 'En effaçant la figure de la mère, elle en prend en même temps la place. La fille se substitue à la folie maternelle, elle tue moins sa mère qu'elle ne la prolonge dans l'hallucination négative d'une identification toujours fidèlement amoureuse' ['In erasing the figure of the mother, she takes her place at the same time. The daughter substitutes herself for maternal madness, she kills her mother less than she prolongs her in the negative hallucination of an identification always faithfully loving'].[21] I am arguing, however, that the daughter does not so much erase and 'take the place' *herself* of the mad mother, as attempt – ultimately in vain – to displace and replace the mother with a feminised, maternalised and love-maddened lover.

But such efforts to displace and replace the mother must remain vexed in light of the mother's oceanic destructiveness, and its threat to engulf the daughter – which we might read as an extreme version of the feminine identification and doubling constantly at work in Duras's oeuvre. Arguing for Lol's perpetual displacement in *Le ravissement de Lol V. Stein*, Karen McPherson goes on to suggest a corollary movement towards replacement of Duras's characters by each other, who occupy, successively, '*a single place*' [*sic*].[22] Similarly, the phantasmatic scene in *L'Amant* involving the trio of the daughter's friend Hélène Lagonelle, the daughter herself and her lover is understood by Hill as a rewrite of the T. Beach scene in *Le Ravissement de Lol V. Stein* ['The Ravishing of Lol V. Stein']; in both scenes, suggests Hill, 'the woman narrator imagines herself giving away the body of her much admired – and keenly desired – girlfriend to her male lover and thrilling at the merging of her own bodily enjoyment with that of her two partners'.[23]

In developing this model of feminine identification and doubling in *L'Amant*, we might notice what lies just beyond the crucial image (the photograph never taken) of the daughter on the ferry; for beyond its absent image lies the Mekong river, bearing with it the danger of being swept out to sea. Indeed, in the ferry scene of the lovers' first encounter, what prompts the daughter to get off the bus and come to the railing where the Chinese gentleman sees her from his limousine, is the fear of this danger: 'Je descends toujours du car quand on arrive sur le bac, la nuit aussi, parce que toujours j'ai peur, j'ai peur que les câbles cèdent, que nous soyons emportés vers la mer' ['I always get off the bus when we get to the ferry, at night too, because I'm always afraid, I'm afraid that the cables will break, that we'll be swept seaward'] (*L'Amant*, p. 18). Duras herself confesses that nothing terrifies her more than the sea, subject of her nightmares.[24] While we might hesitate at Leslie Hill's claim for the fundamental ambivalence of the sea as provoking 'a yearning for bodily submersion', the sea is indeed, as he suggests, construed in the *Amant* narratives as metaphor 'for that most primal and archaic of all ambivalent love objects in Duras's writing', the mother's body.[25]

Pursuing such an insight, however, we understand that the sea represents not only the body of the mother, but by extension, the threat of the daughter's own engulfment within her mother's madness. The sea has effectively destroyed the mother through its constant flooding of the property sold to her by corrupt officials, relentlessly drowning possible arable land. The sea that destroyed her mother also threatens to engulf the daughter in that mother's madness: a threat the daughter cannot escape, despite her flight into the lover's arms and apartment. Unsurprisingly, just as the spectre of the mother is present in the lover's bachelor retreat, so is the sound of the sea.[26] In *L'Amant de la Chine du Nord*, the daughter, evoking her memories, 'entend encore le bruit de la mer dans la chambre' ['still hears the noise of the sea in the room'] (*L'Amant de la Chine du* Nord, p. 78); similarly, she imagines the lover's bachelor apartment as 'immergée' ['immersed'] within the city's cacophony (*L'Amant*, p. 47). A description of the lovers falling asleep is followed by an invasive, overflowing image of the Mekong. Reinscribing the source of the mother's madness in the sea floods that rendered her property sterile, as well as the daughter's terror of being dragged into the river, the overflowing river image not only brings the engulfing mother into the lover's bachelor refuge; it also implicitly sweeps away the lovers by taking their place. 'Le fleuve. Loin. Ses méandres entre les rizières. Il prend la place des amants' ['The river. Far away. Its meanderings among the rice fields. It takes the place of the lovers'] (*L'Amant de la Chine du Nord*, p. 135).[27]

Such imbrication of the mother and the sea – wrought by the daughter's terror at being engulfed by the sea of her mother's madness – undermines critical claims for the decisiveness of the daughter's crossing on the Mekong ferry. Understanding the Mekong as an 'arm' separating the domain of the mother from that of the lover, Went-Daoust suggests that crossings, whether of rivers or seas, correspond to 'a change in mode of existence'.[28] For Ellison as well, the Mekong crossing represents 'the crossing from childhood to womanhood accomplished in the act of love'.[29] Similarly, Hill emphasises the decisiveness of the girl's 'mythic journey across the Mekong … toward desire, sexual knowledge, prostitution, and subsequent exile'.[30] In a more explicitly colonial context, the Mekong crossing is also understood as crucial by Panivong Norindr, who argues for importance of the urban division of colonial Saigon into the city centre and periphery. In Norindr's claim, the young heroine is able to transform herself into 'Other' and 'to circulate, cross and transgress different boundaries in the colonial city', 'dislocating in scandalous fashion fraudulent and venal notions of colonial propriety'.[31] My purpose in this chapter, however, is not only to explore further the daughter's spectacle and its ultimate meaning, but to question whether the daughter actually succeeds in crossing the most powerful, daunting and intimate boundary: that releasing her from crippling bondage to the mad, destroyed, mother.

Other critics indeed question the decisiveness of the Mekong crossing; suggesting that a river crossing 'signals no definitive departure from one place to another', Susan Cohen points out that the daughter's 'rite of passage takes place on a ferry, which rather than transporting one to a permanent destination, shuttles back and forth. The ferry has neither point of origin nor end port'.[32] Cohen does conclude, however, that while the daughter 'will never consign herself, either symbolically or concretely, to one or the other of the river banks', she will leave both her lover and her family for writing.[33] Yet the writing itself belies the daughter's claim that she no longer remembers her mother's laughter and cries, and thus is able to write so easily about her (*L'Amant*, p. 38); for it is through the mother's discourse that the daughter construes herself, referring to herself as 'she', and 'the child', in the mother's idiom – which remains, as Went-Daoust puts it, 'desperately alive in the discourse of the writer'.[34]

Contributing yet further, I would argue, to the psychic weight and power of the mother's omnipresence in the daughter's flight into display is the mother's link with the narrative's mad beggar. For the mother's own madness and destitution are evoked in this somewhat sinister, surrogate figure, seen by Madeleine Borgomano as a 'generative cell' for Duras's entire oeuvre.[35] Haunted by the memory of an itinerant beggar trying to sell her child, Duras speaks in an interview of having tried to process this memory in her work, but with agonising difficulty. She recognises the peculiar obsessiveness of the memory, suggesting it has driven her to writing.

> L'acte est restée en moi dans une opacité dont il ne sortait jamais … et c'est depuis que mon enfant est grand … que la chose s'est représentée à mes yeux … comme un problème à résoudre avec les seuls moyens que j'aie, c'est-à-dire l'écriture … Cet acte monstrueux et adorable … j'ai essayé de le faire entrer dans la literature … et je n'ai pas réussi.

> [The act has remained within me, amidst an opacity from which it never emerged … and it's since my child has grown up … that this has taken shape for me … as a problem to resolve through the only means I have, writing … This monstrous and adorable act … I've tried to render it in my work … and I have not succeeded.][36]

Pointing to the psychic resonance of this memory, Borgomano suggests that the child witnessing this event relived, indirectly, 'le traumatisme le plus archaïque et l'angoisse la plus insoutenable: l'abandon par la mère, répétition du traumatisme de la naissance et préfiguration de tous les abandons futurs' ['the most archaic trauma and the most unbearable anguish: abandonment by the mother, repetition of the birth trauma and the prefiguration of all abandonments to come'].[37] Borgomano, however, immediately cancels the trauma of this abandonment by understanding it as mere, 'reassuring' substitution; this doubling of mothers, with its compensatory and recuperative adoption, establishes – in Borgomano's claim – the phantasm of a chain of love and inaugurates the long series of Durassian displacements.[38] Yet, the impossibility of psychic compensation for such abandonment – such indelibly 'archaic trauma' – would explain the insurmountable ambivalence provoked in the *Amant* texts by the mad mother in her daughter. Abandoned, in effect, by the mother's favouritism for her destructive older son, and threatened by engulfment within the mother's madness, the daughter remains psychically crippled by this troubled bond. Tellingly, in *L'Amant*, the anecdote about the mother's sudden, alienating otherness is surrounded by fragments that feature the mad beggar. In a scene that is, ambiguously, either remembered or hauntingly fantasised, the daughter describes being pursued along dark streets by the madwoman. 'Tout en courant je me retourne et je vois. C'est une très grande femme, très maigre, maigre comme la mort et qui rit et qui court. Elle est pieds nus, elle court après moi pour me rattraper. Je la reconnais, c'est la folle du poste, la folle de Vinhlong' ['As I run, I turn around and see her. She's a very tall woman, very thin, thin as death, laughing, running. She's barefoot, she runs after me to catch me. I recognise her, she's the madwoman of the town, the madwoman of Vinhlong'] (*L'Amant*, p. 103). Evoking her great fear of the beggar's madness, the daughter tells us, 'Ce que l'on peut avancer, c'est le souvenir que si la femme me touche, même légèrement, de la main, je passerai à mon tour dans un état bien pire que celui de la mort, l'état de la folie' ['What one might be sure of is the memory that if this woman touches me, even lightly, with her hand, I, too, will be plunged into a state much worse than death, the state of madness'] (*L'Amant*, p. 104).[39] Immediately following this scene in *L'Amant*, confirming the association of the mother and madness, is the account of the mother's sudden, dazed, unrecognisable otherness: itself followed in the text by a return to the beggarwoman, this time explicitly associated with the mother, who cares for the beggar's infected foot and her unwanted little child.

Cast out by her own mother because of her pregnancy, the beggarwoman thus displays, through her expanding belly, the shame and persecuted motherhood of the narrator's mother herself in the *Amant* texts. The unwanted pregnancy, source of humiliation and disgrace for the beggarwoman, becomes an emblem of the narrator's mother's humiliation and disgrace through her children: her 'bad' son, her scandalous daughter, her half-wit son. Even more crucially, however, the beggarwoman sells her daughter: 'elle n'en veut plus du tout, elle la donne, allez, prends' ['she doesn't want anything more to do with her, she gives her, here, take her'] (*L'Amant*, p. 106). The beggar's rejection of her own daughter thus figures the inadequate, problematic love of the narrator's mother for her daughter. Tellingly, in *L'Amant*, it is only her destructive oldest son that the mother calls 'mon enfant' ['my child']; she calls the others, 'les plus jeunes' ['the youngest ones'] (*L'Amant*, p. 75). In Annaud's film version and in *L'Amant de la Chine du Nord*, this imbalance is more explicitly rendered, with the daughter begging her mother tearfully to explain why she loves the older son so much more than the others. The mother at first denies this, then admits that she does not know why and has never known (*L'Amant de la Chine du Nord*, pp. 25–6). Emphasising the extreme implications of such rejection by the mother, Borgomano argues that abandoning a child is the shocking limit of dispossession, with its implications not only of misery, but of madness.[40]

The mad beggar also appears in *Le Vice-Consul* ['The Vice Consul'], published eighteen years before *L'Amant*, where the beggarwoman's tormented bond with a mother who has rejected her, is developed as motivating and shaping her very wanderings.[41] As she wanders, the beggar is haunted by obsessive, vengeful thoughts of her mother:

> Revoir cette femme entre toutes la plus méchante qu'elle ait connue, sans cela qui va-t-on devenir? … A l'enfant, elle parlait. A qui maintenant? A la vieille mère de Tonlé-Sap, origine, cause de tous les maux, de sa destinée de travers, son amour pur … Comme il est tard pour retourner chez sa mère, retourner jouer, retourner dans le Nord pour dire bonjour et rire avec les autres, se faire battre par elle et mourir sous ses coups.

> [To see again this meanest of all the women she's ever known, or else what will become of her? … She used to talk, to the child. To whom, now? To the old mother of Tonlé-Sap, the origin and cause of all her troubles, of her unfortunate fate, her pure love … How late it is to go home to her mother, to go home to the North to say hello and laugh with the others, to be beaten by her and die beneath her blows.][42]

As Borgomano puts it, 'à travers un système complexe d'abandon, de renoncement, d'intercession et d'échange, se joue et se rejoue le jeu de la maternité, et de la féminité' ['through a complex system of abandonment, renunciation, intercession and exchange, the game of maternity and femininity is played and replayed'].[43] The story of the beggarwoman, however, as Selous demonstrates, is overwhelmingly shaped less by her maternity than by her ambivalent feelings for her own mother. All the beggar's emotion is invested in the mother who rejected her, not in her unborn child; even on the point of giving birth, the beggarwoman thinks of her mother, wishing to give her the child. After the beggar gives her child to the white woman, instead, the beggar's mother – in Selous's suggestion – still 'remains the only addressee of her thoughts, now that the baby is gone; her mother is the beggar woman's only guarantor of her own sanity as a separate, thinking subject'. Selous concludes that since return to the mother is impossible, the beggarwoman sinks into madness, unable to find a substitute for her mother: an object 'in relation to which she can be a subject of desire and build an identity'.[44] We might theorise that, similarly, the daughter of the *Amant* narratives is ultimately unable to find a maternal substitute, even in her feminised, maternalised Chinese lover.

Beyond establishing a troubling bond between maternity and alterity, the beggarwoman's madness is explicitly developed in *Le Vice-Consul*. 'Sous le lampadaire, grattant sa tête chauve, elle, maigreur de Calcutta pendant cette nuit grasse, elle est assisse entre les fous, elle est là, la tête vide, le coeur mort, elle tend toujours la nourriture. Elle parle, raconte quelque chose que personne ne comprendrait' ['Under the streetlamp, scratching her bald head, she, the thinness itself of Calcutta on this heavy evening, she's sitting among the mad, she's there, her head empty, her heart dead, she's still waiting for food. She talks, recounts something that no one would understand].[45] In another scene in *Le Vice-Consul*, the beggarwoman chases a fleeing Charles Rossett: an episode prefiguring the madwoman's pursuit of the daughter in *L'Amant*. In this scene from Duras's earlier novel, however, the beggarwoman takes a live fish from between her breasts, and, laughing, bites off its head:

> Le poisson guillotiné remue dans sa main. Elle doit s'amuser
> de faire peur, de donner la nausée. Elle avance vers lui.
> Charles Rossett recule, elle avance encore, il recule encore,
> mais elle avance plus vite que lui et Charles Rossett jette

la monnaie par terre, se retourne et fuit vers le chemin en courant.

[The guillotined fish flops in her hand. She must enjoy scaring him, making him sick. She walks towards him. Charles Rossett backs away, she advances again, he backs away again, but she advances faster than he and Charles Rossett throws the change on the ground, turns around and flees towards the road, running.][46]

Rossett's fear of and flight from the beggarwoman anticipate the narrating daughter's haunted fear in *L'Amant* that with one touch, the madwoman of Vinhlong's madness will be transmitted to her, the narrator (*L'Amant*, pp. 103–4) – contaminating the daughter with her mother's madness, disgrace and persecution. In *L'Amant de la Chine du Nord*, the Chinese lover implicitly links the beggar to the mother, via the image of the sea. Referring to the daughter's fear of beggars as part of a persistent, childish terror, of 'tout' ['everything'], the lover goes on to connect the beggar and the sea, as well as, by implication, the spectre of the mad mother profiled in the sea: 'de tout, des orages, du noir, des mendiants, de la mer' ['of everything, of storms, of the dark, of beggars, of the sea'] (*L'Amant de la Chine du Nord*, p. 162). This complex of the beggar, madness and the sea is also evoked in 'une troisième musique … entrecoupée de rires fous, stridents, de cris. C'est la mendiante du Gange qui traverse le poste comme chaque nuit. Pour toujours essayer d'atteindre la mer' ['a third sort of music … punctuated with wild, strident laughter, with cries. It's the beggar of the Ganges, crossing the town the way she does every night. Always trying to reach the sea'] (*L'Amant de la Chine du Nord*, p. 22). Later in that narrative, the daughter speaks of Indian beggars rendered mad by fear (*L'Amant de la Chine du Nord*, p. 107); the Chinese lover responds by mentioning a specific beggar 'qui crie en riant, qui fait des discours, qui chante. Qui fait peur' ['who shrieks while laughing, who makes speeches, who sings. Who frightens'] (*L'Amant de la Chine du Nord*, p. 107).

This image of the mad beggarwoman with her unwanted child shadows, even haunts, that of the narrating daughter's mother throughout the various versions of *L'Amant*. The daughter suggests the link of homelessness, madness and poverty in saying about her mother, 'Je la vois comme une sorte de reine, vous voyez … une reine … sans patrie … de … comment dire ça … de la pauvreté … de la folie, voyez' ['I see her as a sort of queen, you see … a queen … without a country … a queen of … how to say it … of poverty … of madness, you see'] (*L'Amant*, p. 117). Linking the beggarwoman's story to those of the mother and the Dame de Savannaket, Marilyn Schuster suggests that 'they embody three figures of motherhood: the outcast, the madwoman, and the woman who bears desire and death'.[47]

This imbrication of maternity, madness and abandonment further figures another Durassian preoccupation: a slow drifting, as Borgomano puts it, in which successive characters displace and replace each other, effacing identities.[48] The beggarwoman's child is given another mother, only to die, nonetheless. As we saw above, Borgomano further points to Anne-Marie Stretter's replacing displacing of Lol at the ball, and Lol's replacing of Tatiana, in *Le ravissement de Lol V. Stein*. Such a system of drifts, substitutions and shifted identities provides a backdrop for the most complex and confused of all imbricated identities, that between mother and daughter.

This imbrication suggests that the daughter's love affair with the Chinese gentleman, far from representing escape and autonomy for her, instead expresses their impossibility. To be sure, Hill argues that it is perhaps the very impossibility of fulfilment within another relation that animates the daughter's desire. In other words, beyond the stamp of cultural, social and racial interdictions, stands the final interdiction, the impossibility of gratification; and this ultimate impossibility is, in Hill's claim, what gives rise to desire. 'It is only ever when there is no possibility of relation between self and other that the other may be grasped as radically different, and thus genuinely desirable.'[49]

Yet what may ultimately block fulfilment of the relation with the Chinese lover, establishing him as forever inaccessible, may not, in the end – as in Hill's suggestion – be related to the lover's own social, cultural, financial and racial difference. Rather, fulfilment within the forbidden affair, I would argue, is blocked by the more primordial, powerful, engulfing relation between mother and daughter. It is therefore difficult to subscribe to claims for the erotic as the vehicle for the daughter's liberation. Hinting at such a difficulty, Brooks suggests that '[o]ne of the prime effects of desire, in this novel, seems to be to make subject into object, to allow or to force the subject to grasp itself as it is for the desire and in the perspective of the other'; Brooks argues, indeed, that the Chinese lover is *an* other, not *the* Other.[50] Yet we might now take a step further; having understood that the lover is merely *an* other, we are able to recognise the true Other: the mother. By making herself object of a *corrected* mother's desire (as mediated through the now transgendered lover's desire) the daughter's self-display becomes legible as an intense effort to displace the suffocating, enveloping threat of the mother's madness.

As we have seen, the spectacle created by the daughter's love affair with the Chinese gentleman has tended to be read as the 'story' of *L'Amant*; yet just how much lies beyond and beneath the daughter's self-display has become increasingly apparent. And yet, what makes this search beyond spectacle difficult is that the novel itself becomes increasingly spectacularised, sensationalised, beginning with its film version. For the daughter's own spectacle is itself appropriated by producer Claude Berri and director Jean-Jacques Annaud for what Hill calls their 'creakingly wooden, exotically voyeuristic screen version' of *L'Amant*.[51] Duras initially collaborated with this screen project, and attempted several screenplays, all rejected by Annaud. Eventually severing all participation, Duras complained that Annaud was filming *The Lover* more as biography than as literary text;[52] that is, sensationalising the narrative itself, rather than attempting a literary, artistic film.

And indeed, Annaud's film might be viewed as a sensationalised version of Duras's *L'Amant*. The novel's implicit lesbian bond with Hélène Lagonelle is suggested more explicitly in the film, where the two girls exchange confidences as they lie in bed together, Hélène saying she would rather end up as a prostitute than be sent to nurse a leper colony; the daughter responds that Hélène's possible future customers would be lucky. The love scenes in the lover's bachelor apartment are more spectacle than sensual. After the restaurant dinner with the daughter's family, during which the lover himself is either ignored or mocked, the pair returns to the bachelor apartment. Here the lover strikes the daughter, then virtually rapes her, in a violent scene that never took place in the novel. Lying, still dressed, on the bed, the daughter asks what it would cost to do in a brothel what they'd just done, saying that her mother needs 500 piastres. In the midst of one sensationalised sex scene, another theme becomes sensationalised: the mother's complicity in her daughter's so-called prostitution. And indeed, in subsequent frames, we see the mother accepting the envelope of money from her daughter. The prostitution theme is furthered when the lover forces the daughter to repeat after him that she had come to his apartment so that he would give her money; and that she has been thinking about money, only, since the instant she saw him on the ferry.

Further spectacularisation of the prostitution topos occurs in *L'Amant de la Chine du Nord* with the mediating episode of Alice's more visible, more crude prostitution, as she services her clients in a ditch outside the boarding house: encounters that occur, moreover, with the voyeuristic complicity of both boarders *and* supervisors, watching from the windows (*L'Amant de la Chine du Nord*, p. 173). Just as the narrator's mother is figured, ominously, both in the beggarwoman eager to sell her child and in the madwoman, so the daughter's implied prostitution is figured and exaggerated in Alice's own.

As Duras withdrew from Annaud's film project, she gathered up her various rejected screenplays, converting them eventually into her rewritten novel, *L'Amant de la Chine du Nord*. Ironically, for all Duras's complaints about Annaud's neglect of literariness, this second *Amant* narrative – manifestly a protest against Annaud's film[53] – has a peculiarly 'screenplay' cast. It is frequently disrupted with directives as to soundtrack, camera angles, and staging. Particularly interesting is the intrusive voice of 'l'auteur' ['the author'], as though Duras herself, frustrated at the appropriation of her story by Annaud, is insisting on reclaiming it as her own.[54] Yet this repossession, ironically enough, occurs at the price of increased sensationalism, increased spectacle. Examples of such spectacularisation include the lover himself, in the seminal scene on the ferry, being described as less fragile, more assured and 'on display' than the man depicted in the earlier novel version, more 'pour le cinéma' ['for the movies'] (*L'Amant de la Chine du Nord*, p. 36). The daughter, similarly, behaves as though she is a film heroine: when she plants a kiss on the window of the limousine, 'ses yeux sont fermés comme dans les films' ['her eyes are closed, as in the movies'] (*L'Amant de la Chine du Nord*, p. 61). Relationships are further sensationalised, with the description of an incestuous sexual relationship between the daughter and her little brother; similarly, the implicit lesbian bond with Hélène Lagonelle in *L'Amant*'s fiction becomes, as we have seen, more explicit in *L'Amant de la Chine du Nord*. Here, the daughter's awareness of the lover's money is much bolder. In Annaud's film version, she had been quite demure, seldom looking directly at the lover; in the rewritten novel, however, she stares boldly at him during the opening scene on the ferry, at his clothes, his car, appearing not to hear what he's saying (*L'Amant de la Chine du Nord*, p. 37). The presence of money, confirming the whiff of prostitution, is far more explicit from the beginning in *L'Amant de la Chine du Nord* – whereas in *L'Amant*, the flow of money is more subtly suggested. Originating with the lover's father, as we have seen, money passes through the lover to the daughter and on to her mother. In *L'Amant de la Chine du Nord*, however, this flow of money is far more explicit. The lover's father offers in a letter to compensate the mother for her daughter's shame; he also offers to pay for the brutal brother's passage home to France. Through such generalised sensationalising of the story, Duras seems to be setting out to outdo Annaud's sensationalising in his film, the very tendency to which she had originally most objected.

From the spectacle no one wants, the spectacle of the destroyed mother's madness, we reach a series of spectacles, plural. These spectacles depict, in increasingly sensational ways, the daughter's effort to correct that original destruction and effacement of her mother. The daughter's selling of herself – wresting her way into visibility, backed by the mother's complicity – increasingly becomes a spectacle that everyone wants to 'buy into'. In selling her daughter, the mother – replicating the beggarwoman's selling of her child – buys into her spectacle, followed by Annaud, followed by Duras herself – each buyer further sensationalising the daughter's story.

The daughter's display, I have argued, must be read as a desperate and futile effort to displace the threat of engulfment within the mother's oceanic madness. The rich Chinese lover functions less as 'Other' than as screen in both senses of the word: as a display surface receiving projected images, as well as an occulting partition. In these ways, the lover 'screens' a more engulfing 'Other': the mad mother. Working towards such identification is not only a certain complicity among mother, lover and daughter, but particularly, the transgendering of the lover. Despite being himself the beneficiary of his father's exploitive, masculinised economy of shrewd, ruthless investment in real estate (*L'Amant*, p. 119) – the very economy that has ruined the mother – the lover is increasingly not only feminised, but construed as an idealised mother: loving to the point of being 'maddened' by his love, tender, gentle. Ironically enough, we realise that the lover, the first buyer of the daughter's spectacle, was the only one to do so for love. The word 'amant' ['lover'] in the two versions of Duras's work – *L'Amant* and *L'Amant de la Chine du Nord* – mocks its various sellers and buyers long after the Chinese lover's death. His silent, nameless inscription within each title stands as a mute accusation, reminding us of what even the daughter herself cannot quite recognise: his love for her, a love that subsumes, transgenders and almost repairs the mother's own toxic love for her daughter, shaming all other buyers of the daughter's display.

Conclusion

'So how should I presume?' wonders T. S. Eliot's plaintive J. Alfred Prufrock, in a question I might borrow as I presume to resume. In these pages, I have argued for ways in which dynamics of spectation and gender construction, along with their reversals, are harnessed as narrative strategies. These have been explored across a wide range of fictions: a canonical work by a Catholic male writer (Mauriac's *Thérèse Desqueyroux*); a coming-of-age narrative by a canonical woman novelist (Colette's *Le blé en herbe*); a detective novel from the 1960s (Japrisot's *Piège pour Cendrillon*); an early novel by Nobel laureate André Gide (*La porte étroite*); a francophone African novel set in colonial Cameroon (Oyono's *Une vie de boy*); and a narrative set in French Indochina by a woman novelist and filmmaker (Duras's *L'amant* and *L'amant de la Chine du Nord*). Yet within the diversity of such a corpus, we find transversal connections across narrative differences. Two narratives are set during the French colonial era, one – Oyono's *Une vie de boy* – recounted as the intimate journal of a Cameroonian houseboy under French colonial rule, the other (Duras's *Amant* texts) filtered through a white French teenager's perspective in French Indochina. Yet, from this remote, exotic, colonial setting, Duras's works find echoes in Brittany as they join Colette's *Le blé en herbe*; each manipulates unexpected gender upsets in a context of adolescent sexual discovery. Two narratives – Mauriac's *Thérèse Desqueyroux* and Japrisot's *Piège pour Cendrillon* – centre upon acts of attempted murder by women; two unfold against oppressive religious backdrops, the landed Catholic bourgeoisie in *Thérèse Desqueyroux* and ascetic Protestant fanaticism in Gide's *La porte étroite*.

Beyond such transversal links across my corpus lies the connection shared by each work: the manipulation of gendered oppositions for purposes of resistance in a context of lime-lit display. The mannish interests of Mauriac's Thérèse are enrolled in the narration's effort to isolate her as monstrously unfeminine. Between-the-lines love between women emasculates the official and virile hunt for the truth in Japrisot, just as feminine tropes in

Colette's novel innocently sabotage normative masculine virility. After serving to feminise the white colonists in Oyono's narrative, gendered differences culminate and explode in a scene opposing two women as the white Commander's wife turns cool, evaluative scrutiny upon a Black potential maidservant – who deftly glances back. Undoing gendered oppositions in more subtle, supple ways in Duras's narrative becomes the daughter's strategy for safely displacing the mad mother's engulfing threat by transgendering her as the daughter's own Chinese lover. Gide's heavily embodied Juliette – whose name alone genders her decisively as feminine – spectacularly self-immolates, disappearing into a predictably corporealised and female destiny of voluminous maternity.

Such gendered tensions and oppositions are enlisted by each narrative to stage scenarios of display that operate, curiously, towards purposes of displacement. Mounted and framed through various devices that heighten their visibility, these scenarios are offered up to spectation, ostensibly confirming the reader or embedded spectator's primacy as viewing subject; yet they actually serve to displace, or occult, the subject they appear to solicit so intently. Through such neutralising power, display becomes a dynamic site of instability and upset, as suggested in Colette's and Oyono's scenes of spectatorial narcissism and reversal: scenes viewed by a complacent, self-assured subject seeking his or her own pleasure or purpose (Colette's cocky young bourgeois, Philippe, or Oyono's narcissistic white colonist, the Commander's wife) who then finds himself or herself toppled from such a privileged, consumerist position, and reduced as the power relation shifts. A daughter's display in Duras's narratives works to neutralise and displace her mad, destroyed mother; Japrisot's narrative flaunts its conformity to virilised paradigms of the detective genre, only to double surreptitiously as a homoerotic love story that subtly yet efficiently displaces the reader's triumphant capture of 'the solution'. Display is also manipulated to isolate within framing mechanisms, 'monstrify', and thus safely occult, its own object: Mauriac's troubled Thérèse Desqueyroux. Ultimately, Gide's novel provides an example of display as self-displacement in the frantic self-eclipsing, melodramatic efforts of two sisters in love with the same man, as each attempts to sacrifice herself on behalf of the other.

Just as display constructs and positions a viewer from whom it implicitly solicits reaction, narrative scenarios involving display construct and position their readers, in an Althusserian 'interpellation', or 'hailing'.[1] Such a 'hailing' or positioning of the reader/spectator, only to occult this viewer, might be crudely diagrammed by certain Cubist portraits. Picasso's portraits of his simultaneous mistresses of the 1930s, Marie-Thérèse Walter – mother of his daughter, Maya – and fellow painter Dora Maar, show each seated in a chair, with shoulders positioned to face the viewer squarely. In 'Portrait de Marie-Thérèse' of 1937, the model (Walter) raises a hand with forefinger outstretched, as though directly apostrophising the viewer in an interlocutor position that her eyes, meeting the viewer's gaze, confirm. Similarly, the portrait of Dora Maar, painted the same year in darker tones of black and red, positions her seated, shoulders and face turned towards the viewer, the irises of both eyes meeting our gaze directly.

Yet, in these and other Picasso portraits, the direct gaze and frontal shoulder position is belied by a superimposed profile of forehead, nose and lips, as though the figure were not only meeting our gaze, but turning away, as well. Is she offering another angle for us to admire, thereby extending her display even as she consolidates her power over us? Or could we read her profile as dismissive, the signal of lost interest: an indifference that contradicts the posture of display inviting our appreciation? In effect, the viewer is simultaneously positioned as spectator, and discarded as the model's face turns away from us; each figure displays herself for our viewing pleasure as she holds our gaze, yet displaces us in glancing elsewhere. Embedded in Picasso's portraits we thus find, in crude form, the dynamic explored in these pages.[2]

Yet these Cubist portraits connect in another way to my argument, and that is through cubism's link to caricature. In an early essay, Adam Gopnik points to such a link, dramatically visible in faces sketched by Picasso: a page compared by Gopnik to the 'intermediate fossil' that is the 'dream and despair of the paleontologist'. In Picasso's sketch, suggests Gopnik, his friend and art critic André Salmon, 'the primitive fetishist, is caricaturized as a primitive fetish' as Picasso elongates Salmon's brow and jaw. Caricature, as Gopnik puts it, 'remains the base camp from which

Picasso makes ever more daring forays into the forests of primitive form'.[3] Caricature, then, with its combination of exaggeration, extremes, imagination, and nightmare, on the one hand – and the familiar, the comfortable and known, on the other – offers a link between the familiar and the alien, the unknown. Caricature, theorise psychologists, works successfully because its forms somehow 'mirror the internal structure of our mental representations, the idealized and schematized imagery that our minds use to "presort" and structure perception'.[4] Cubist portraits such as Picasso's, with their heavy outlines and exaggerated yet streamlined features – images that are both recognisable and alien, familiar yet other – are consonant with the extremes of display explored in these pages. Such liminality makes caricature a strategy for attracting attention; it lies somewhere between the familiar and the unknown, the 'normal' and the strange. For caricature obtains its effects through display; it nudges the familiar into hypervisibility, swathing it in the 'otherness' of lime-lit glare; it oscillates between the known and the alien, the familiar and the different.

Turning back now to my cover illustration, we might read the Larry Rivers work as a caricature of Manet's 1863 'Olympia'. Ultimately, we realise that Manet's painting itself contained aspects of caricature – as Mina Curtiss noted in pointing to its 'flattened and simplified forms, the outlined and underlined contours'.[5] Like the Freudian uncanny, caricature is the return of the familiar, but in a different guise; it is a means of distancing the familiar, setting it apart.

Yet Rivers' piece offers more than a caricature of a caricature, and more than the upset accomplished by stolen limelight: the flash of unexpected illumination that seizes our attention, only to discard it, subsequently. Rivers' sculpture also engages a certain 'gimmickiness' in its slick efficacy, its adroit scrambling of power relations at work within spectation. Such a move strikes us, in Ivor Brown's definition of the gimmick, as a 'trick or a dodge', a 'tactical device', 'a poor kind of artifice'.[6] Pursuing Brown's definition, Sianne Ngai argues that the gimmick 'irritates because it "abbreviates" work and time'. Gimmicks, she continues, are 'bits of business for performing aesthetic operations'; they are '[r]epulsive if also in an important way attractive, maintaining a degree of charm we often acknowledge grudgingly'. Ngai notes that a gimmick 'is both a wonder *and* a trick. It is a form we marvel at *and* distrust, admire *and* disdain, whose affective intensity for us increases precisely because of this ambivalence'.[7] She goes on to argue for the importance of 'suspicion' and 'contempt' in defining our relationship to the gimmick. Distinguishing between the gimmick and the device, Ngai emphasises the importance of affect, of 'distrust and aversion'; for the gimmick, argues Ngai, is 'always enchanting and repulsive at once'.[8]

Particularly pertinent for my 'stolen-limelight' argument is the gimmick's 'enchanting and repulsive' capacity for abbreviation, its short-cutting sleight of hand. Saving the viewer/reader's time and labour, it obliges us to 'acknowledge grudgingly' – in Ngai's formulation – its charm and accomplishment as it overtakes and condenses the labour of interpretation. Indeed, the gimmick offers a shorthand capture of the very labour of such a theft of visibility. In this way, for our purposes, the act itself of stealing the limelight becomes a gimmick, a kind of cheating: a deft, covert, illicit, wildly successful shortcut that we cannot help but admire reluctantly. Appropriately, the gimmick's possible link to magic is embedded in its rough anagram of this older word.

To what extent does the idea of the gimmick contribute to our understanding of the narrative devices we have been exploring? Dynamics of display as displacement might be viewed as narrative gimmicks, themselves stolen from practices of spectation. Obtaining certain effects through the 'shorthand labour' of reversals, our texts manipulate gendered scenarios for purposes of repression or resistance. Colette's narrative culminates in a display scene of feminine tropes, whose very spectacle displaces the viewer's masculinist gaze; the particular charge carried by the scene is heightened through its positioning as the narrative's closing episode. It takes place on a balcony, moreover, thus engaging an entire intertextual resonance of other, renowned, balcony scenes. The scene's simplicity and density, sketched in a few lines – its deft, womanly displacement of the adolescent male gaze – inspires in Phil, we might presume, both admiration and dismay. 'Je ne lui aurai donné que cela … que cela' ['I will only have given her that … just that'], he realises in humiliated epiphany. The lime-lit glare trained upon Mauriac's Thérèse Desqueyroux by the narrating voice with its framing, isolating devices, operates as gimmick; it works as an illicit, covert, shorthand tactic to displace and thus effectively neutralise and occult the threat incarnated by Thérèse. Japrisot's virilised, masculinist detective narrative bent upon its predatory quest for the truth is neatly undermined by a covert, homoerotic love story; the laboured, spectacularised conquest of the truth is undermined, its conclusions revisited, by such a narrative 'gimmick'. Again, we admire the deftness, the sleight-of-writing-hand that engineers such an upset, even as we deplore having succumbed to its tricks. In Duras's *Amant* narratives, it is the love story itself that works as the lure, the marketing presentation that neatly packages the narrative; yet, again, surreptitious effects of transgendering displace our reading of the love story's primacy. Rather, more fraught, more tormented than the young French colonist's affair with a Chinese gentleman living off his father's real-estate investments, is the daughter's anguished relationship with her destroyed mother. The 'gimmick' of transgendering works to sidestep the theatrics of the daughter's highly visible and transgressive affair, taking us behind the commotion of scandal to show us a more fundamental, more tangled, more anguished love story: that between mother and daughter. The feminised Chinese lover becomes the destroyed mother rehabilitated: tender, sensitive, caring. For Gide's sisters in love with the same man, spectacular self-effacement must fail; the limelight each so desperately sought to avoid is unwillingly self-inflicted, spectacularised by melodramatic devices – gimmicks – conveying meaning through gesture and muteness. In Oyono's *Une vie de boy*, specular gazes ignite a charged scene between two women, the French commander's narcissistic wife and the Black woman she evaluates as a potential maidservant. Here, however, the indifferent maidservant gazes back in blank, unfocused disinterest that nonetheless effortlessly diagnoses the white woman's pathology. Such refracted limelight – the cold glare of evaluative scrutiny flung back against its source, collapsing the hierarchy separating the two women – might be read as gimmicky, a 'poor device' to abbreviate the time and labour of interpretation. For Kalisia dares to pronounce, in deft summary, the verdict Toundi has not been able to face: the white goddess's narcissistic promiscuity.

Exploring the narrative 'gimmick' of stolen limelight has been the project of these pages. Our frenzied visual culture is saturated with viewing practices, sharpened through the ubiquity of the image in daily life. Bringing these practices with us to the study of narrative illuminates the ways narrative implicitly manipulates spectation as it cues the reader. Scenarios of display shaping the relation between reader and text become newly legible. Attention to such dynamics of display and displacement confers, as I hope to have demonstrated, greater visibility and definition upon a range of tensions – gendered, racial, cultural – at work within narrative.

Notes

Preface

1. Jules Supervielle, 'A mon livre', *Brumes du passé* (1901) (Paris: Gallimard, Bibliothèque de la Pléiade, 1996), p. 44; with the kind permission of Daniel Bertaux.
2. Marcel Proust, *A la recherche du temps perdu*, ed. Jean-Yves Tadié (vol. 3) (Paris: Gallimard, 1988), p. 667.
3. Virginia Woolf, 'Preface', *Orlando: A Biography* (New York: Harcourt, Brace and Co., 1928), p. viii.

Introduction

1. In his study of eighteenth-century French painting, Michael Fried makes a similar argument for the work's 'neutralisation' of the viewer, via depictions of absorption in subjects painted by Greuze, Chardin and others. While I am indebted to Fried's arguments, I situate my own in a context of display, not absorption: a difference that sharpens the paradox of the displaced viewer. For the notion of display would appear precisely calculated to solicit, even force, the viewer's attention – thus rendering all the more startling and unexpected display's effective displacement of the very viewer it sought to intrigue. However, scenes depicting subjects absorbed in their own activities – as studied by Fried – would appear from the outset to signal these subjects' indifference to the viewer; it is therefore scarcely surprising that the viewer is effectively 'displaced', as Fried argues in *Absorption and Theatricality: Painting and Beholder in the Age of Diderot* (Berkeley CA: University of California Press, 1980).
2. Larry Rivers, 'I Like Olympia in Blackface', painted relief (Paris: Musée National d'Art Moderne, Centre Georges Pompidou, 1970). While the Black Lives Matter movement has increased our awareness of the regrettable racist insensitivity reflected by such a title, the work itself offers a powerful illustration of the display-as-displacement dynamic studied in these pages.
3. Barbara Bolt, 'Shedding Light for the Matter', *Hypatia: A Journal of Feminist Philosophy*, 15/2 (Spring 2000), 204.

[4] Susan Harrow, *The Art of the Text: Visuality in Nineteenth and Twentieth-Century Literary and Other Media* (Cardiff: University of Wales Press, 2013), p. 257.

[5] Harrow, *The Art of the Text*, p. 252.

[6] Judith Butler, *Gender Trouble: Feminism and the Subversion of Identity* (New York and London: Routledge, 1990).

[7] Naomi Schor, *Bad Objects: Essays Popular and Unpopular* (Durham NC and London: Duke University Press, 1995), p. 163.

[8] Schor, *Bad Objects*, p. 163.

[9] Harrow, *The Art of the Text*, p. 257.

[10] Stephen Greenblatt, 'Resonance and Wonder', in Ivan Karp and Steven D. Lavine (eds), *Exhibiting Cultures: The Poetics and Politics of Museum Display* (Washington DC and London: The Smithsonian Institution Press, 1991), p. 49.

[11] Svetlana Alpers, 'The Museum as a Way of Seeing', in Karp and Levine (eds), *Exhibiting Cultures*, pp. 26–7.

[12] Peter Brooks, *Reading for the Plot* (New York: Knopf, 1984).

[13] In *The Female Grotesque: Risk, Excess and Modernity* (New York: Routledge, 1995), Mary Russo attempts to correct what she calls the 'normalization of feminism' by investigating 'the strange, the risky, the minoritarian, the excessive, the outlawed, and the alien' (vii), which she understands as the 'female grotesque'. Russo's project is to rehabilitate the grotesque by inverting its cultural position as 'low' to link it, instead, to what she views as 'the "high" registers of modernism, the sublime, and discourses of liberation' (viii).

[14] The link between the gendered and the everyday is explored by Laurie Langbauer in *Women and Romance: The Consolations of Gender in the English Novel* (Ithaca NY: Cornell University Press, 'Reading Women Writing' Series, 1990). Inspired by Henri Lefebvre's work on 'le quotidien', Langbauer argues that women culturally embody the domestic quotidian, in that 'each [women and the domestic everyday] comes to represent the very forces that create subjects, both in literally producing them and then normalizing them into culture' (p. 51). However, as Langbauer also claims, any attempt to define the everyday disfigures it. The everyday is elusive, opaque; it cannot become an object of knowledge without being transformed. 'By making the invisible visible', as Langbauer puts it, 'by giving form and content to an experience so vague and seemingly natural that part of its significance is that its subjects cannot define it, by defining, or *theorizing*, the everyday, it is transformed into what it is not' (p. 50).

15   Such epistemological confusion is explicitly linked to gender by Mary Ann Doane in *Femmes Fatales: Feminism, Film Theory and Psychoanalysis* (New York: Routledge, 1991). Doane argues that 'femininity in modernity has become very much a question of hypervisibility. As soon as the relation between vision and knowledge becomes unstable or deceptive, the potential for a disruption of the given sexual logic appears'. Doane goes on to link such epistemological disruptiveness specifically to the *femme fatale*, whom she sees as precisely 'the figure of a certain discursive unease, a potential epistemological trauma. For her most striking characteristic, perhaps, is the fact that she never really is what she seems to be. She harbors a threat which is not entirely legible, predictable, or manageable' (p. 1). However, one might hesitate at Doane's claim that the epistemological threat posed by the gendered is confined to the *femme fatale*. For in many ways, the *femme fatale* – Circe – is so culturally over-coded, her script so familiar, as to be entirely domesticated. We know her artifices, her seductions; indeed, she incarnates artifice and seduction, and thus belongs squarely and entirely in the realm of theatre. As Baudrillard argued in *De la séduction* (Paris: Editions Galilée, 1979), seduction is always a matter of artifice, sign and ritual (p. 8). The *femme fatale*'s operations occur within recognisable rituals. Her *function* as temptress, of course, is dangerous, threatening; but it is a threat that we recognise immediately: a familiar, known danger following an established script. Essentially, she is threatening as temptress, but not as object of knowledge. Instead, more disruptive than the *femme fatale*, I would argue – because more illegible, more enigmatic, sowing more epistemological confusion – is what occurs in the liminal, ambiguous space between the maternal and the *femme fatale*.

16   By way of understanding what is so disconcerting about this blurred boundary between the natural and the artificial, one might recall the Platonic notion of the simulacrum, as reworked by Jean Baudrillard in *Simulacres et simulation* (Paris: Editions Galilée, 1981). At the level of the simulacrum, we would seem to be quite removed from what is understood as the natural or normal, what is intuited as the real. Yet Baudrillard argues that the simulacrum does not – merely – slavishly imitate and replicate the real. For in doing so, the simulacrum effaces and eclipses the real; it collapses all difference between itself and the real, usurping the real's claim to be, precisely, reality. Ultimately, the simulacrum jettisons the real as a poor imitation of itself, the artificial; the reassuring distinction between artificial and real thus disintegrates. In this way, the fake 'natural' comes to seem more real to us than the

true natural itself. Yet this utter eclipsing of the real by the more perfect fake, the simulacrum, is less threatening, I would argue, than the point at which this model falters. What is unsettling here is the flaw in the Baudrillardian simulacrum: the instant at which we become aware that we are not looking at what we *thought* we were looking at. A crack in the artificial reveals the natural; a crack in the natural reveals the artificial. The difference between the two opens up what I am calling the 'space of display', when a familiar figure – ordinary and quotidian – strikes us suddenly as other, different; and I am arguing that this otherness occurs as a sort of excess. We sense something excessive about this ordinariness, something that oversteps an intuitive boundary, marking the ordinary suddenly as the other. Thus, whereas the simulacrum collapses all difference between itself and the real – incinerates the real – the space of *trompe l'oeil* maintains that difference; it prances upon the very border of the real and the simulacrum, invoking both, scrambling both, flirting with both.

17   Joan Riviere, 'Womanliness as a Masquerade', *International Journal of Psychoanalysis*, 10 (1929), 303.

18   Riviere, 'Womanliness as a Masquerade', 306. Despite her argument that the gendered and masquerade are 'the same thing', Riviere's masquerade has nonetheless been read as *mask*, separable and apart from genuine femininity. Mary Ann Doane in *Femmes Fatales*, for instance, argues that: '[t]he masquerade, in flaunting femininity, holds it at a distance. Womanliness is a mask which can be worn or removed. The masquerade's resistance to patriarchal positioning would therefore lie in its denial of the production of femininity as closeness, as presence-to–itself, as, precisely, imagistic' (p. 82). As Doane continues, however, we see that her understanding of the masquerade appears to be limited to its most extreme, hyperbolic variation, that of – again – the *femme fatale*. Similarly, Emily Apter, in *Feminizing the Fetish: Psychoanalysis and Narrative Obsession in Turn-of-The-Century France* (Ithaca NY and London: Cornell University Press, 1991), argues for a distinction, or separability, between the masquerade and femininity. She then claims that the masquerade might *not* provide an 'enabling articulation of femininity,' for 'with its language of veils, masks, and sexual travesty, the discourse of the masquerade seems always to participate in the very obfuscation of femininity that it seeks to dispel' (p. 90). Apter goes on to ask, 'How did woman come to be identified with womanliness and then trapped behind the mask of the masquerade?' (p. 90). For Doane and Apter, then, the masquerade, emblematised by the *femme fatale*, is theatre – that is, an assumed mask, and thus a convention, an artifice,

the unreal. Both Doane and Apter seem to search Riviere for an essential gendered identity trapped *beneath* the masquerade, forgetting that Riviere understands femininity as inseparable from masquerade – forgetting that, in Riviere's argument, 'they are the same thing' (Riviere, 'Womanliness', 306). A more probing analysis of Riviere, it seems to me, is Geraldine Harris's discussion in *Staging Femininities: Performance and Performativity* (Manchester and New York: Manchester University Press, 1999):

[T]his masquerader plays both subject and object, active and passive, at the same time … it is the fact that this female subject apparently *successfully* occupies the 'masculine' place of speaking subject which creates the threat and the subsequent necessity for a defence. To some extent, then, this masquerade could be seen as a double bluff in which the female subject manipulates both masculine and gendered roles, using one to disguise the other so that there is, as it were, always one mask too many, creating an 'excess' which potentially defamiliarises both. (p. 123)

However, although I want to put the masquerade to a different use – reading it as an offensive rather than defensive tactic – Apter's discussion of Riviere, Heath and Doane on the masquerade is useful, and her conclusion suggestive: 'we might reread the theory of the masquerade as corrected, so to speak, by sartorial female fetishism, which supplants the notion of femininity as empty content or infinitely layered veil, to replace it with a theory of materialized social construction' (p. 98).

[19] Butler, *Gender Trouble*, p. 140.

[20] For an analysis of gendered excess in the context of British and American women's fiction, see Barbara Claire Freeman's fascinating work in *The Feminine Sublime: Gender and Excess in Women's Fiction* (Berkeley CA: University of California Press, 1995) on what she calls 'the gendered sublime': 'a domain of experience that resists categorization, in which the subject enters into relation with an otherness – social aesthetic, political, ethical, erotic – that is excessive and unrepresentable' (p. 2). Freeman and I differ in our approaches to gendered excess, however; whereas she links it to 'a radical alterity that remains unassimilable to representation', my effort here is to trace its energies *within* representation.

21 Barbara Freedman, 'Frame-Up: Feminism, Psychoanalysis, Theatre', in Sue-Ellen Case (ed.), *Performing Feminisms: Feminist Critical Theory and Theatre* (Baltimore MD: Johns Hopkins University Press, 1990), p. 56.

22 Judith Butler, 'Performative Acts and Gender Constitution: An Essay in Phenomenology and Feminist Theory', in Case (ed.), *Performing Feminisms*, p. 278. Such implications for theatre are developed by Octave Mannoni, who argues in *Clefs pour l'imaginaire* (Paris: Seuil, 1969) – via the Freudian concept of *Verneinung*, denial – for theatre as stamped by an absolute negation. In theatre, he points out, 'ce qui est représenté le plus possible comme vrai est en même temps présenté comme faux' ['what is represented to the greatest extent possible as true is, at the same time, presented as false'] (p. 304). It is by virtue of this negation that, while the imagination is exhorted, it is also controlled, kept in check; there is no possibility of illusion, or scrambling between theatre and the real (p. 304). Mannoni goes on to distinguish between, on the one hand, such a notion of theatre as consummate emblem of denial, and, on the other hand, acts of purgation, catharsis and ritual. In theatre, an actor kills in a gesture that is unrestrained, undertaken as 'real' – but is not real; and in this way, theatre is based on *Verneinung* – denial – which separates it from ritual (p. 308).

23 Emma Barker (ed.), *Contemporary Cultures of Display* (New Haven CT and London: Yale University Press, 1999), p. 15.

24 Barker, *Contemporary Cultures*, p. 15.

25 Karl Toepfer, *Theatre, Aristocracy and Pornocracy* (New York: PAJ Publications, 1991), p. 24.

26 As Marian Hobson argues in 'Du Theatrum Mundi au Theatrum Mentis', *Revue des Sciences Humaines*, 167 (1977), the formulation 'theatricality outside theatre', in evoking the transgression of a boundary between art and life, 'établit en fait deux lieux bien distincts, qu'elle fait communiquer et qu'elle tient séparés dans le moment de la transgression même' ['in fact establishes two very distinct sites, which it holds in communication and yet separately in the very moment itself of transgression'] (379).

27 Joseph Litvak, *Caught in the Act: Theatricality in the Nineteenth-Century English Novel* (Berkeley CA: University of California Press, 1992), xii. Litvak goes so far as to understand theatricality as the very ground of selfhood, in a move suggestive of Butler's argument for gender as performance. 'The trope of theatricality,' he claims, 'enables us both to unpack subjectivity as performance and to denaturalize – to read as *scene* – the whole encompassing space in which that subjectivity gets constituted … if the self is treated here as not just a text but a

contingent cluster of theatrical roles, then it becomes possible to make a spectacle of the imperious domestic, sexual, and aesthetic ideologies for which, and in which, it is bound' (xii).

28 Butler, 'Performative Acts and Gender Constitution', p. 278.

29 Terry Castle, *Masquerade and Civilization: The Carnivalesque in Eighteenth-Century English Culture and Fiction* (Stanford CA: Stanford University Press, 1986), p. 33.

30 Castle, *Masquerade*, p. 253.

31 Nina Auerbach, *Private Theatricals* (Cambridge MA: Harvard University Press, 1990), p. 4.

32 Auerbach, *Private Theatricals*, p. 114. Such an idea of the theatricality of sincerity itself offers an interesting parallel to the notion of the masquerade of femininity; essentialised notions of sincerity and of gendered norms are replaced by the conviction that each is inseparable from its own appearance.

33 Kimberly Benston, 'Being There: Performance as Mise-en-Scène, Abscene, Obscene and Other Scene', *PMLA*, 107/3 (1992), 446–7.

34 Benston, 'Being There', 436.

35 Barbara Freedman, *Staging the Gaze: Postmodernism, Psychoanalysis, and Shakespearean Comedy* (Ithaca NY and London: Cornell University Press, 1991), p. 1.

36 Norman Bryson, *Vision and Painting: The Logic of the Gaze* (New Haven CT and London: Yale University Press, 1983), p. 106. The political implications of such a reversed gaze – in which the beholder is suddenly, uncomfortably, beheld – are studied here in Chapter Two in the context of Oyono's francophone narrative, where the masterful white viewing subjects become himself and herself objects of the native Black gaze.

37 Freud, *Standard Edition* (vol. 7), p. 222.

38 Freedman, *Staging the Gaze*, p. 70.

39 Breaking free of claustrophobic intimacy, as we will see in the context of Duras's narratives, is precisely the agenda behind the young heroine's transgressive liaison with a Chinese lover. The hypervisibility she creates through self-display is an attempt, I argue, to explode the suffocating, failed intimacy of destructive family bonds.

40 Richard Schechner, 'Performers and Spectators, Transported and Transformed', *The Kenyon Review*, 3/4 (Autumn 1981), 84.

41 Norman Bryson, *Looking at the Overlooked: Four Essays on Still Life Painting* (Cambridge MA: Harvard University Press, 1990), pp. 58–9.

42 Bryson, *Looking at the Overlooked*, p. 59.

43 Bryson, *Looking at the Overlooked*, p. 143.

44 Bryson, *Looking at the Overlooked*, p. 66. Similar to the mechanism of *trompe l'oeil*, the play of narrative with gendered excess disrupts the reader's sense of bearings, confounding the reader's 'intimate knowledge' of his or her relation to the text. In Japrisot's narrative, *Piège pour Cendrillon* – to be discussed later in these pages – for instance, one believes oneself to be reading a detective novel; by the end, however, we are disconcerted to find that beneath our very noses, the detective narrative has been overtaken by a love story. We're no longer comfortably established within the genre that we thought we were reading; and the values of that genre, which guide its search for the solution to the mystery, are suddenly, subtly but disconcertingly displaced. In Gide's novel *La porte étroite*, as we will see, the drama we are reading displaces and obscures an even more searing and poignant one, until we are made to recognise and respect a different, silent but nonetheless spectacular theatricality.

45 Doane, *Femmes Fatales*, p. 194.

46 Doane, *Femmes Fatales*, pp. 194–5.

47 Freud, *Standard Edition* (vol. 7), p. 245.

48 Freud, *Standard Edition* (vol. 7), p. 243.

49 Freud, *Standard Edition* (vol. 7), p. 226.

50 The peculiar threat posed by a *gendered* automaton is detailed by Andreas Huyssen in *After the Great Divide: Modernism, Mass Culture, Postmodernism* (Bloomington IN: Indiana University Press, 1986). Huyssen argues that the fears provoked by machines 'are recast and reconstructed in terms of the male fear of female sexuality, reflecting, in the Freudian account, the male's castration anxiety' (p. 70). The machine as either controllable or uncontrollable becomes linked to gender, as either docile or treacherous; '[t]he myth of the dualistic nature of woman as either asexual virgin-mother or prostitute-vamp is projected onto technology which appears as either neutral and obedient or as inherently threatening and out-of-control' (p. 73).

51 Freud, *Standard Edition* (vol. 7), p. 236.

52 Castle, *Masquerade and Civilization*, p. 5.

53 Castle, *Masquerade and Civilization*, p. 25. Symptomatic of this threatened integrity of the habitual self is fascination, as John Gregg argues in *Maurice Blanchot and the Literature of Transgression* (Princeton NJ: Princeton University Press, 1994); for fascination dismantles the difference between interiority and exteriority. 'When fascinated, writers are outside themselves, "beside themselves" when they give themselves up to the image, which provokes the transformation from the personal to the impersonal' (p. 29).

54 A discussion of Caillois's analyses of ritual and the sacred in *L'homme et le sacré* (Paris: Gallimard, 1950) is offered by Terry Castle in her *Masquerade and Civilization*, p. 53.

55 In his chapter 'On Some Motifs in Baudelaire', in *Illuminations* (New York: Harcourt, Brace and World, Inc., 1955), Walter Benjamin quotes Baudelaire's sonnet 'A une passante' ['To a Passerby']. Here, the stranger's 'fugitive beauté/Dont le regard m'a fait soudainement renaître' ['fugitive beauty/through whose glance I was suddenly reborn'] provides an erotic shock for the poet. Yet, as Benjamin suggests, 'it is not love at first sight, it is love at last sight. It is a farewell forever in the poem which coincides with the moment of enchantment' (pp. 170–2). We might surmise that this sort of *Liebestod* mixing the familiar and the strange in the fleeting encounter of a farewell instant is consonant with the vertigo of lost bearings we have been exploring.

56 Escher's 'The Print Gallery' depicts such a destabilising of the spectator's look in which the framed becomes the framing, the subject becomes the object, in slippages among and transgression of boundaries. Here a framed representation of the cityscape overflows its frame and curves around to create the container, the print gallery itself. We see the depicted beholder himself framed, the gazer become object of our own gaze, as we see the gazer through a framing window in the structure of the print gallery. In her *Staging the Gaze*, Freedman emphasises that '[j]ust as the windowpane of the gallery through which we see the young man frames him, so the print the young man beholds is constructed so as to escape the boundaries of its frame' (p. 124).

57 Freedman, 'Frame-Up', p. 74.

58 Jean Comolli, 'Machines of the Visible', in Teresa De Lauretis and Stephen Heath (eds), *The Cinematic Apparatus* (London: MacMillan, 1980), pp. 122–3.

59 György Lukàcs, *The Theory of the Novel: A Historico-Philosophical Essay on the Forms of Great Epic Literature*, trans. Anna Bostock (Boston MA: Massachusetts Institute of Technology Press, 1971).

60 Michel de Certeau, *L'invention du quotidien, I: Arts de faire* (Paris: Gallimard, 1990), p. 120. Certeau's claim notwithstanding, we realise that this apparent bedrock everyday experience – the normal, real, quotidian – is itself highly shaped, highly constructed. We think of Althusser's argument for interpellation in the landmark essay 'Idéologie et positions idéologiques d'Etat' of his work *Positions 1964–75* (Paris: Editions Sociales, 1976), whereby the individual is defined and positioned by social forces: a positioning the individual accepts as

'normal', as 'natural' (p. 113). Similarly, cinema positions us as spectators, creating ready-made subjectivities for us: subjectivities from within which we react to what happens onscreen. It is thus not surprising to consider that narrative, presenting itself as the genre of the ordinary, also shapes and positions us as readers. 'Much as social formations and representations appeal to and position the individual as subject in the process to which we give the name of ideology', argues Theresa de Lauretis in *Alice Doesn't: Feminism, Semiotics, Cinema* (Bloomington IN: Indiana University Press, 1984), 'the movement of narrative discourse shifts and places the reader, viewer, or listener in certain portions of the plot space' (p. 121). The reader is positioned to accept an 'ordinary' that is, in fact, highly shaped and defined by the narrative; and yet, just as our understanding of the ordinary is ideologically shaped and manipulated by convention, so, increasingly, is our understanding of narrative. Studies of narrative such as Genette's *Figures III: Discours du récit* (Paris: Editions du Seuil, 1972) have separated the 'real' from the constructed – distinguishing, in other words, between the (fictional) 'real' events described by the narrative, and the way in which these are recounted. This difference implicitly reproduces the distinction between what is natural, normal, quotidian, real – and what is artificial, contrived, constructed, assumed, manipulated. Yet Genette, having made use of this distinction, will eventually come to argue in *Nouveaux discours du récit* (Paris: Editions du Seuil, Collection Poétique, 1983) that the act of recounting – the narration – produces not one, but two creations, or constructions: not only the crafted, organised 'story' itself, but the equally crafted, manipulated illusion of a natural source, or raw material, available to be organised as 'story'. Increasingly, the natural, the 'what really happened', is itself seen as artefact, as an artificially created naturalness: a careful illusion crafted by the narration. Similarly, of course, in Riviere's argument, the 'natural', gendered self is always already assumed, a creation.

[61] Another such effort to domesticate gendered transgressiveness, particularly in scenarios such as Oyono's that involve a gazed-upon object suddenly returning that gaze, might be read in Bram Dijkstra's depiction of gendered evil in *Idols of Perversity: Fantasies of Feminine Evil in Fin-de-Siècle Culture* (New York: Oxford University Press, 1986). For Dijkstra, such evil seems peculiarly bound up with narcissistic self-absorption – which ultimately becomes not really so evil, for such energies, turned narcissistically in upon themselves, are safely contained. One might also hesitate at Dijkstra's reading of Manet's painting 'Nana', as self-absorbed, 'largely unmoved by the concerns of the men around

her' (p. 140). However, Nana's glance at the viewer is not 'casual and only mildly curious', Dijkstra puts it, but focused, intent; it therefore ruptures any claim for total self-absorption. Even as we gaze at Nana primping before her looking-glass, she returns our gaze, fixing us intently and insistently, destabilising our controlling, voyeuristic position as spectators.

Staging the Hyperfeminine

[1] Colette, *Le blé en herbe, Œuvres* (3 vols), ed. Claude Pichois (Paris: Gallimard, Bibliothèque de la Pléïade, 1984–6). Page numbers in the text refer to vol. 2 of this edition.

[2] Colette, *Mes apprentissages, Œuvres* (vol. 3), p. 1050.

[3] Colette, *Le pur et l'impur, Œuvres* (vol. 3), p. 586.

[4] Colette, *Mes apprentissages, Œuvres* (vol. 3), p. 1023.

[5] Colette, *Mes apprentissages, Œuvres* (vol. 3), p. 1042.

[6] Colette, *Mes apprentissages, Œuvres* (vol. 3), p. 1046.

[7] Colette, *Mes apprentissages, Œuvres* (vol. 3), p. 1051.

[8] Colette, *Mes apprentissages, Œuvres* (vol. 3), p. 1697.

[9] Colette herself plays her character 'Claudine' at L'Alcazar in Brussels in November 1908; at La Scala in Lyon that December; she performs the role in Toulouse in April 1909 and, at last, at the Moulin Rouge in Paris in November 1910. She will later play another of her most memorable characters, Léa, as of the hundredth performance of 'Chéri', created in December 1921 at the Théâtre Michel; Maïté Albistur and Daniel Armogathe, *Histoire du féminisme français* (Paris: Editions des femmes, 1977), p. 159.

[10] *Mes apprentissages, Oeuvres* (vol. 3), p. 1052.

[11] Monique Cornand and Madeleine Barbin, *Colette*, Catalogue de l'exposition (Paris: Bibliothèque nationale, 1972). The first stage production of 'Claudine' – 'Claudine à Paris', subsequently augmented with a prologue, 'Claudine à l'école' – opened on 21 January 1902 at the Buffes-Parisiens, with runaway success resulting in 123 consecutive performances (p. 15).

[12] *Le nouveau journal*, 8 November 1907.

[13] Maurice Mignon, *Willy, Colette et Polaire* (Clamecy: Imprimerie générale de la Nièvre, 1960), p. 7. In her *Colette and the Fantom Subject of Autobiography* (Ithaca NY: Cornell University Press, 1992), Jerry Flieger also points to the 'hall of mirrors' of these circulating identities (the actress Polaire, the author Colette and Colette's character

Claudine, played by Polaire) (p. 5). Whereas Flieger analyses Colette's work as autobiographical fiction, my purpose here, instead, is to emphasise the theatricality of Colette's own displaced, appropriated identities in the surrogates of Claudine and Polaire.

14 Polaire [Emilie Marie Bouchard], *Polaire par elle-même* (Paris: Figuière, 1933), pp. 116–17. Quoted in Herbert Lottman, *Colette: A Life* (Boston MA: Little, Brown, 1991), p. 55.

15 Colette, *Mes apprentissages, Oeuvres* (vol. 3), p. 1066.

16 Colette's imaginary dialogue with Claudine is quoted by Maurice Mignon in *Willy, Colette et Polaire*, p. 5. If Colette did not immediately get to play the onstage role of Claudine, she nonetheless plays a supreme role in front of her mother: the charade of married happiness, with its struggle to resist the temptation to take flight and go home to Sido: 'de revenir tout écorchée, obscure et sans argent, peser sur la fin de sa vie' ['to go home scorched, bruised and penniless, to weigh down the end of her life'] (*Mes apprentissages, Oeuvres* (vol. 3), p. 1028).

17 Colette, *Gribiche, Oeuvres* (vol. 3), p. 1175. In contrast to Colette herself, however, Nicole Ward Jouve argues in *Colette* (Bloomington IN: Indiana University Press, 1987) for such music-hall mime performances not as an escape for the actress from her own identity, but as her accession through 'a language rooted in the body' to more direct self-expression (p. 106).

18 Colette, *L'envers du music-hall, Oeuvres* (vol. 2), p. 224. Such hesitation and reluctance before her own image is implied in *La vagabonde* ['The Vagabond'], the 1910 novel inspired by Colette's years on the music-hall stage. Opening upon its protagonist in her dressing room, the narrative details actress Renée Néré's not-so-playful dread of finding herself alone across from her own image as she confronts her mirror (Colette, *La vagabonde, Oeuvres* (vol. 1), p. 1067–9). Once home alone, she finds herself obliged to face the interview with her mirror once again as she contemplates 'l'image d'une femme de lettres qui a mal tourné' ['the image of "a woman of letters who has gone astray"'] (Colette, *Oeuvres* (vol. 1), pp. 1072–5). This topos of the confrontation with her mirrored self becomes explicitly antagonistic as Renée and her image size each other up 'en adversaires dignes l'une de l'autre' ['as adversaries worthy of each other'] (Colette, *Oeuvres* (vol. 1), p. 1078).

19 Albert du Moulin, *Paris-Lumière*, December 1906.

20 The fact that a marquise should go upon the stage was viewed as only slightly less scandalous than the kiss she exchanged, in her role as a besotted archaeologist, with Colette, as press reactions suggest:

La marquise de Belboeuf qui, depuis son divorce, avait repris son nom de marquise de Morny, trouvant insuffisante la notoriété qui s'attachait déjà à son nom, a imaginé de monter sur les planches d'un music-hall, en compagnie de Madame Colette Willy, pour y jouer une pantomime soi-disant de sa composition, et qu'il est vraiment cruel, par surcroît, de lui attribuer!

[The marquise of Belboeuf, who, since her divorce, had taken back the name of Marquise of Morny, finding insufficient the notoriety already attached to her name, took it into her head to go upon a music-hall stage, in the company of Madame Colette Willy, to perform there a pantomime of her own creation, and which it is truly painful, moreover, to attribute to her!] (*La libre parole*, 6 January 1907)

Missy's family succeeded in obtaining a court order preventing further performances of 'Rêve d'Egypte'. Renamed 'Songe d'Orient' ['Oriental Reverie'] with the mime Georges Wague replacing Missy as the archaeologist who falls in love with the mummy played by Colette, the production continued, with measured acceptance. The replacement of Missy by Wague, in one opinion, 'évitera aux spectateurs le sentiment de gêne que l'on a toujours lorsqu'on assiste à quelque chose qui ne vous regarde pas' ['will spare spectators the feeling of unease one has around something that doesn't concern one'] (*L'intransigeant*, 6 January 1907).

21   Gaston Calmette, quoted in *Le matin*, 5 January 1907. In an effort to palliate the scandal produced by 'Rêve d'Egypte', an appeal is made in the press to the historical precision of this 'évocation très exacte des moeurs de l'Egypte d'autrefois' ['very precise evocation of Egyptian mores of the past'], with the claim that Colette spent several days at the Louvre studying Egyptian mosaics for the purpose of rendering the production more historically accurate (*L'Evénement*, December 1906; *La liberté*, 3 January 1907).

22   Interestingly, it was Willy who masterminded the production of 'Rêve d'Egypte' ['Egyptian Dream']. The lesbian club to which Colette and Missy belonged occasionally staged pantomimes for the amusement of its members. Curious, Willy attended; with an eye always out for a profit, he persuaded Missy to perform. Subsequently enlisting Colette's pantomime teacher and mentor, Georges Wague, along with their pianist, Willy – according to Tristan Rémy in his *Georges Wague, Le*

Mime de la Belle Epoque (Paris: Girard, 1964), p. 67 – eventually interested the director of the Moulin-Rouge in the production (quoted in Joanna Richardson, *Colette*, p. 37).

23   Programme de l'Olympia, Paris, 21–29 September 1910):

Yulka vit avec la farouche contrebandier Hokartz qui l'aime de toute la force de son âme sauvage, mais Yulka lui est infidèle de toute la force de sa beauté. Elle reçoit, en l'absence d'Hokartz, les visites d'un jeune sous-officier dont elle est amoureuse. Le contrebandier surprend leur rendez-vous, et surgit tout à coup; il désarme et assomme à moitié le séducteur, qu'il jette ensuite dehors. Restés seuls, l'amant exige une explication, il veut savoir. Yulka reste muette; il la tuerait peut-être si, dans la lutte, son vêtement se déchirant, ne laisse apparaître 'La Chair' dont il est sauvagement épris. Yulka fuit, épouvantée, tandis que dans la folie de son désespoir et l'impossibilité de la posséder encore il se tue devant la porte irrévocablement fermée.

[Yulka lives with the wild outlaw Hokartz, who loves her with all the force of his untamed soul, but Yulka is unfaithful to him with all the force of her beauty. In Hokartz's absence, she receives a young petty officer, with whom she is in love. The outlaw surprises their *rendez-vous*, and suddenly appears; he disarms and partly knocks out the seducer, whom he then throws out. Alone now, the lover demands an explanation, he wants to know. Yulka is mute; he would kill her, perhaps, if, in the struggle, her garment hadn't ripped, revealing 'the Flesh' that he wildly adores. Yulka flees, terrified, while in the madness of his despair and the impossibility of possessing her again, he kills himself in front of the irrevocably shut door.]

24   *La république*, 3 November 1907.

25   Kursaal de Lausanne, summer 1911.

26   Armand Massard, *La presse*, 5 November 1907. Whatever the interpretation of just how Yulka's clothes came to be ripped in 'La chair', Colette was successful in the role, as hyperbolic descriptions of her performance suggest. Theatre critics admired the range of her 'nuances de sentiment' ['nuances of feeling'], nuances that culminated in 'la joie cruelle de la triomphatrice, inaccessible à la pitié' ['the cruel joy of the triumphant one, unmoved by pity'] (Lionel de Nestaques, *Paris-théâtre*, 25 April 1908); 'son talent si personnel, fait de charme et

de fantaisie' ['her very personal talent, comprised of charm and fantasy'] (*Le Gil Blas*, 2 November 1907); her 'verve fougueuse' ['fiery verve'] (*L'Officiel des théâtres*, 10 November 1907). Advance publicity fawns over 'les grâces prenantes de son geste et l'harmonieuse souplesse de ses attitudes' ['the appealing grace of her gestures and the harmonious suppleness of her poses'] (*Le journal*, 13 October 1907); 'la souplesse d'un corps qu'anime la double flamme de l'art et de la vie' ['the suppleness of a body animated by the double flame of art and life'] (*Le Figaro*, 13 October 1907). A more specifically corporeal tongue-in-cheek review compares the firmness of Colette's breasts to that of the Alpes-Maritimes' prefect's order (*Nouveau journal*, 21 February 1908) that she cover them for performances at Monte Carlo:

Madame Colette jouait 'la Chair', en chair, ses moyens le lui permettent. Elle était donc peu vêtue; ses jambes, d'un galbe si fin, étaient nues de la cheville aux hanches, et ses seins, véritables coupes d'albâtre, se montraient fraternellement, encore plus fermes que le ministère.

[Madame Colette played 'The Flesh' in the flesh itself, her charms allowing it. She was scantily clothed; her legs, so finely shaped, were naked from ankle to hips, and her breasts, veritable alabaster bowls, appeared fraternally – firmer, even, than the prefect's office.] ('Snob' [signed], 'Les Potins de Paris', *Le rire*, 266, 7 March 1908, p. 2).

27 In curious contrast to her coquettish, styled self-depictions and self-veilings, Colette's stage creations were lauded in her time for their sincerity and spontaneity. One admirer emphasised her 'sincérité complète dans l'expression quasi impulsive de sensations réellement éprouvées. Elle se donne toute à son personnage, elle le vit plus qu'elle ne le joue' ['complete sincerity in the virtually impulsive expression of sensations truly felt. She gives herself over to her character; she lives, more than plays, her character'] (*Album comique*, October 1908). In similar idiom, as Rachilde was to write years after Colette's début role as a little faun, '[i]l était à la fois malicieux et gauche, mais si pur de lignes, si chastes de gestes et un tel rythme de poésie cadençait ses moindres mouvements, qu'on le sentait en chair et en os dans ce décor de vil carton et qu'on y croyait, malgré le rayon de lune électrique' ['he was both awkward and mischievous, and yet so pure in his lines, so chaste in his gestures, and so poetic in the rhythm of his slightest movements, that one felt he was flesh and blood in this cheap

cardboard setting. One believed in him, despite the electric moonbeam. He was no longer dancing. He was living his dream'] (*Mercure de France*, 1 December (1913), p. 588; quoted in Joanna Richardson, *Colette*, p. 32).

28   Further masterminding of feminine tropes might also be read in the beauty and cosmetic enterprise Colette ran for a year. She mentions the pleasure her writer's fingers took in working with 'la vivante substance humaine, dont ils rehaussent la couleur, masquent la défaillance' ['living human substance, whose colour they accented, whose deficiencies they masked'] (quoted by Nicole Ferrier-Caverivière in *Colette et la mode*, ed. Ferrier-Caverivière (Paris: Editions Plume, 1991), p. 27).

29   Jouve, *Colette*, p. 112.

30   *Le Figaro*, 20 January 1954, p. 10; reprinted as 'Allocution de Colette (1954)' in Colette, *Oeuvres* (vol. 2), p. 1275. Colette's own preference for *Le blé en herbe* over her other novels is echoed by her readers; '*Chéri* est un livre bien fait' ['*Chéri* is a well-executed book'], runs one opinion, 'Mais le livre riche (entre autres), c'est *Le Blé en herbe*' ['But the richest book (among others) is *Le blé en herbe*'], (Claude-Michel Cuny, *Les lettres françaises*, 2 February 1967.) A helpful summary by Claude Pichois and Madeleine Raaphorst-Rousseau of critical reactions to the novel may be found in Colette, *Oeuvres* (vol. 2), pp. 1705–8.

31   In her discussion of what she calls Colette's 'study of sex roles, their limits, overlap, and evolution', Joan Hinde Stewart in *Colette* (Boston MA: Twayne Publishers, 1983) cites this image of Phil smeared with lipstick to demonstrate that 'explicit designations of femininity and masculinity, attached to traits, gestures, and actions, permeate the lexical atmosphere' (p. 59).

32   Alain Virmaux and Odette Virmaux (eds), *Colette au cinéma: chroniques, dialogues, scénarios* (Paris: Flammarion, 1975), pp. 89–92.

33   Gabriel René, 'En marge de *Julie de Carneilhan*', in *L'Ecran française*, 3–4/248 (1950). Quoted in Virmaux and Virmaux (eds), *Colette au cinema*, p. 19.

34   Virmaux and Virmaux (eds), *Colette au cinéma*, p. 11. In addition to her cinematic interests, Colette's lasting commitment to the theatre continued as, over the course of five years – from 1933 to 1938 – she attended dress rehearsals so as to write weekly theatre reviews for *L'éclair*, *La revue de Paris*, *Le journal* and *Le petit parisien*. Her success was such that newspaper sales jumped the day her reviews appeared. For one reader, her theatrical instinct for the faintest flaw, either in

the work or in its interpretation, was so acute as to inspire the analogy of a cat lying in wait to pounce, then, having seized its prey, cleaning the fishbone thoroughly. 'Ici la cruauté est délicate, toujours voilée, parfois presque imperceptible' ['Here, the cruelty is delicate, always veiled, at times almost imperceptible'] (François Porché, *Le jour*, 16 August 1934).

35 Laura Mulvey, 'Visual Pleasure and Narrative Cinema,' *Screen*, 16/3 (1975).

36 At the time of her 1975 discussion in 'Visual Pleasure and Narrative Cinema', Mulvey did not speculate as to the implications of such a pleasure-producing apparatus for a *female* spectator; rather, her argument served to render apparent the heavily masculinised sort of pleasure provided by mainstream cinema. In her subsequent *Visual and Other Pleasures* (Bloomington IN: Indiana University Press, 1989), Mulvey theorised an inherent female bisexuality that, together with cultural coercion, provides for feminine identification with the male spectator's perspective. 'Trans-sex identification,' she argued, 'is a *habit* that very easily becomes *second nature*. However, this Nature does not sit easily and shifts restlessly in its borrowed transvestite clothes' (p. 33).

37 Colette, *Le blé en herbe*, illustrated by G. Bernard (Paris: Livre imprimé, 1928).

38 Mulvey, *Visual and Other Pleasures*, p. 21. Mulvey develops such masculine, narcissistic viewing pleasure to argue for its exhibitionist implications. Not only does one admire in narcissistic gratification the antics of one's more perfect, screen-image self – one also derives exhibitionist pleasure in admiring the antics of this idealised self-projection.

39 Malcolm Offord, 'Imagery in Colette's *Le blé en herbe*', *Nottingham French Studies*, 25/1 (1986), 52.

40 In parallel to Phil's fragile, developing masculinity, Vinca's tomboy outfit and demeanour are portrayed as equally tentative, fleeting and provisional, with the important exception of her woman's eyes: 'sauf ces yeux anxieux, jaloux, éloquents, elle ressemblait à un collégien déguisé pour une charade' ['but for these anxious, jealous, eloquent eyes, she looked like an adolescent disguised for play-acting'] (Colette, *Le blé en herbe, Oeuvres*, p. 1198).

41 This line describing Madame Dalleray's 'corps de femme' ['woman's body'] (Colette, *Le blé en herbe, Oeuvres*, p. 1224) has been read by Marcelle Biolley-Godino in *L'homme objet chez Colette* (Paris: Klincksieck, 1972) as a marker of the older woman's masculinity, for, argues Biolley-Godino, the notions of abduction, capture and rape are specific to masculine rather than feminine eroticism (p. 74).

42 Madame Dalleray's 'feminisation' could be read as consonant with a possible normative cultural punishment for her virile, gender-bending, transgressive appropriation of the gaze. 'There is always a certain excessiveness,' writes Mary Ann Doane in 'Film and the Masquerade: Theorizing the Female Spectator', *Screen*, 23/3–4 (1982), 'a difficulty associated with women who appropriate the gaze, who insist upon looking'. As Doane argues in the context of the horror genre, 'the woman's active looking is ultimately punished. And what she sees, the monster, is only a mirror of herself – both woman and monster are freakish in their difference – defined by either "too much" or "too little"' (p. 83).

43 Malcolm Offord, 'Colours in Colette's *Le blé en herbe*', *Nottingham French Studies*, 22/2 (1983), 51.

44 Jouve, *Colette*, p. 112.

45 Offord, 'Imagery', *Nottingham French Studies*, 25/1 (1986), 38.

46 In a letter to her friend Marguerite Moreno of 1 August 1922, Colette implies that her own daughter, Bel-Gazou, provided inspiration for Vinca's boyishness (*Colette: Lettres à Marguerite Moreno*, ed. Claude Pichois (Paris: Flammarion, 1959), p. 62.

Me voilà seule … avec ma fille et mon grand lévrier de garçon, qui commence à prendre une bonne gueule de campagne. Quant à ma fille … elle vaut le voyage, non seulement à cause d'un corps singulièrement beau et robuste, d'un visage insolent couleur de brugnon brun-mais à cause de l'indépendance abominable dont la Bretagne l'imprègne. Par tout temps elle est sur les routes, les sentiers et les rocs, elle traîne une flopée de guenilleux, qu'elle commande; elle disparaît des heures, reparaît cauteleuse, pleine de cambouis et d'une docilité sournoise … Elle est abominable, je te répète, et comme à Dorian Gray, ses péchés fleurissent sur ses joues. Elle déterre des oignons dans les champs et les mange … [L]a vie d'une mère, quel calvaire!

[Here I am alone … with my big girl and my greyhound of a boy, who's taking on a good country complexion. As for my daughter … she's worth the trip, not only for her singularly lovely and robust body, with its insolent face the colour of a dark nectarine, but for the abominable independence that Bretagne imbues her with. In all weather, she's out and about, on the paths and rocks, dragging a little crowd of ragged creatures that she tyrannises; she disappears for hours, reappearing slyly, filthy and full of crafty docility … She's abominable, I repeat, and like those of Dorian Gray, her sins blossom on her cheeks. She unearths onions in the fields and eats them … [W]hat martyrdom, the life of a mother!]

47 *Le Figaro*, 9–10 January 1954, p. 10.
48 *Le Figaro*, 9–10 January 1954, p. 10.
49 While gender construction is accomplished otherwise – and far less daringly – in Autant-Lara's film than it is in the novel, the gaze, instrument of gender definition, is nonetheless heavily thematised in the film. The opening beach scene, for instance, with its gust of wind scattering bathers and strollers, includes a photographer under his black camera cape, as though to emphasise the importance of vision. Additionally, after Phil and Vinca set off for a film being shown by an outdoor travelling cinema, Vinca changes her mind during a dispute and returns home; arriving at the cinema, Phil is projected onto the screen in silhouette, to riotous disturbance, distracting the accompanying pianist and violinist. He sits down with Margot, until Vinca unexpectedly returns, to be projected onscreen in the same spectacular fashion; recognising Vinca's silhouette, Phil jumps up to join her, reaching her in the aisle just as the projector superimposes upon the film their own two silhouettes united in a larger-than-life kiss. Such an episode serves further to foreground the primacy of vision, the gaze and spectacle in Autant-Lara's film.
50 Despite its careful respect of convention, the film version of *Le blé en herbe* was nonetheless judged as scandalous. 'Le thème, jugé provocateur, scandaleux, inadmissible par les défenseurs de l'ordre moral, faisait peur aux commerçants' ['The theme, deemed provocative, scandalous, inadmissible by defenders of moral order, frightened merchants'], writes Freddy Buache in *Claude Autant-Lara* (Paris: Editions L'Age d'Homme, 1982). Buache points out that in the publicity brochure, director Autant-Lara reflected on what he saw as the hypocrisy of such reactions, emphasising what he considered to be the film's frankness and delicacy of feeling, expressed with simplicity for an effect of 'indiscutable pureté' ['indisputable purity'] (pp. 64–5).
51 Yannick Resch, *Corps féminin, corps textuel: essai sur le personnage féminin dans l'oeuvre de Colette* (Paris: Klincksieck, 1973), p. 40.
52 E. Ann Kaplan, *Women and Film: Both Sides of the Camera* (New York and London: Methuen, 1983).
53 The importance of this closing scene for Colette herself is suggested in a letter to Marguerite Moreno of May or June 1923, in Claude Pichois, ed. (Paris: Flammarion, 1959), p. 65:

J'ai fini – que je crois – 'Le Seuil' [titre d'origine]. Non sans tourments! La dernière page, exactement, m'a coûté toute ma première journée de Castel-Novel – et je te défie bien, en la lisant, de t'en douter. Quoi, ces vingt lignes où il n'y a ni cabochon ni ciselure … Hélas, c'est comme ça. C'est la *proportion* qui m'a donnée du mal. J'ai une telle horreur de la grandiloquence finale.

[I've finished – I think – 'The Threshold' [the novel's original title]. Not without suffering! The last page cost me, exactly, my whole first day at Castel-Novel – and I defy you, in reading it, to guess that. What, these twenty lines where there is neither stopping nor chiselling … Alas, that's the way it is. It's the proportion that gave me trouble. I so dislike closing grandiloquence.]

[54]   Mulvey, *Visual and Other Pleasures*, p. 21.
[55]   Studying the 'two structural moments' of gender's 'double trajectory' in texts by Stendhal, Balzac, Flaubert and Rachilde, Dorothy Kelly writes in *Fictional Genders: Role and Representation in Nineteenth-Century French Narrative* (Lincoln NE: University of Nebraska Press, 1989) that 'the first is that of aporia and ambiguity when the two genders cannot be distinguished from each other; the second is a repositioning of the genders into their original, traditional definitions' (pp. 2–3).
[56]   Luce Irigaray, *Speculum de l'autre femme* (Paris: Minuit, 1974).
[57]   Irigaray, *Speculum*, pp. 73–4.
[58]   Kimberly Devlin, 'En-gendered Choice and Agency in *Ulysses*', in Michael Patrick Gillespie and A. Nicholas Fargnoli (eds), Sebastuab D. G. Knowles (foreword), Ulysses *in Critical Perspective* (Gainesville FL: University Press of Florida, 2006), p. 71.
[59]   In *Sexual/Textual Politics: Feminist Literary Theory* (London and New York: Routledge, 1988), Toril Moi argues that:

Irigaray's mimicry in *Spéculum* becomes a conscious acting out of the hysteric (mimetic) position allocated to all women under patriarchy. Through her acceptance of what is in any case an ineluctable mimicry, Irigaray doubles it back on itself … Hers is a fundamentally paradoxical strategy that reflects that of the mystic: if the mystic's abject surrender becomes the moment of her liberation, Irigaray's undermining of patriarchy through the overmiming of its discourses may be the one way out of the straitjacket of phallocentrism. (p. 140)

60 Judith Butler, *Bodies that Matter: On the Limits of 'Sex'* (New Brunswick and London: Routledge, 1993), pp. 47 *et passim*.

61 On masculine-scripted femininity, see Mary Russo, 'Female Grotesques: Carnival and Theory', in Teresa de Lauretis (ed.), *Feminist Studies/Critical Studies* (Bloomington IN: Indiana University Press, 1986); Judith Butler, 'Lacan, Riviere and the Strategies of the Masquerade', in *Gender Trouble*, pp. 43–57; and Sue-Ellen Case, 'Toward a Butch-Femme Aesthetic', in Lynda Hart (ed.), *Making a Spectacle* (Ann Arbor MI: University of Michigan Press, 1988).

62 If Vinca cannot be read as mimicking in subtle irony the feminine stereotype, thereby mocking its reductiveness, can she be read as a hyperbolisation of the feminine? Is Vinca the archetypal Woman? Indeed, the scene's very profusion of feminine tropes would seem to suggest – as Mary Ann Doane puts it in 'Film and the Masquerade' – the flaunting or 'hyperbolisation of the accoutrements of femininity' (p. 82). Vinca's behaviour appears to proclaim her womanliness in a decisive, wholesale embracing of its most culturally overdetermined signifiers. Exploring the notion of feminine archetype, Kimberly Devlin asks of Joyce's Molly Bloom, 'Is her womanliness wonderfully quintessential or shamefully derivative?' – in other words, 'can she be defended as an archetype or should she be stigmatized as a stereotype?' ('Engendered Choice', p. 73). Such questions may be raised for Vinca, whose nascent femininity indeed becomes, as we have seen in this closing episode, a profusion of ultrafeminine clichés. However, whether we construe Vinca as a primordial Eve, archetypal Woman, in the fresh, seaside dawn of the novel's closing episode, or as a copy – a reductive, derivative stereotype, a pastiche of weary clichés of femininity – is inconsequential; for, as Devlin demonstrates, the definitions of archetype and stereotype too easily collapse into the same. More pertinently, it is the impact – instead – of this womanly archetype/stereotype on Phil's voyeuristic gaze that interests me here.

63 Colette, *The Ripening Seed*, trans. Roger Senhouse (New York: Penguin Books, 1996), p. 121.

64 Well before the novel's closing events, the very possibility of a sexual relation between Phil and Vinca was seen as sufficiently scandalous at the time as to suspend serialised publication – which had begun in the summer of 1922 – of the novel in *Le Matin*. Interestingly, we find gendered norms again at work in the fact that public reaction to Phil's own loss of virginity, earlier in the novel, was less indignant.

65 Colette, *Oeuvres* (vol. 2), p. 1730.

66 Mulvey, *Visual and Other Pleasures*, p. 19.

67 Mulvey, *Visual and Other Pleasures*, p. 21.

68 Predictably, the film closes with a far more conventional scene in which Phil and Vinca surreptitiously attend a wedding – miming in the back pew, the exchange of vows and rings. Far from the ingenious and subversive overturning of gendered scripts carried out by the novel's closing episode, the film closes with a pious preview of what – we infer – is considered the only 'appropriate' ending for Phil and Vinca: marriage. In Freddy Buache's opinion in *Claude Autant-Lara* (Paris: Editions L'Age d'Homme, 1982), the mimed wedding scene does not add much, and the film would have done better to conclude with the novel's more powerful ending of 'la joyeuse harmonie corporelle de Vinca, le matin, contemplée avec une surprise vaguement inquiète par Phil' ['Vinca's joyous corporeal harmony in the morning, contemplated in vaguely worried surprise by Phil'] (p. 62).

69 Colette, *Oeuvres* (vol. 2), p. 1275.

Dismantling Gender

1 Ferdinand Oyono, *Une vie de boy* (Paris: Editions Julliard, 1956). Page numbers in the text refer to this edition.

2 Edward Said, 'Representing the Colonized: Anthropology's Interlocutors', *Critical Inquiry*, 15/2 (1989), p. 210.

3 Christopher Miller, *Blank Darkness: Africanist Discourse in French* (Chicago IL: University of Chicago Press, 1985), p. 296. For a subtle and persuasive demonstration of such a mutually enriching encounter between Africa and 'the West', see Eileen Julien's analysis of reciprocal illumination produced by reading Gide's *L'immoraliste* ['The Immoralist'] against Oyono's *Une vie de boy* in 'Of Colonial and Canonical Encounters: A Reciprocal Reading of *L'immoraliste* and *Une vie de boy*', in Josef Gugler, Hans-Jurgen Lusebrink, Jurgen Martini (eds), *Literary Theory and African Literature* (Hamburg: Lit Verlag, 1994).

4 Edouard Glissant, *Poétique de la relation* (Paris: Gallimard, 1990).

5 Edouard Glissant, Interview with Frédéric Joignot, *Le Monde*, 2 (2005); republished 3 February 2011.

6 David Chioni Moore, 'An African Classic in Fourteen Translations: Ferdinand Oyono's *Une vie de boy* on the World Literary Stage', *PMLA*, 128/1 (January 2013), 103.

7 In his *Blank Darkness*, Miller details the example of anthropologist Leo Frobenius, whose European-orientated projections of Africa produced, claims Miller, 'a mirror in which a European can contemplate his own

idea of beauty' (p. 17). Frobenius's projected Africa, ironically enough, was adopted in various ways by the founders of the Négritude movement: Léopold de Senghor, Aimé Césaire and Léon Damas.

8   Miller, *Blank Darkness*, p. 121.

9   Jacques Bourgeacq, 'The Eye Motif and Narrative Strategy in Ferdinand Oyono's *Une vie de boy*: An Ethno-Cultural Perspective', *The French Review*, 66/5 (1993), 789.

10   Bourgeacq, 'The Eye Motif', 789. What may once have been understood by the West merely as 'a psychological mechanism', in Bourgeacq's claim, has now been greatly scrutinised. The power relations at work within the gaze having been uncovered and examined by Western feminist film theory, we now more fully understand the gender manipulation that subtends these relations – as I seek to show in the case of Oyono's novel.

11   Bourgeacq, 'The Eye Motif', 789.

12   Bourgeacq, 'The Eye Motif', 797.

13   Said, 'Representing the Colonized', 212. While the problem of themselves as observers remains under-analysed by contemporary anthropologists, it is true, however, that 'revisionist anthropological currents' actively scrutinise past anthropologists as observers. See Mark Rogin Anspach's discussion of this displacement of the object of anthropology in his 'When American Anthropologists Go "Postmodern"', *Stanford French Review*, 15/1–2 (1991).

14   Said, 'Representing the Colonized', 212.

15   Said, 'Representing the Colonized', 216–17.

16   Christopher Miller, *Theories of Africans* (Chicago IL: University of Chicago Press, 1990), p. 260. Extending beyond the cultural mediation at work in the encounter of Western attention and African text is the dynamic itself of reading, the active animation and production of any text by any reader. One might here note a doubly thick mediation or overlap, involving not only an encounter of cultures, but that encounter itself as scripted differently by every reader of every text.

17   Miller, *Blank Darkness*, p. 139.

18   Said, 'Representing the Colonized', 214.

19   Camara Laye, *L'enfant noir* (Paris: Plon, 1953).

20   Christopher Miller, 'Francophonie and Independence', in Hollier *et al.*, (eds), *A New History of French Literature* (Cambridge: Harvard University Press, 1989), p. 1030.

21   Miller, *Theories of Africans*, p. 28.

22   Miller, 'Francophonie and Independence', pp. 130–1.

23   Arthur Flannigan, '"The Eye of the Witch": Non-Verbal

Communication and the Exercise of Power in *Une vie de boy*', *The French Review*, 56/1 (1982), 61.

24 Jean-Paul Sartre, 'Orphée noir', *Situations III* (Paris: Gallimard, 1949), p. 229.

25 Maxwell Okolie, 'Le regard et le drame de Toundi dans *Une vie de boy*', *Ethiopiques*, 5/1 (1988).

26 Oyono is considered a 'comic satirist' by Richard Bjornson in 'Cameroonian Writing and the National Experience,' *The African Quest for Freedom and Identity* (Bloomington IN: Indiana University Press, 1991), p. 79, while Flannigan maintains that 'much, if not all, the humor' of the novel can be ascribed to the difference between knowing reader and innocent narrator ('The Eye of the Witch', 51). For Douglas Alexander in 'Le tragique dans les romans de Ferdinand Oyono', *Présence francophone*, 7 (1973), this difference at least creates a somewhat sinister 'comique' (27). But the detailing of Toundi's violent death at the outset of the novel makes claims for the narrative's 'comic' resonance problematic. Contributing yet further to the weight and solemnity of the death scene is the projection by lamplight of two spiders, whose enormous shadowy legs are likened to the branches of a weeping willow falling upon the shadow of the dying Toundi's head (12). Citing this image, Alexander himself argues that its very exaggeration anticipates the extreme dimension ('démesure') of Toundi's destruction ('Le tragique', 26). Indeed, the inexorability and 'démesure' with which Toundi is crushed by the whites make it difficult to read much humour into his story. Similarly, such 'démesure' on the part of the white colonists poses a challenge to a different claim, that Toundi's destruction is in some ways his own 'fault'. Reading Toundi's gluttony as a sort of tragic flaw, marking him as always needing more, Claire Dehon in *Le roman camerounais d'expression française* (Birmingham AL: Summa Publications, 1989) appears to see a logical extension to Toundi's belief in his own superiority: 'Il est gourmand, donc il lui faut toujours plus que les autres et il se croit supérieur à ses compatriotes' ['He's a glutton, so he always needs more than others and he believes himself superior to his compatriots'] (p. 12). Dehon unproblematically espouses the Commander's wife's judgement of Toundi as an 'esprit chimérique enclin à la folie des grandeurs ['a chimerical spirit inclined to delusions of grandeur'] (*Le roman camerounais*, p. 12), without seeming to question the wife's own motives to discredit Toundi. As such a 'chimerical spirit', continues Dehon, Toundi loses contact with reality, even as he describes it in his journal. And Dehon is severe in her judgement of Toundi, arguing that

it is not out of strength or courage that he disrupts white mastery, but out of personal faults of vanity and curiosity; she concludes by seeing Toundi as an anti-hero 'who makes no attempt to control his own destiny' (*Le roman camerounais*, pp. 71–2). However, the vicious mobilisation of the entire white community to crush Toundi seems entirely disproportionate to the innocent behaviour of a naive adolescent – and renders such readings problematic.

27 Okolie, 'Le regard', 210.

28 Bjornson, 'Cameroonian Writing and the National Experience', p. 79.

29 In another context, Ella Shohat in 'Imagining terra incognita', *Public Culture*, 3/2 (1991), offers a subtle rehearsal of the various gendered tropes that inhabit colonialist discourse (notions of the 'dark continent', 'virgin territory', 'the untamed colony' as 'libidinous, wild femininity', for example).

30 The plight of the native woman (to be pursued later in this discussion à propos of a culminating scene between a white woman and a Black one) is particularly worthy of attention in that even Frantz Fanon, most vehement of colonialism's critics, 'does not analyze the double oppression – racist and sexist – of the colonized woman', as Ketu Katrak points out in 'Decolonizing Culture: Toward a Theory for Postcolonial Women's Texts', *Modern Fiction Studies*, 35/1 (1989), 162. Studying Fanon's omission, Gwen Bergner in 'Who is That Masked Women? or, The Role of Gender in Fanon's *Black Skin, White Masks*', *PMLA*, 110/1 (1995) goes further in arguing for Fanon's 'own desire to circumscribe black women's sexuality and economic autonomy in order to ensure the patriarchal authority of black men' (81).

31 Julien, 'Of Colonial and Canonical Encounters', p. 83.

32 Interestingly, Toundi himself is uncircumcised, having left home before his ritual initiation into manhood. Dehon argues for the importance of this lack, and for another lack that it bespeaks: the consequent lack of Toundi's connection with the oral Cameroonian tradition, which is transmitted through instruction at the time of initiation. Removed thus from his own culture, Toundi is not equipped to cope – suggests Dehon – with his own discovery of white flaws; 'il n'a pas appris la sagesse nécessaire pour recevoir ces informations et pour savoir qu'en faire' ['he hasn't learned the wisdom necessary to process such information and to know what to do with it'] (p. 74).

33 Critics (Bjornson, Alexander) have pointed to Toundi's grave mistake in supposing, now that he has discovered that the Commander is uncircumcised, that there is nothing to fear from him. In transposing African standards of manliness – or their absence, in the case of

circumcision as a mark of manhood – to a European, Toundi is blinded, suggests Douglas Alexander in 'Le tragique dans les romans de Ferdinand Oyono', *Présence francophone*, 7 (1973), 'par son africanité même et condamné à subir les conséquences' ['by his Africanness itself and condemned to suffer the consequences'] (25).

34 Does his 'seeing' diminish Toundi, rendering him merely a vulgar voyeur? In both the voyeur's and Toundi's gaze, it is true, a process of reduction is at work. The voyeur reduces the feminine to object, an object then held for display under the voyeur's power. But Toundi's native gaze, rather than reducing the feminine to dominated object, transforms the virile to the effeminate; and the operative motive, for Toundi, is not prurient sexual pleasure for its own sake, but political resistance.

35 Bjornson, in 'Cameroonian Writing', reads the engineer Magnol's jealousy of Toundi somewhat differently, emphasising instead Magnol's anxiety over his own sexual potency. 'By discharging his anger on the innocent Houseboy', runs Bjornson's claim, 'he can evade the truth about his own fears' (p. 79). Such a reading, however, in shifting emphasis to Magnol's own self-doubts, neglects what I feel to be more crucial, generalised fears among the white colonists, and ones that will ultimately destroy Toundi: white fears of his transgressive and therefore, threatening, manhood.

36 In her discussion of the marked, inscribed colonised body in 'Transfiguring: Colonial Body into Postcolonial Narrative,' *Novel*, 26/3 (1993), Elleke Boehmer points to such self-pastiching behaviour as a form of resistance. 'Devices such as mimicry or, more than that, what might be called excessive self-replication, are used to indicate the weightiness and oppressiveness of the body's status as sign' (p. 275). In this politically charged context of the body as sign, argues Boehmer, 'representing its own silence, the colonized body speaks; uttering its wounds, it negates its muted condition' (p. 272).

37 In '"Boy!": The Hinge of Colonial Double Talk', *Studies in Twentieth-Century Literature*, 15/1 (1991), Anne Menke analyses Toundi's love song as a 'hybrid lyric', combining 'elements of the asexual courtly love tradition' as well as 'African terms of ebony, ivory, and antilopes'. She further proposes that Toundi's lyric might be read as 'an exemplary, Christian response to (illicit) love' (21).

38 The closest Toundi manages to come to pronouncing a judgement of Madame is to praise the wisdom of an ancestral proverb on the promiscuity of women. 'Nos ancêtres' ['Our ancestors'] writes Toundi, 'étaient des gens bien sages qui disaient: "La femme est un épi de mais

à la portée de toute bouche pourvu qu'elle ne soit pas édentée''' ['were wise people indeed, to say "woman is an ear of corn available to every mouth, as long as it isn't toothless"'] (p. 108). Yet such a pronouncement is highly mediated, and, consequently, attenuated, by its status as quotation; as though Toundi quotes such a thought – rather than pronouncing the idea himself – specifically to distance himself from it. Furthermore, as a general assertion about *all* women, such a claim essentially relieves Madame herself of the responsibility to behave otherwise. One might even understand Toundi's quoted line as an implicit exculpation of Madame's own promiscuity, elevated as it is by this proverb to a universal feminine condition.

39 I echo Eileen Julien's assertion here that it is ultimately via Madame, the white woman, 'that excessive claims for white masculinity and the pretense of a superior European civilisation are debunked' ('Of Colonial and Canonical Encounters', p. 85). In this chapter, I have attempted to demonstrate the specific mechanisms of display that operate such 'debunking'.

40 Dehon, *Le roman camerounais d'expression française*, p. 72.

41 Laura Mulvey, *Visual and Other Pleasures* (Bloomington IN: Indiana University Press, 1989), p. 25.

42 Okolie, in 'Le regard et le drame de Toundi', describes this particular 'reifying' gaze, reducing its colonised, exploited object to a pure vehicle of service to the whites: 'la plupart des Blancs n'ont de regard que pour "perquisitionner" la personne du Noir afin de savoir s'il est "voleur", s'il est "propre", s'il n'a pas de "gales" ou de "chiques"' ['most of the Whites only have eyes to examine the Black's person to see whether he's a "thief", whether he's "clean", whether he has "scabies" or "fleas"'] (p. 208).

43 Norman Bryson, *Vision and Painting: The Logic of the Gaze* (New Haven CT and London: Yale University Press, 1983), pp. 93–4.

44 Bryson, *Vision and Painting*, p. 122.

45 Mary Ann Doane, *Femmes Fatales: Feminism, Film Theory and Psychoanalysis* (New York: Routledge, 1991), p. 231. In the chapter 'Dark Continents: Epistemologies of Racial and Sexual Difference in Psychoanalysis and the Cinema', Doane analyses the situation of the invisible Black woman in the context of Fanon's erasure of the Black female subject in favour of Black *male* subjectivity.

46 Boehmer, 'Transfiguring', p. 271.

47 Boehmer, 'Transfiguring', p. 271.

48 One might point to a similar scene in which Toundi's gaze might be argued to 'mark' and defile Madame's body: a 'grotesque' moment,

argues Eileen Julien, in which Toundi accidentally perceives Madame asleep, sprawled on her bed, a fly on her cheek. 'The craving, sexual body', suggests Julien, 'is here exposed, in a vulgar disposition as the ironic fly takes the place of a "grain de beauté"' ('Of Colonial and Canonical Encounters', p. 85). The defiling presence of the fly is symptomatic of Toundi's 'marking' gaze. However, whereas Julien argues that 'the door is open and Toundi does see', I maintain that Toundi, to the end, sees but cannot *acknowledge* what he sees. And this is why Kalisia's more penetrating, lucid gaze – free of the desire that cripples Toundi's – becomes necessary.

49   Miller, *Blank Darkness*, p. 139.

50   Miller, *Theories*, p. 262.

Disappearance as Display

1   André Gide, *La porte étroite*, in Y. Davet and J.-J. Thierry (eds), *Romans, Récits et Soties* (Paris: Gallimard, Bibliothèque de la Pléiade, 1958). Page numbers in the text refer to this edition.

2   In a letter to Gide, Edmund Gosse was sensitive to the extremes that Alissa represents: 'I can witness to the penetration, the truth, the bitter sweetness of your searching analysis of Calvinistic pietism, so far more tragic, so far more hopeless and desolating than any of the ecstasies of the Catholic Church. What are the sufferings of S. Catherine of Sienna, of S. Fina of San Gimigniano, by the side of the slow and cruel suicide of Alissa?' (Edmund Gosse, Letter to André Gide, in Linette F. Brugmans (ed.), *The Correspondence of André Gide and Edmund Gosse, 1904–1928* (London: Peter Owen, 1960), p. 45).

3   As defined by the *Oxford Dictionary of English* (2nd edition, revised) (Oxford: Oxford University Press, 2003,), *logos* – meaning 'The Word of God … incarnate in Jesus Christ' – understood as the manifestation, or embodiment, of a discourse, will become particularly significant later in this chapter in the analysis of Juliette's word-made-flesh 'embodiment'.

4   This verse from Luke XIII, 24 – 'Efforcez-vous d'entrer par la porte étroite' ['Strive to enter through the strait gate'] – is not only the novel's epigraph but integrated within the narrative when Jérôme ponders a pastor's sermon inspired by Christ's exhortation, and resolves to be among the few who succeed (pp. 505–6).

5   Emily Apter, *André Gide and the Codes of Homotextuality* (Stanford CA: Stanford University Press, Anma Libri, 1987), p. 132.

6   My emphasis on the importance of absence is anticipated by Gide's remark in his journal about the writing of *La porte étroite*. When a friend objects to him that this novel lacks 'les qualités qui faisaient la séduction de quelques-uns des autres' ['those qualities that rendered some of the others so appealing'], Gide tries to convince his friend that the difficulty in writing *La porte étroite* was precisely to omit such reader-pleasing charms. As Gide wrote in his journal 'L'important, le difficile, était précisément de ne pas les y mettre, ici, ces qualités qui n'étaient pas celles qui convenaient à ce roman' ['The important and difficult thing was precisely not to put them in, here – such qualities not being appropriate to this novel'] (*Journal I*, p. 275).

7   Kevin Newmark, 'Love's Cross in *La porte étroite*', *MLN*, 99/5, (1984), 1095. Gide was adamant in his claim that his wife Madeleine was not the model for Alissa: 'Mais quelle erreur, celui qui croirait que j'ai tracé son portrait dans ma *porte étroite*! Il n'y eut jamais rien forcé ni d'excessif dans sa vertu' ['But what an error, he who would believe that I have traced her portrait in my *porte étroite*! There was never anything forced or excessive about her virtue'] (*Journal I*, p. 1078). In her chapter on *La porte etroite*, however, Armine Kotin Mortimer argues for a different sort of 'truth' revealed in Gide's fiction. She quotes Gide's coquettish assertion that since memoirs are always only partially sincere, and since things are always more complicated that one claims, perhaps one gets closer to the truth via fiction (André Gide, *Si le grain ne meurt* p. 547; quoted in Armine Kotin Mortimer, *Plotting to Kill* (New York: Peter Lang Publishing, 1991), p. 78). Mortimer suggests that the failure of Alissa and Jérôme to marry in Gide's novel might be read as an indirect sort of wish-fulfillment, a record of Gide's regret over having married his cousin Madeleine. Such a regret is explicitly expressed in his journal: 'Si je m'étais écouté … j'aurais fait quatre tours du monde … et je ne me serais pas marié. En écrivant ces mots j'en tremble comme d'une impiété' ['If I had listened to myself … I would have gone around the world four times … and I would not have married. In writing these words, I tremble as though at an impiety'] (*Journal I: 1939–49*, 9 September 1940, p. 53). In 'plotting to kill' its heroine (Alissa), argues Mortimer, a novel such as *La porte etroite* reaches 'a truth that is better, though it radically departs from biography, than the truth we might arrive at by intending to tell the truth' (p. 78).

8   The 'eccentricity' of *La porte étroite* is further suggested by Gide's own view of it as 'anachronistic': 'Ce qui me donne tant de mal à l'écrire, ce livre, c'est aussi ce qui leur donne (je songe principalement à Ghéon) assez de mal à l'écouter: il reste en anachronisme avec ce que

nous pensons, sentons et voulons aujourd'hui' ['What gives me such trouble in writing this book is also what makes it so hard for them (I'm thinking mainly of Ghéon) to listen to it: it remains anachronistic to what we think, feel and want today'] (André Gide, *Journal I*, p. 581).

8   Newmark, 'Love's Cross', 1110. Newmark refuses the status of recollection to Jérôme's text, claiming that Jérôme's resistance to any sort of interpretive work upon his past produces a narration that is 'the unreflective process of mere recording' (1111). Jérôme's text is condemned by Newmark as 'an unthinking and inessential *enumeration*'. Newmark's claim for the unreflective, fixed past of Jérôme's narration is shared by Eric Marty, who sees it similarly as 'enferré dans le passé' ['ossified within the past'], 'privée de cette liberté d'une écriture au présent qui va toujours de l'avant, dans une présence indéfectible à soi' ['deprived of that liberty of a discourse in the present that always moves forward, in unfailing presence-to-itself'] (Eric Marty, 'A propos de *La porte étroite*: Répétition et remémoration: Le nouvel Abelard', *Revue des sciences humaines*, 70/199 (1985), 83).

9   Apter, *André Gide*, p. 106.

10   Apter, *André Gide*, pp. 129–33.

11   Marty, 'A propos de *La porte étroite*', 97.

12   Jérôme's devotion to his studies and the scholarly life – a devotion he mentions pointedly and repeatedly – acquires nuance when read in a context of sublimated narcissism, according to Jean Laplanche and J. B. Pontalis in *Vocabulaire de la psychanalyse* (Paris: Presses Universitaires de France, 1967): 'on retrouverait, au niveau de l'objet visé par les activités sublimées, le même caractère de belle totalité que Freud assigne ici au moi' ['one would find, at the level of the object at which sublimated activities are directed, the same character of beautiful totality that Freud assigns here to the ego'] (p. 466).

13   Greene, Robert, 'Fading (Sacred) Texts and Dying (Guiding) Voices in Gide's Early Récits', *French Forum*, 12/1 (1987), 86.

14   Even critics who claim a presence-to-itself for Alissa seem implicitly to recognise Alissa's theatricality. Alissa, writes Marty, 'joue merveilleusement le rôle du *Maître* … Si Alissa est maîtresse des signes et la seule maîtresse du sens, c'est parce que comme tout être de tragédie, elle est l'être du *déjà*; elle sait *toujours déjà*, elle est … déjà derrière lequel s'essoufle Jérôme qui déjouant un piège en trouve aussitôt un nouveau sur sa route' ['plays the role of Master marvellously … If Alissa is mistress of signs and the sole mistress of meaning, it's that, like all tragic beings, she is a being of the "already"; she "always already" knows, she is already the one Jérôme struggles to keep up with as he

eludes traps only to find another in his path'] (Marty, 'A propos de *La porte étroite*, 90). This 'toujours déjà' context recalls the tragic character as understood by Georg Lukacs, who saw the figure as stranded onstage, compelled in tragic dignity and resignation to play out a role that he or she knows is futile.

15 Albert Sonnenfeld, 'Strait is the Gate: Byroads in Gide's Labyrinth', *Novel*, 1/2 (1968), 130.

16 Sonnenfeld, 'Byroads', 131.

17 Might Alissa have been right to fear that she was 'too old' for Jérôme? The fact that she is two years older than Jérôme is – perhaps significantly – the first detail Jérôme himself provides about her (p. 497).

18 Marty, 'A propos de *La porte étroite*', 94.

19 Other indications suggest Alissa as a being of absence, of renunciation. When Jérôme asks her if she'd like to travel, Alissa answers that it is enough to know that such countries exist, that they are beautiful, and that others may visit them (p. 519). She later tells Jérôme, who has come to her room to finalise their engagement, that she has no need of so much happiness (p. 521). Exchanging letters with her while at the Ecole Normale, Jérôme cannot help but suspect that Alissa's missives, rather than transparently conveying her thoughts, in fact obscure them.

20 Lacan, Jacques, *Les Quatre Concepts fondamentaux de la psychanalyse*, in Jacques-Alain Miller (ed.), *Le Séminaire de Jacques Lacan* (Paris: Editions du Seuil, 1973), p. 201.

21 'Nous choisissons l'être, le sujet disparaît, il nous échappe, il tombe dans le non-sens – nous choisissons le sens, et le sens ne subsiste qu'écorné de cette partie de non-sens qui est, à proprement parler, ce qui constitue, dans la réalisation du sujet, l'inconscient' ['We choose the being, the subject disappears, it eludes us, it falls into non-sense – we choose meaning, and meaning only subsists in being deprived of that part of non-sense that is, properly speaking, what constitutes, in the production of subjectivity, the unconscious'] (Lacan, *Les Quatre concepts*, pp. 191–2).

22 Lacan, *Les Quatre concepts*, p. 99.

23 One reading of this masquerade, this relationship mediated by words in a perversion of *logos*, is Newmark's claim for a pedagogical, cognitive bond linking Alissa and Jérôme. This pedagogical relationship, suggests Newmark, is what 'disturbs the *affective* specular rapport', which 'is allowed to become increasingly pedagogic at the expense of its romance' (Newmark, 'Love's Cross', 1100). But the pedagogical,

however, would seem to be not so much an end in itself as yet another expression of the novel's theatricality: a masquerade of screens and quotations whose purpose is not to instruct, but to dissimulate, to disguise. The reader must remain wary of accepting the pedagogical masquerade as an authentic definition of Alissa and Jérôme's relationship.

24 This notion, that a profusion of quotations only serves to mask an underlying absence, is also argued by Robert Greene. Noting the naming of Corneille even as he goes unquoted, Greene points to 'the great textual emptiness that is located where a great textual fullness ought to be found … One finally gets the impression from reading *La porte etroite* that texts always enclose other texts, and that the act of quotation involves an infinite regression, an endless quest for an original, authenticating citation' (Greene, 'Fading (Sacred) Texts', 89).

25 Marty, 'A propos de *La porte étroite*', 101–2.

26 Clifford Geertz, *The Interpretation of Cultures* (Chicago IL: Basic Books, 1973), p. 126. Quoted in Brooks, *The Melodramatic Imagination*, p. 18.

27 Brooks, *The Melodramatic Imagination*, p. 18.

28 Geertz, *The Interpretation of Cultures*, p. 126.

29 Brooks, *The Melodramatic Imagination*, p. 18.

30 Edmond de Rostand, *Cyrano de Bergerac*, line 2486.

31 Octave Mannoni, *Clefs pour l'imaginaire* (Paris: Seuil, 1969), p. 176.

32 Pierre Fédida, *L'absence* (Paris: Editions Gallimard, 1978), p. 80.

33 Fédida, *L'absence*, p. 81.

34 Fédida, *L'absence*, p. 55.

35 Fédida, *L'absence*, p. 70.

36 Fédida, *L'absence*, p. 77.

37 Fédida, *L'absence*, p. 88.

38 Fédida, *L'absence*, p. 89.

39 Freud, *Complete Works*, vol. XVIII, p. 132.

40 Freud, *Complete Works*, vol. XVIII, p. 132.

41 Melanie Klein, 'Mourning and Its Relation to Manic-Depressive States', in *Contributions to Psychoanalysis, 1921–1945* (London: Hogarth Press, 1948), p. 311.

42 Klein, 'Mourning', p. 317.

43 Marty, 'A propos de *La porte étroite*', 102.

44 Klein, 'Mourning', pp. 317–19.

45 Klein, 'Mourning', p. 320.

46 Klein, 'Mourning', p. 337–8.

47 Newmark, 'Love's Cross', 1104.

48 Geertz, *The Interpretation of Cultures*, p. 98.

49 Newmark, 'Love's Cross', 1101.

50 Roddey Reid, 'Modernist Aesthetics and Familial Textuality: Gide's Strait is the Gate', *Studies in Twentieth-Century Literature*, 13/2 (1989), 158.

51 Reid, 'Modernist Aesthetics', p. 164.

52 Thomas Cordle, *André Gide, Updated Edition* (New York: Twayne Publishers, 1993), p. 80.

53 Doris Kadish, '"Alissa dans la vallée": Intertextual Echoes of Balzac in Two Novels by Gide', *French Forum*, 10/1 (1985), 79.

54 Albert Sonnenfeld, 'Strait is the Gate: Byroads in Gide's Labyrinth', *Novel* 1/2 (1968), 121.

55 Without pursuing further the melodramatic 'descent from the cross' implications that interest me in this scene and that will be explored further in this chapter, Thomas Cazentre considers Juliette's fainting – which brings to a close the novel's first four chapters – 'un *finale* éminemment théâtral' (Thomas Cazentre, 'Les comédiens sans le savoir: L'inconscient dramatique dans *La porte étroite*', *Bulletin des Amis d'André Gide*, XXXII, 141, January 2004, 20).

56 Brooks, *The Melodramatic Imagination*, p. 41.

57 Brooks, *The Melodramatic Imagination*, p. 56.

58 Brooks, *The Melodramatic Imagination*, p. 48.

59 Juliette's collapse is suggestive of Rogier Van der Weyden's 'Descent from the Cross' (c. 1435) in several ways. We might here note, moreover, Gide's appreciation for Van der Weyden's works; describing a museum visit in Brussels, he writes in his journal entry of 29 September 1929, 'les Van Der Weyden me paraissent plus admirables que jamais' ['The Van Der Weydens seem to me more admirable than ever'] (Gide, *Journal I*, p. 937).) As I will argue later in this chapter, Juliette and Christ are further linked in that each incarnates sacrifice.

60 Brooks, *The Melodramatic Imagination*, p. 67.

61 Brooks, *The Melodramatic Imagination*, p. 10.

62 Brooks, *The Melodramatic Imagination*, p. 199.

63 Brooks, *The Melodramatic Imagination*, p. 80.

64 I am grateful to Dorothy Stegman for this reading of Juliette's significant use of the verb 'se réfugier'.

65 Kadish, 'Alissa dans la vallée', 79.

66 Brooks, *The Melodramatic Imagination*, p. 77.

67 Sonnenfeld, 'Byroads', 132.

68 Kadish, 'Alissa dans la vallée', 80.

69 In Rome in 1935, Gide found himself in a group in which his works were much discussed; knowing how interested all present were in

Caravaggio, Gide brought the painter up in conversation, and the group decided to take a tour the next day of Caravaggio works in Rome (Alan Sheridan, *André Gide: A Life in the Present* (London: Hamish Hamilton Ltd, 1998), p. 475).
70   Gide, *Journal II*, p. 1061.
71   Gide, *Journal I*, p. 1187.
72   Gide, *Journal I*, p. 1187.
73   Sonnenfeld, 'Byroads', 171.

Framing Monstrosity

1   François Mauriac, *Thérèse Desqueyroux*, in Jacques Petit (ed.), *Oeuvres romanesques et théâtrales* (vol. 2) (Paris: Gallimard, 1979). Page numbers in the text refer to this edition.
2   Marie-Hélène Huet, *Monstrous Imagination* (Cambridge MA: Harvard University Press, 1993) p. 6.
3   Thérèse's story was largely inspired by the Canaby scandal, in which a respectable bourgeois housewife attempted to poison her wine-broker husband, in Bordeaux in 1906, when Mauriac was twenty years old. Through forged prescriptions, Madame Canaby had acquired excessive quantities of aconitine, digitalin and chloroform; her husband, already ill, worsened after drinking his morning hot chocolate. At first, she refused to let anyone see him, but he was eventually hospitalised, where he recovered; he was able to testify in favour of his wife at the trial, even denying certain facts that seemed to establish her guilt. Thanks to an impassioned speech pleading for the honour of the family, Maître Peyrecave (whose name Mauriac uses directly in *Thérèse Desqueyroux*), obtained an acquittal for Madame Canaby, though she was sentenced for forgery. For further details of the scandal, see J. S. T. Garfitt's account of the incident in *Mauriac: Thérèse Desqueyroux* (London: Grant and Cutler, Ltd, 1991), pp. 40–1.
4   Mauriac's strange obsession with Thérèse's 'monstrosity' is understood by David O'Connell in *François Mauriac Revisited* (New York: Twayne Publishers, 1995) as an expression of his Catholicism: '[a]s a Catholic novelist, [Mauriac] does not see evil as a mere concept, but as an incarnation – Satan'. O'Connell quotes Thérèse's question to Dr Schwartz in Mauriac's later short fiction, 'Thérèse chez le docteur', where Thérèse asks the doctor whether he believes that evil is a person. O'Connell sees such a question as expressive of 'Mauriac's deepest convictions as a novelist' (p. 105).

5 Staging this scene in his 2012 eponymous film of Mauriac's novel, director Claude Miller instead places Thérèse to the side and behind the two men, who appear oblivious to her presence. Such removal of Thérèse from the confines of the male frame depicted in the text is contrary, however, to the framing effect emphasised by the narration.

6 The 'monstrous' connection with Thérèse Raquin is pointed out by J. S. T. Garfitt, who observes that the name Thérèse 'évoque à la fois le monstre et la sainte, Thérèse Raquin aussi bien que Thérèse de l'Enfant Jésus' ['evokes at once the monster and the saint, Thérèse Raquin as well as Thérèse of the Child Jesus'] ('Clés pour *Thérèse Desqueyroux*: Onomastique et Calendrier Liturgique', *Présence de François Mauriac, Actes du colloque organisé à Bordeaux pour le Centenaire de Mauriac* (10–12 October 1985) (Pessac: Presses Universitaires de Bordeaux, 1986), p. 205. Another intertextual reference, this time to Racine's *Phèdre*, is also pointed out by Garfitt, who notices that the line rendering Thérèse's dilemma over what to say to Bernard – 'Que lui dirait-elle? Par quel aveu commencer?' ['What would she say to him? With what avowal to begin?'] – echoes Phèdre's: 'Ciel! Que vais-je dire? Et par ou commencer?' ['Oh God! What will I say? And where to begin?'] (Racine, *Phèdre*, line 247). Pursuing the 'Phèdre' resonance, Garfitt in his *Mauriac: Thérèse Desqueyroux* (London: Grant and Cutler, 1991) also points to Thérèse's characterisation of Bernard as an 'Hippolyte mal léché' ['uncouth Hippolyte'] (p. 38). Garfitt unquestioningly accepts the text's handling of monstrosity, calling Thérèse a 'fascinating and complex "monster"' (p. 41), and asserting Thérèse's own embracing of such an identity: monstrosity as Thérèse's 'own self-assessment' (p. 30).

7 Edward Gallagher, *Textual Hauntings: Studies in Flaubert's Madame Bovary and Mauriac's Thérèse Desqueyroux* (Lanham MD: University Press of America, 2005), p. 78.

8 André Joubert, *François Mauriac et Thérèse Desqueyroux* (Paris: Nizet, 1982), p. 88.

9 Jacques Derrida, *La vérité en peinture* (Paris: Editions Flammarion, 1978), p. 73.

10 The epigraph reprises the closing lines of Baudelaire's poem 'Mademoiselle Bistouri' from his collection *Petits poèmes en prose* in *Oeuvres complètes*, ed. Claude Pichois (Paris: Gallimard, 1954).

11 Sandra Gilbert and Susan Gubar, *The Madwoman in the Attic: The Woman Writer and the Nineteenth-Century Literary Imagination* (New Haven CT: Yale University Press, 1979), p. 28.

12 Huet, *Monstrous Imagination*, p. 33.

13 Jeffrey Jerome Cohen, 'Monster Culture (Seven Theses)', in Cohen

(ed.), *Monster Theory: Reading Culture* (Minneapolis MN: University of Minnesota Press, 1996), p. 19.

[14] Cohen, 'Monster Culture', p. 19.

[15] Cohen, 'Monster Culture', p. 17.

[16] David O'Connell, *François Mauriac Revisited* (New York: Twayne Publishers, 1995), p. 75.

[17] Jacques Petit, 'Notice', in Mauriac, *Œuvres romanesques et théâtrales* (vol. 2), p. 918.

[18] William Kidd, 'Oedipal and Pre-Oedipal Elements in *Thérèse Desqueyroux*', in John E. Flower and Bernard C. Swift (eds), *François Mauriac: Visions and Reappraisals* (Oxford: Berg Publishers, 1989), p. 25.

[19] Gallagher, *Textual Hauntings*, p. 39.

[20] Diana Festa-McCormick, 'Mauriac's Thérèse: an Androgynous Heroine', in *Writing in a Modern Temper: Essays in French Literature and Thought in Honor of Henri Peyre* (Saratoga CA: Anma Libri, 1984), p. 184.

[21] Timothy J. Williams, 'Thérèse and Anne: Mauriac's Mimetic Rivals', *Romance Quarterly*, 48/2 (Spring 2001), 79.

[22] Williams, 'Thérèse and Anne', 79.

[23] Garfitt, *Mauriac*, p. 41.

[24] Joubert, *François Mauriac*, p. 105.

[25] Joubert, *François Mauriac*, p. 109.

[26] Williams, in 'Thérèse and Anne', argues for the importance of Thérèse and Anne's 'mimetic rivalry' to the understanding of Thérèse's actions, a crucial moment in this 'rivalry' being Anne's letter to a honeymooning Thérèse.

If one person cannot obtain the object of desire seen (or believed to be) in the hands of another, that individual will attempt to deprive the other of its possession as well, becoming an obstacle to the other's realization of the desire. The ensuing rivalry commences a downward spiral that is increasingly hostile and can end in outright violence (p. 76).

In Williams's argument – inspired by René Girard's work on mimetic desire in *Mensonge romantique et vérité romanesque* (Paris: Grasset, 1961) – Thérèse's violent actions (sticking the photo of Jean Azevedo with a pin and attempting to poison Bernard) are provoked by her desire to have what Anne has. The difficulty with this Girardian reading, however, is that, at the time of Anne's letter, Anne does not precisely 'have' what she assumes Thérèse does: that is, sexual fulfilment; nor is Thérèse's violence directed at 'depriv[ing] the other of its possession as well'. Rather, Anne's letter serves to remind Thérèse of what she, Thérèse, *should* have, but does not: 'Et moi, alors? Et moi? Pourquoi pas moi?' ['And me, then? And me? Why not me?'] (p. 54).

27   Mary Ann Caws, *Reading Frames in Modern Fiction* (Princeton NJ: Princeton University Press, 1985), p. 6.

28   Meyer Shapiro, 'On Some Problems in the Semiotics of Visual Art: Field and Vehicle in Image-Signs', *Simiolus: Netherlands Quarterly for the History of Art*, 6/1(1972–3), 11.

29   A comparable use of framing as 'othering' tactic is found in Cocteau's 1946 film *L'éternel retour* ['The Eternal Return'], where the evil Natalie – who will betray Patrick/Tristan by lying to him, thus precipitating his death before the arrival of the good Natalie/Iseult – is heavily framed by the wooden support beams of a boat hangar as she eavesdrops upon a plan to summon the good Natalie/Iseult to the dying hero.

30   Jean Racine, *Phèdre*, Comédie Française, Palais Royal, Paris, 19 March 2013.

31   Shapiro, 'On Some Problems', 12.

32   Intriguingly, Bertha Mason in Charlotte Brontë's *Jane Eyre* also embodies an association of madness and conflagration – like *Thérèse Desqueyroux*'s construction of Thérèse's monstrosity – dying in a fire she herself ignites at her husband Mr Rochester's estate of Thornfield.

33   When a more humane explanation for Thérèse's actions is offered, it is at the cost of falsifying her. William Kidd argues that through Thérèse, Mauriac 'has regressively re-created the psychological dynamics which may have been attendant on his own loss of his father' (p. 45). This reading relies, however, on seeing Thérèse's nostalgia for her dead mother as, in fact, a son's ambivalent feeling for his father. As Kidd writes, 'a major, if not the major, emotional characteristic of Thérèse is an ambivalent nostalgia for the mother. In that sense, it is the father who is the true 'absent' of the novel' (p. 45). Again, the difficulty with such an argument is that it contorts Thérèse and her mother into a heavily Freudian father/son dynamic.

34   Some critics, however, refuse to accept the legitimacy of a 'sympathetic' reading of Thérèse, conceding only that she may evoke sympathy in 'a certain type of reader': implicitly, a female reader like Thérèse herself. 'While accepting that Thérèse is representative of a certain provincial womanhood, and that she elicits thereby the

sympathetic complicity of a certain type of reader, [Mauriac] emphatically rules out any equally clear-cut motive for his own heroine' (Kidd, 'Oedipal and Pre-Oedipal Elements', p. 26). My argument, of course, has been that a masculinised narrating apparatus, in 'monstrifying' Thérèse, works to block any 'sympathetic complicity' on the part of her reader.

35 Barbara Claire Freeman, *The Feminine Sublime: Gender and Excess in Women's Fiction* (Berkeley CA: University of California Press, 1995), p. 75.

36 François Mauriac, *Thérèse Desqueyroux* (Paris: Editions Grasset, 1927).

37 Mauriac will again, some years after the 1927 publication of *Thérèse Desqueyroux*, pick up Thérèse's narrative in three short stories: 'Thérèse chez le docteur' ['Thérèse at the Doctor's'] (1933); 'Thérèse à l'hôtel' ['Thérèse at the Hotel'] (1934); and 'La fin de la nuit' ['The End of the Night'] (1935). As Mauriac explained in his forward to 'La fin de la nuit', he had difficulty letting go of his complex character, Thérèse. However, because he published *Thérèse Desqueyroux* in 1927 with the conviction that her story was complete, I have chosen to respect his original vision for the novel and will not discuss the subsequent short stories here.

Genre, Masquerade and Displacement

1 Sébastien Japrisot, *Piège pour Cendrillon* (Paris: Editions Denoël, 1965). Page numbers in the text refer to this edition.

2 Shoshana Felman, 'De Sophocle à Japrisot (via Freud), ou pourquoi le policier?', *Littérature*, 49 (1983), 26.

3 Uri Eisenzweig, 'Présentation du genre', *Littérature*, 49 (1983).

4 Fredric Jameson, *The Political Unconscious: Narrative as a Socially Symbolic Act* (Ithaca NY: Cornell University Press, 1981), pp. 106–7; quoted in Jack Zipes, *Fairy Tales and the Art of Subversion* (New York: Wildman Press, 1983), p. 4.

5 Michel Butor, *L'emploi du temps* (Paris: Editions du Minuit, 1956).

6 Butor, *L'emploi*, quoted without reference in Tzvetan Todorov, 'Typologie du roman policier', *Poétique de la prose* (Paris: Seuil, 1971), p. 57.

7 Jameson, *The Political Unconscious*, pp.106–7.

8 Laura Mulvey, *Visual and Other Pleasures* (Bloomington IN: Indiana University Press, 1989), p. 199.

9 Zipes, *Fairy Tales*, p. 1.

10   Zipes, *Fairy Tales*, p. 7.

11   Bruno Bettelheim in *The Uses of Enchantment: The Meaning and Importance of Fairy Tales* (New York: Knopf, 1976) suggests a similar understanding of the fairy tale as touching upon universal sensibilities, though he goes further in arguing for it as therapeutic solution, not merely – as Todorov does – template; he understands the fairy tale as a problem-solving story for children, helping them work through certain problems of identity. Arguing that gender in the fairy tale is irrelevant, Bettelheim suggests that hero and heroine are 'two (artificially) separated aspects of one and the same process which *everybody* has to undergo in growing up … children know that, whatever the sex of the hero, the story pertains to their own problems' (p. 226) (quoted in Kay Stone, 'The Misuses of Enchantment: Controversies on The Significance of Fairy Tales', in Rosanna A. Jordan and Susan J. Kalcik (eds), *Women's Folklore, Women's Culture* (Philadelphia PA: University of Pennsylvania Press, 1985), p. 129).

12   Zipes, *Fairy Tales*, p. 27. Zipes is alluding here to Charles Perrault's *Histoires ou contes du temps passé: Avec des Moralitez* (1697), in Jean-Pierre Collinet (ed.), *Contes* (Paris: Gallimard, 1981).

13   Zipes, *Fairy Tales*, p. 11.

14   Zipes, *Fairy Tales*, p. 30.

15   Stone, 'The Misuses of Enchantment', p. 134.

16   Zipes, *Fairy Tales*, p. 30.

17   Zipes, *Fairy Tales*, p. 25.

18   Zipes, *Fairy Tales*, p. 30.

19   Stone, 'The Misuses of Enchantment', p. 135.

20   Simone de Beauvoir, *Le deuxième sexe* (vol. 2) (Paris: Gallimard, 1949), p. 40.

21   Carol De Dobay Rifelj, 'Cendrillon and The Ogre: Women in Fairy Tales and Sade', *Romanic Review*, 81/1 (1990), 16.

22   Huang Mei, *Transforming the Cinderella Dream* (New Brunswick and London: Rutgers University Press, 1990), p. 4.

23   Perrault, *Histoires*, p. 171.

24   Perrault, *Histoires*, p. 175.

25   Mei, 'Transforming the Cinderella Dream', p. 5.

26   In *A Psychiatric Study of Myths and Fairy Tales: Their Origin, Meaning and Usefulness* (Springfield IL: Charles C. Thomas, Publisher, 1974), Julius Heuscher claims that – consonant with the standard passive, patient, 'feminine' reading – 'Cinderella is the individual who is able willingly to restrict her enjoyment of the prince's palace and feast, until she has grown sufficiently, until the slipper fits perfectly' (p. 55) (quoted in

Stone, 'The Misuses of Enchantment', p. 140). However, in light of Cinderella's obvious gusto and abandon to the moment during her earlier evenings at the Palace ball, such a claim is unconvincing.

27 Perrault, *Histoires*, p. 177.

28 Indeed, a 'feminist' reading of an active, resourceful Cinderella has been argued by Leah Kavablum in *Cinderella: Radical Feminist, Alchemist* (Guttenberg NJ: Guttenberg, 1973), where she suggests that Cinderella's prince is merely an emblematic recuperation of her own inner strength. Kavablum further asserts the Freudian symbolism of Cinderella's slipper as her own vagina; in this reading, Cinderella's rightful recovery of the slipper represents the attaining of her own independent identity (quoted in Kay Stone, 'Feminist Approaches to the Interpretation of Fairy Tales', in Ruth B. Bottigheimer (ed.), *Fairy Tales and Society: Illusion, Allusion, and Paradigm* (Philadelphia PA: University of Pennsylvania Press, 1986), p. 231).

29 Perrault, *Histoires*, p. 172.

30 Perrault, *Histoires*, p. 172.

31 Perrault, *Histoires*, p. 174.

32 Peter Brooks, *Body Work: Objects of Desire in Modern Narrative* (Cambridge MA: Harvard University Press, 1994), p. 6.

33 Eisenzweig, 'Présentation du genre', 12.

34 Joseph Litvak, *Caught in the Act: Theatricality in the Nineteenth-Century English Novel* (Berkeley CA: University of California Press, 1992), xiii.

35 Todorov, 'Typologie', p. 62.

36 Felman does, however, despite her detective-genre framework, note traces of a love story in the novel. She observes that the amnesiac's first hope of deriving a story other than the one recounted by Jeanne comes from love letters received at the hospital. Eluding Jeanne, the amnesiac heroine sets off in search of the mysterious François Roussin whose name appears on the letterhead: a move that opens up other explanations of the mystery beyond those offered by Jeanne. Felman recognises, parenthetically, that the narrative involves 'un triangle d'amours jaloux et de désirs conflictuels' ['a triangle of jealous love and conflicting desire'] ('De Sophocle à Japrisot', p. 26) ; she suggests a love relationship between Do and Mi (whereas the text points instead to one of envy and possession) (p. 27) ; and she mentions the love that unites the survivor and Jeanne at the trial and ultimate inculpation (p. 30). Yet, while Felman mentions such love elements in the novel, they are not engaged systematically in her oedipal model.

37 Felman, 'De Sophocle à Japrisot, p. 40.

38 Felman, 'De Sophocle à Japrisot, p. 40. Overlooked by this argument

for the unconscious as figured by the criminal's knowledge and its effort to escape detection, however, is that the unconscious – the force that undoes the detective's victory – might more accurately be modelled as 'the criminal's *desire*'. For what the criminal knows is merely the consequence of a crime motivated by a certain desire; the criminal knows, indeed, but such knowledge emerges from actions driven by an original desire or intent. Felman does point to the workings of desire for the detective – as opposed to the criminal – when she writes that 'the detective is more radically subverted in his desire itself *as* a detective, in other words, his desire as an interpreter: the desire to produce the *end* of the quest, that is, the truth, the certainty of absolute knowledge' (p. 38). But desire is recognised here only to be immediately subsumed, channelled, as an intellectual appetite for truth. As such, desire – in Felman's reading – remains unthreateningly consonant with and contained within the imperatives of the detective model.

39   Felman, 'De Sophocle à Japrisot', p. 39.

40   Felman, 'De Sophocle à Japrisot', p. 39.

41   In subverting not only the genre of the detective novel as Felman argues, but the very idea of 'genre' itself – as I claim – the novel places Felman in the position she has analysed for Oedipus: unconsciously working from within oppositions to which one believes oneself to be exterior, thus unwittingly entangled within the very terms one believes to be scrutinising from a safe, analytical distance.

42   The Grimm Brothers' version of the tale also depicts Cinderella crying over her mother's tomb; her tears water a tree that grows to be inhabited by birds giving Cinderella anything she wishes.

43   The prince is clearly construed as lovestruck, entreating Cinderella to return the next evening to the ball (Perrault, *Histoires*, p. 175), praising her constantly (p. 175) and, after her hasty departure, spending the rest of the evening gazing at the lost little slipper: 'assurément il était fort amoureux de la belle personne à qui appartenait la petite pantoufle' ['most assuredly, he was very much in love with the beautiful owner of the little slipper'] (p. 176).

44   Edgar Allan Poe, 'The Purloined Letter', *Tales* (London: Wiley and Putnam, 1845).

45   Jacques Lacan, *Les Quatre Concepts fondamentaux de la psychanalyse*, in Jacques-Alain Miller (ed.), *Le Séminaire de Jacques Lacan* (Paris: Editions du Seuil, 1973), p. 38.

46   Felman, 'De Sophocle à Japrisot', p. 42.

47   Arthur Rimbaud, Letter to Paul Demeny, 15 May 1871.

48	Felman, 'De Sophocle à Japrisot', p. 41.
49	Felman, 'De Sophocle à Japrisot', p. 41.
50	Roland Barthes, *Le plaisir du texte* (Paris: Editions du Seuil, 1973).
51	The Dora case models a 'scientific' quest in conflict with desire. As Martha Noel Evans points out in *Masks of Tradition* (Ithaca NY: Cornell University Press, 1987), Freud's very writing and publication of Dora's case violated her wishes so as to privilege what he viewed as his obligation to knowledge. As Evans summarises, '[t]he domain of the personal, the literary, is assigned to women, while men claim the superior realm of knowledge and science' (p. 161).
52	Eric Berne, *What Do You Say After You Say Hello? The Psychology of Human Destiny* (New York: Bantam Books, 1973), p. 238.
53	Felman, 'De Sophocle à Japrisot', p. 31.
54	Felman, 'De Sophocle à Japrisot', p. 31.
55	Felman, 'De Sophocle à Japrisot', p. 35.
56	In uncovering the multiple voices that inhabit Piège's narration, dismantling any façade of univocity, we are reminded of Litvak's claims that treating the self as a collection of theatrical roles helps lay bare certain coercive ideologies within which it is bound (*Caught in the Act*, xii).
57	Defining such a hysterical identity in *Masks of Tradition*, Evans argues for a dynamic emphasising the direction of activity, rather than its source. Rather than originating from 'a self-defining, autonomous subject', hysterical actions are instead, suggests Evans, 'linked by their direction toward the potential receiver of their message' (p. 171).
58	What produces this refusal to know, argues Freud in his 'Early Drafts on Hysteria', is the traumatic 'return of a psychical state which the patient has already experienced earlier – in other words, *the return of a memory*' (*Standard Edition* (vol. 1), p. 152): an idea that Freud pursues in 'Studies on Hysteria' with the claim that 'hysterics suffer mainly from reminiscences' (*Standard Edition* (vol. 2), p. 7). According to this claim, the amnesia depicted in *Piège* would be the hysterical symptom of the heroine's desire to divest herself of an intolerable criminal past. Every case of hysteria, Freud asserted, presents a degree of such 'double conscience' (*Standard Edition* (vol. 2), p. 12).
59	Felman, 'De Sophocle à Japrisot', p. 35.
60	Freud, *Standard Edition* (vol. 7), pp. 1–122, quoted in Evans, p. 162).
61	Freud, *Standard Edition* (vol. 7), p. 16.
62	Evans, *Masks of Tradition*, p. 163.
63	Freud, *Standard Edition*, p. 114.
64	Litvak, *Caught in the Act*, vii.

65 Evans, *Masks of Tradition*, p. 186.

66 Jean Laplanche and J. B. Pontalis, *Vocabulaire de la Psychanalyse* (Paris: Presses Universitaires de France, 1967), p. 7.

67 Pierre Fédida, *L'absence* (Paris: Editions Gallimard, 1978), p. 92.

68 Octave Mannoni, *Clefs pour l'imaginaire* (Paris: Seuil, 1969), p. 302.

69 Mannoni, *Clefs*, p. 306.

70 Pierre Briquet, *Traité de l'hystérie* (Paris: Baillière, 1859), p. v; quoted in Jacques Gasser, *Jean-Martin Charcot (1825–1893) et le système nerveux: étude de la motricité, du langage, de la mémoire et de l'hystérie à la fin du XIXème siècle*, Thèse de doctorat, 3ème cycle, 3 vols (vol. 2) (Paris: Ecole des Hautes Etudes en Sciences Sociales, 1990), p. 430.

71 Jean-Martin Charcot, *Œuvres complètes* (4 vols) (vol. 1) (Paris: Bureau du Progrès Médical, 1885–94), p. 301; quoted in Gasser, *Jean-Martin Charcot* (vol. 2), p. 443.

72 One might note here Charcot's reluctant admiration for the ingenuity and ruse of the hysteric, in what he viewed as her toying with the doctor (*Oeuvres Complètes* (vol. 1), pp. 281–2; quoted in Gasser, *Jean-Martin Charcot* (vol. 2), p. 437).

73 Charcot, *Oeuvres completes* (vol. 1), p. 288.

74 Gasser, *Jean-Michel Charcot* (vol. 2), p. 438.

75 Jacqueline Sonolet, *Charcot et l'hystérie au XIXème siècle* (Paris: Catalogue de l'exposition à la Salpêtrière, 2–18 June 1982), p. 12.

76 Sigmund Freud, quoted in A. R. G. Owen, *Hysteria, Hypnosis and Healing: The Work of J.-M. Charcot* (London: Dennis Dobson, 1971).

77 Jean-Martin Charcot and Paul Richer, *Les démoniaques dans l'art* (Paris: Delahaye et Lecrosnier, 1887).

78 Gasser, *Jean-Michel Charcot* (vol. 2), p. 465.

79 Martha Noel Evans, *Fits and Starts: A Genealogy of Hysteria in Modern France* (Ithaca NY: Cornell University Press, 1991), p. 21.

80 Nina Auerbach, *Private Theatricals* (Cambridge MA: Harvard University Press, 1990), p. 81.

81 Paul Richer, *L'etude descriptive de la grande attaque hystéro-épileptique et de ses principales variétés* (Paris: V. Adrien Delahaye, 1879).

82 Albert Londe, 'La photographie en médecine', in *La nature*, 523 (1883), 215.

83 Evans, *Fits and Starts*, p. 24.

84 Georges Guillain, *J.-M. Charcot 1825–93, His Life-His Work*, trans. P. Bailey (New York: Paul B. Hoeber, 1959), p. 174n; quoted in Evans, *Fits and Starts*, p. 41.

85 Evans, *Fits and Starts*, p. 41.

86 Joseph Babinski, *Démembrement de l'hystérie traditionnelle: pithiatisme*

(Paris: Imprimerie de la Semaine Médicale, 1909), p. 214. Babinski also quotes Edouard Brissaud in articulating a sceptical view of hysteria (p. 218).

87	Anatole Chauffard, quoted in Babinski, *Démembrement*, p. 218.

88	In *Fits and Starts*, Evans discusses Babinski's revision of hysteria as 'pithiatism': his neologism for 'curable by persuasion' (pp. 54–6).

89	Charles Richet, 'Les Démoniaques d'aujourd'hui et d'autrefois', *La revue des deux mondes*, 37 (1880), 346; quoted in Evans, *Fits and Starts*, p. 30.

90	Evans, *Fits and Starts*, p. 31.

91	Paul Hartenberg, *L'hystérie et les hystériques* (Paris: Alcan, 1910), pp. 14–15; quoted in English only by Evans, *Fits and Starts*, p. 69.

92	Maria Ramas, 'Freud's Dora, Dora's Hysteria', in Charles Bernheimer and Claire Kahane (eds), *In Dora's Case: Freud – Hysteria – Feminism* (New York: Columbia University Press, 1985), p. 150.

93	Ramas, 'Freud's Dora', p. 152.

94	Richard Schechner, 'Performers and Spectators', p. 84.

95	Naomi Schor, 'Female Fetishism: The Case of George Sand', *Poetics Today*, 6, 1/2 (1985), 307.

96	Schor, 'Female Fetishism', 308.

Spectacular Scripts

1	Marguerite Duras, *L'Amant* (Paris: Editions de Minuit, 1984) and *L'Amant de la Chine du Nord* (Paris: Editions Gallimard, 1991). Page numbers in the text refer to these editions. Written by Duras during her dispute with filmmaker Jean-Jacques Annaud over his vision for *L'Amant*'s 1992 film adaptation, *L'Amant de la Chine du Nord* is Duras's attempt to correct what she perceived as Annaud's misinterpretation.

2	Julia Kristeva, *Soleil Noir: Dépression et mélancolie* (Paris: Gallimard, 1987), p. 249.

3	As David Ellison suggests in *Of Words and the World: Referential Anxiety in Contemporary French Fiction* (Princeton NJ: Princeton University Press, 1993), 'Marguerite defines herself in relation to a mother whose *originalité* as described in the early pages of the book is, in fact, the sign of an evolving, increasingly visible madness' (p. 82).

4	The ambiguity of this double negative must be respected; it is too often overlooked in the frequent claim that this is the instant at which the narrator recognises her love for the Chinese gentleman. In an opposing assertion, Kristeva in *Soleil noir* understands this line as a momentary hesitation from within the narrator's decisive conviction that she does *not* love him: 'la jeune fille se persuade de ne pas aimer et ne se laisse troubler par un écho de sa passion délaissée que par un air de Chopin sur le bateau qui l'emmène en France' ['the young girl persuades herself that she doesn't love [him], and is only troubled over an echo of her abandoned passion by a Chopin melody on the boat taking her to France'] (p. 248).

5   Peter Brooks, *Body Work: Objects of Desire in Modern Narrative* (Cambridge MA: Harvard University Press, 1994), p. 271. Brooks goes on to mention a connection to Bataille's notion of expenditure, and an erotics that is 'fundamentally transgressive of taboos and limitations' (p. 274).

6   Leslie Hill, *Marguerite Duras: Apocalyptic Desires* (London: Routledge, 1993), p. 40.

7   One is reminded, in this context, of Susan Gubar's discussion of Magritte's surrealist pornography in her 'Representing Pornography: Feminism, Criticism and Depictions of Female Violation', *Critical Inquiry*, 13/4 (Summer 1987). Gubar links Magritte's headless, obscured, disfigured women to the traumatic impact of Magritte's sight of his drowned mother, her nightgown pulled up over her face. Similarly, I am suggesting that what the text construes as socially, culturally and racially transgressive – the daughter's affair – is symptomatic of pain, loss, mourning.

8   Anne Hermann in 'Travesty and Transgression: Transvestism in Shakespeare, Brecht, and Churchill', in Sue-Ellen Case (ed.), *Performing Feminisms* (Baltimore MD: Johns Hopkins University Press, 1990) understands the spectacle of the daughter's ensemble as one produced by 'proliferating contradictions'. Hermann points to the narrator's liminal cultural and social situation – her poverty despite being a coloniser in French Indochina – and the emblematic transgression of the man's hat. '[The narrator] transgresses the boundaries of age, nationality, and sexual difference signified by a single item of clothing meant for someone else. The result is not an androgynous figure but an anomalous one; the object, for her, is not to resolve the contradictions, but to proliferate them' (p. 295).

9   Drawing on Martin Heidegger's original use of the idea of 'under erasure' to refer to an inadequate yet necessary term in *Fundamental Concepts of Metaphysics: World, Finitude, Solitude*, trans. William McNeill and James Walker (Bloomington IN: Indiana University Press, 1995), Jacques Derrida extends this reflection in *De la grammatologie* (Paris: Editions de Minuit, 1967).

10   Critics have dwelt at length on the importance of this absent yet
     central photograph. In *Women and Discourse in the Fiction of Marguerite
     Duras: Love, Legends, Language* (Amherst MA: University of
     Massachusetts Press, 1993), Susan D. Cohen argues that this absence
     enables the play of desire in the work of memory: 'what [the narrator]
     remembers of her appearance combines with her preferred imaginary
     vision of herself to compose the image' (p. 93).

11   In her 'L'histoire de la mendiante indienne: une cellule génératrice
     de l'oeuvre de Marguerite Duras', *Poétique* (1981), Madeleine
     Borgomano reads *L'Amant* as a quest for the lost centre (p. 70); she
     further suggests a link that binds the beggar, the daughter and the
     mother in pointing to the spaces devoid of centre that characterise
     the Indian beggar, the centreless life of the narrator, and the deserts
     of the mother's life (p. 72). Borgomano sees the crossing on the ferry,
     if not as offering a centre to the daughter's narrative, at least as
     instituting a decisive, meaningful split between the past and the future,
     the family and life (p. 72). I argue, however, that underlying this
     crossing, literally and figuratively, is the danger for the daughter of
     being swept out to the 'mer/mère' ['sea/mother'], that is, the danger
     of engulfment within the mother's madness. In another discussion of
     Duras's line about the absence of a life story, David Ellison in *Of Words
     and the World* suggests that it be read not only as the personal claim
     that 'the story of one's life as faithful depiction of recovered reality is
     radically impossible', but that it also be understood as a densely
     theoretical meditation on the problematic nature of autobiography
     (pp. 71–2).

12   Trista Selous, *The Other Woman: Feminism and Femininity in the Work of
     Marguerite Duras* (New Haven CT and London: Yale University Press,
     1988), p. 193.

13   Brooks, *Body Work*, p. 268.

14   Hill, *Marguerite Duras*, p. 79.

15   Hill, *Marguerite Duras*, p. 79.

16   Ellison, *Of Words and the World*, p. 85.

17   Françoise Lionnet, Review of Leah Hewitt, *Autobiographical Tightropes*,
     SubStance, 21/2, Issue 68 (1992), 135.

18   Panivong Norindr, *Phantasmatic Indochina: French Colonial Ideology in
     Architecture, Film and Literature* (Durham NC: Duke University Press,
     1996), p. 126.

19   For readings of flowing spaces as liberating in *L'Amant*, see Ellison, *Of
     Words and the World*, p. 85; and Leah D. Hewitt, *Autobiographical
     Tightropes: Simone de Beauvoir, Nathalie Sarraute, Marguerite Duras,*

Monique Wittig, and Maryse Condé (Lincoln NE: University of Nebraska Press, 1990), p. 126.

[20] For Ellison in *Of Words and the World*, Duras's text itself represents an overcoming of borders and limits through art; he views Duras's works as '*prepositional exercises*' governed by 'the possibility of crossing *through* and going *beyond* the limitations – both conceptual and concrete – imposed on the human perception by the strictures of family, society, and good manners in general' (p. 86). I would like to argue, however, for the ultimate failure of any crossing of boundaries in the *Amant* texts – that the affair with the Chinese gentleman and its representation in writing only affirm the failure, rather than success, of separating from and thus 'going beyond' the mad, destroyed mother.

[21] Kristeva, *Soleil Noir*, p. 250.

[22] Karen McPherson, *Incriminations: Guilty Women / Telling Stories* (Princeton NJ: Princeton University Press, 1994), p. 86.

[23] Hill, *Marguerite Duras*, pp. 78–9. Further pursuing the connection between Lol in *Le ravissement de Lol V. Stein* and Hélène Lagonelle in the *Amant* narratives, Hill quotes Duras's own claim that Hélène was 'obviously' Lol V. Stein (*Le nouvel observateur*, 14–20 November 1986; quoted in Hill, *Marguerite Duras*, p. 169).

[24] Marguerite Duras, *Les lieux de Marguerite Duras* (Paris: Editions de Minuit, 1977), p. 84.

[25] Hill, *Marguerite Duras*, p. 148. Hill does, however, imply a negative association with the sea in linking it not only to the mother, but additionally (if perhaps too ambitiously, considering the range of connections claimed) to 'the theme of incestuous identification with the brother, and the theme of death, loss and guilt' (p. 146).

[26] Yvette Went-Daoust notes a further analogy linking the mother and the sea in that, with its imbrication of birth and death, the sea carries out the cycle of life (p. 155).

[27] The sea's dangers of madness and immersion, its haunting presence within the lover's apartment, compromise critical claims made for what Norindr in *Phantasmatic Indochina* calls the 'pleasure and desire' (p. 128) the apartment represents.

[28] Yvette Went-Daoust, 'L'écriture au féminin singulier: *L'amant* de Marguerite Duras', *French Literature Series*, XVI (1989), 157.

[29] Ellison, *Of Words and the World*, p. 82.

[30] Hill, *Marguerite Duras*, p. 119.

[31] Norindr, *Phantasmatic Indochina*, pp. 120–1.

[32] Susan D. Cohen, *Women and Discourse in the Fiction of Marguerite Duras:*

Love, Legends, Language (Amherst MA: University of Massachusetts Press, 1993), p. 96.

33   Cohen, *Women and Discourse*, p. 97.

34   Went-Daoust, 'L'écriture au féminin singulier', 155.

35   Borgomano, 'L'histoire de la mendiante indienne', p. 479.

36   'Marguerite Duras parle: "Elle a vendu un enfant"', Alliance Française: Collection *Français de notre temps*, 37. Quoted by Borgomano, 'L'histoire de la mendiante indienne', p. 492.

37   Borgomano, 'L'histoire de la mendiante indienne', p. 492.

38   Borgomano, 'L'histoire de ma mendiante indienne', p. 492.

39   In the context of the mad beggarwoman's dangerously contaminating touch, Leslie Hill mentions Duras's use of the leprosy trope in other works (e.g., *Le Vice-consul* and *India Song*) as 'a figure of infection by touch' (*Marguerite Duras*, p. 99).

40   Borgomano, 'L'histoire de la mendiante indienne', p. 488.

41   Marguerite Duras, *Le Vice-Consul* (Paris: Gallimard, 1966), p. 28.

42   Duras, *Le Vice-Consul*, p. 67.

43   Borgomano, 'L'histoire de la mendiante indienne', p. 482.

44   Selous, *The Other Woman*, p. 224.

45   Duras, *Le Vice-Consul*, p. 149.

46   Duras, *Le Vice-Consul*, p. 205.

47   Marilyn Schuster, *Marguerite Duras Revisited* (New York: Twayne Publishers, 1993), p. 117.

48   Borgomano, 'L'histoire de la mendiante indienne', p. 489.

49   Hill, *Marguerite Duras*, p. 139.

50   Brooks, *Body Work*, pp. 268–9.

51   Hill, *Marguerite Duras*, p. 118.

52   Schuster, *Marguerite Duras Revisited*, p. 124.

53   Leslie Hill in *Marguerite Duras* offers another explanation for Duras's rewrite of *L'Amant*; reading *L'Amant de la Chine du Nord* as symptomatic of 'the anxiety of dispossession associated with authorship', Hill sees such anxiety as a source of 'Duras's continual rewriting of her own texts' (p. 16).

54   An alternative claim is made by Anne Freadman in '… You Know, The Enunciation …', *The Canadian Review of Comparative Literature*, 22/2 (June 1995). Freadman suggests that 'the choice between writing and film is a major concern of this text', but that by the end of the novel, the choice in favour of writing has been made – 'as if the writing had to be wrested from the images'. Ultimately, Freadman views *L'Amant de la Chine du Nord* as 'the autobiography of the writing, not of the author' (p. 309).

Conclusion

[1] Louis Althusser, *Positions 1964–75* (Paris: Editions Sociales, 1976).

[2] By way of contrast, we might note composer Milton Babbitt's effort, in a 1958 essay originally entitled 'The Composer as Specialist' but subsequently more melodramatically retitled by an editor as 'Who Cares if You Listen?', to defend his work. Here, Babbitt argues for the importance of a musical idiom inaccessible to most listeners, where the composer is indifferent, from the outset, to the public's reactions. In such a context, display addresses only other, like-minded, rarified composers in an effort to build exchange and dialogue within such a select group of interlocutors; it makes no pretence of communicating with the public. We notice that there is no surprise here, no unexpected displacement of the audience's primacy, as the audience for whom the display is intended has been switched at the outset; the composer writes for other composers, not for the musical public. The narrative dynamics I have been exploring in these pages, however, work differently, in construing scenarios of display that, in various ways, displace the subjects that they have, precisely, construed.

[3] Adam Gopnik, 'High and Low: Caricature, Primitivism, and the Cubist Portrait', *Art Journal*, 43 (1983), 375.

[4] Gopnik, 'High and Low', 373.

[5] Curtiss, Mina, 'Manet Caricatures: Olympia', *The Massachusetts Review*, 7/4 (Autumn 1966), 728.

[6] Ivor Brown, *Words in Our Time* (London: Alden Press,1958), p. 58.

[7] Sianne Ngai, 'Theory of the Gimmick', *Critical Inquiry*, 43 (Winter 2017), 466–9.

[8] Ngai, 'Theory of the Gimmick', 472.

Bibliography

Ajuriaguerra, Julian, 'Le problème de l'hystérie', *L'Encéphale*, 1 (1951), 50–87.

Albistur, Maïté, and Daniel Armogathe, *Histoire du féminisme français* (Paris: Editions des femmes, 1977).

Alexander, Douglas, 'Le tragique dans les romans de Ferdinand Oyono', *Présence francophone*, 7 (1973).

Alpers, Svetlana, 'The Museum as a Way of Seeing', in Ivan Karp and Steven D. Lavine (eds), *Exhibiting Cultures: The Poetics and Politics of Museum Display* (Washington DC and London: The Smithsonian Institution Press, 1991), pp. 25–41.

Althusser, Louis, *Positions 1964–75* (Paris: Editions Sociales, 1976).

Anspach, Mark Rogin, 'When American Anthropologists Go "Postmodern"', *Stanford French Review*, 15/1–2 (1991).

Apter, Emily, *Feminizing the Fetish: Psychoanalysis and Narrative Obsession in Turn-of-The-Century France* (Ithaca NY and London: Cornell University Press, 1991).

— *André Gide and the Codes of Homotextuality* (Stanford CA: Stanford University Press, Anma Libri, 1987).

Auerbach, Nina, *Private Theatricals* (Cambridge MA: Harvard University Press, 1990).

Autant-Lara, Claude, *Le Blé en herbe*, Centre National de la Cinématographie, Service des Archives du film, Bois d'Arcy, France, 1954.

Babinski, Joseph, *Démembrement de l'hystérie traditionnelle: pithiatisme* (Paris: Imprimerie de la Semaine Médicale, 1909).

Bakhtin, Mikhail, *The Dialogic Imagination*, Michael Holquist (ed.), trans. C. Emerson and M. Holquist (Austin TX: University of Texas Press, 1981).

Barker, Emma (ed.), *Contemporary* Cultures *of Display* (New Haven CT and London: Yale University Press, 1999).

Barthes, Roland, *Le plaisir du texte* (Paris: Editions du Seuil, 1973).

Baudelaire, Charles, *Oeuvres complètes* (Paris: Gallimard, 1954).

Baudrillard, Jean, *De la séduction* (Paris: Editions Galilée, 1979).

— *Simulacres et simulation* (Paris: Editions Galilée, 1981).

Beauvoir, Simone de, *Le deuxième sexe* (2 vols) (Paris: Gallimard, 1949).

Benstock, Shari, *Women of the Left Bank* (Austin TX: University of Texas Press, 1986).

Benston, Kimberly, 'Being There: Performance as Mise-en-Scène, Abscene, Obscene and Other Scene,' *PMLA*, 107/3 (1992).

Bergner, Gwen, 'Who is That Masked Woman? or, The Role of Gender in Fanon's *Black Skin, White Masks*', *PMLA*, 110/1 (1995), 75–88.

Berne, Eric, *What Do You Say After You Say Hello? The Psychology of Human Destiny* (New York: Bantam Books, 1973).

Bettelheim, Bruno, *The Uses of Enchantment: The Meaning and Importance of Fairy Tales* (New York: Knopf, 1976).

Biolley-Godino, Marcelle, *L'homme objet chez Colette* (Paris: Klincksieck, 1972).

Bjornson, Richard, 'Cameroonian Writing and the National Experience', in *The African Quest for Freedom and Identity* (Bloomington IN: Indiana University Press, 1991).

Boehmer, Elleke, 'Transfiguring: Colonial Body into Postcolonial Narrative', *Novel*, 263 (1993).

Bolt, Barbara, 'Shedding Light for the Matter', *Hypatia: A Journal of Feminist Philosophy*, 15/2 (Spring 2000), 202–16.

Borgomano, Madeleine, 'L'histoire de la mendiante indienne: une cellule génératrice de l'oeuvre de Marguerite Duras', *Poétique*, 48 (November 1981), 479–93.

— 'L'amant: Une Hypertextualité illimitée', *Revue des Sciences Humaines*, 202 (1986).

Bourgeacq, Jacques, 'The Eye Motif and Narrative Strategy in Ferdinand Oyono's *Une vie de boy*: An Ethno-Cultural Perspective', *The French Review*, 66/5 (1993).

Bovenschen, Silvia, 'Is There a Feminine Aesthetic?', *New German Critique*, 10 (1977).

Briquet, Pierre, *Traité de l'hystérie* (Paris: Baillière, 1859).

Brissaud, Édouard, 'Les troubles nerveux post-traumatiques', *Revue clinique médico-chirurgicale*, 6 (1 June 1909).

Brody, Jennifer DeVere, 'Black Cat Fever: Manifestations of Manet's 'Olympia', 'Theatre and Visual Culture', *Theatre Journal*, 53/1 (March 2001), 95–118.

Brooks, Peter, *The Melodramatic Imagination* (New Haven CT: Yale University Press, 1976).

— *Reading for the Plot* (New York: Knopf, 1984).

— *Body Work: Objects of Desire in Modern Narrative* (Cambridge MA: Harvard University Press, 1994).

Brown, Ivor, *Words in Our Time* (London: Alden Press, 1958).

Bryson, Norman, *Vision and Painting: The Logic of the Gaze* (New Haven CT and London: Yale University Press, 1983).

— *Looking at the Overlooked: Four Essays on Still Life Painting* (Cambridge MA: Harvard University Press, 1990).

Buache, Freddy, *Claude Autant-Lara* (Paris: Editions L'Age d'Homme, 1982).

Butler, Judith, *Gender Trouble: Feminism and the Subversion of Identity* (New York and London: Routledge, 1990).

— *Bodies that Matter: On the Limits of 'Sex'* (New Brunswick and London: Routledge, 1993).

— 'Performative Acts and Gender Constitution: An Essay in Phenomenology and Feminist Theory', in Sue-Ellen Case (ed.), *Performing Feminisms: Feminist Critical Theory and Theatre* (Baltimore MD and London: Johns Hopkins University Press, 1990).

Butor, Michel, *L'emploi du temps* (Paris: Editions de Minuit, 1956).

Cagnetta, Franco, *Nascita della fotografia psichiatrica* (Venezia: La Biennale, 1981).

Castle, Terry, *Masquerade and Civilization: The Carnivalesque in Eighteenth-Century English Culture and Fiction* (Stanford CA: Stanford University Press, 1986).

Caws, Mary Ann, *Reading Frames in Modern Fiction* (Princeton NJ: Princeton University Press, 1985).

Cazentre, Thomas, 'Les comédiens sans le savoir: L'inconscient dramatique dans *La porte étroite*', *Bulletin des Amis d'André Gide*, XXXII, 141 (January 2004).

Certeau, Michel, *L'invention du quotidien, I: Arts de faire* (Paris: Gallimard, 1990).

Charcot, Jean-Martin, *Œuvres complètes* (Paris: Bureau du Progrès Médical, 1885–94).

Charcot, Jean-Martin, and Paul Richer, *Les démoniaques dans l'art* (Paris: Delahaye et Lecrosnier, 1887).

Chasseguet-Smirgel, Janine, 'Feminine Guilt and the Oedipus Complex', in J. Chasseguet-Smirgel (ed.), *Female Sexuality: New Psychoanalytic Views* (Ann Arbor MI: University of Michigan Press, 1970).

Chauffard, Anatole, 'Stabilité et conditions de variation des espèces morbides', in *La presse médicale* (17 January 1912), 65.

Cohen, Jeffrey Jerome, 'Monster Culture (Seven Theses)', in Cohen (ed.), *Monster Theory: Reading Culture* (Minneapolis MN: University of Minnesota Press, 1996).

Cohen, Susan D., *Women and Discourse in the Fiction of Marguerite Duras: Love, Legends, Language* (Amherst MA: University of Massachusetts Press, 1993).

Colette, Sidonie Gabrielle, *L'envers du music-hall* (Paris: Flammarion, 1913).

— *La vagabonde* (Paris: Ollendorf, 1910).

— *Œuvres* (3 vols), ed. Claude Pichois (Paris: Gallimard, Bibliothèque de la Pléïade, 1986).

— *Le blé en herbe*, Bois en couleurs de G. Bernard (Paris: Livre imprimé, 1928).

— *Colette: Lettres à Marguerite Moreno*, ed. Claude Pichois (Paris: Flammarion, 1959).

— *The Ripening Seed*, trans. Roger Senhouse (New York: Penguin Books, 1996).

Comolli, Jean, 'Machines of the Visible', in Teresa De Lauretis and Stephen Heath (eds), *The Cinematic Apparatus* (London: MacMillan, 1980).

Cornand, Monique and Madeleine Barbin, *Colette*, Catalogue de l'exposition (Paris: Bibliothèque nationale, 1972).

Cordle, Thomas, *André Gide: Updated Edition* (New York: Twayne Publishers, 1993).

Cox, Marian, *Cinderella: Three Hundred and Forty-Five Variants* (London: Nutt, 1893).

Curtiss, Mina, 'Manet Caricatures: Olympia', *The Massachusetts Review*, 7/4 (Autumn 1966), 725–52.

De Dobay Rifelj, Carol, 'Cendrillon and The Ogre: Women in Fairy Tales and Sade', *Romanic Review*, 81/1 (1990).

Dehon, Claire L., *Le roman camerounais d'expression française* (Birmingham AL: Summa Publications, 1989).

De Lauretis, Teresa, *Alice Doesn't: Feminism, Semiotics, Cinema* (Bloomington: Indiana University Press, 1984).

— *Technologies of Gender: Essays on Theory, Film and Fiction* (Bloomington IN: Indiana University Press, 1987).

Derrida, Jacques, *La vérité en peinture* (Paris: Editions Flammarion, 1978).

Deutelbaum, Wendy, and Cynthia Huff, 'Class, Gender and Family System: The Case of George Sand', in *The (M)Other Tongue: Essays in Feminist Psychoanalytic Interpretation* (Ithaca NY: Cornell University Press, 1985).

Devlin, Kimberly, 'En-gendered Choice and Agency in *Ulysses*', in Michael Patrick Gillespie and A. Nicholas Fargnoli (eds), *Ulysses in Critical Perspective* (Gainesville FL: University Press of Florida, 2006).

Didier, Béatrice, *L'Ecriture-femme* (Paris: Presses Universitaires Françaises, 1981).

Dijkstra, Bram, *Idols of Perversity: Fantasies of Feminine Evil in Fin-de-Siècle Culture* (New York: Oxford University Press, 1986).

Doane, Mary Ann, 'Film and the Masquerade: Theorizing the Female Spectator', *Screen* 23/3–4 (1982).

— Linda Williams and Patricia Mellencamp (eds), *Revision: Feminist Essays in Film Analysis* (Frederick MD: University Publications of America, 1984).

— *Femmes Fatales: Feminism, Film Theory and Psychoanalysis* (New York: Routledge, 1991).

Duras, Marguerite, *L'Amant* (Paris: Editions de Minuit, 1984).

— *L'Amant de la Chine du Nord* (Paris: Gallimard, 1991).

— *Le Vice-Consul* (Paris: Gallimard, 1966).

Eisenzweig, Uri, 'Présentation du genre', *Littérature*, 49 (1983).

Ellison, David, *Of Words and The World: Referential Anxiety in Contemporary French Fiction* (Princeton NJ: Princeton University Press, 1993).

Escarpit, Denise, *La littérature d'enfance et de jeunesse en Europe* (Paris: Presses Universitaires de France, 1981).

Evans, Martha Noel, *Masks of Tradition* (Ithaca NY: Cornell University Press, 1987).

— *Fits and Starts: A Genealogy of Hysteria in Modern France* (Ithaca NY: Cornell University Press, 1991).

Fédida, Pierre, *L'absence* (Paris: Editions Gallimard, 1978).

Felman, Shoshana, 'De Sophocle à Japrisot (via Freud), ou pourquoi le policier?', *Littérature*, 49 (1983).

Ferrier-Caverivière, Nicole, 'Colette et la mode', in Colette, *Colette et la mode* (Paris: Editions Plume, 1991).

Festa-McCormick, Diana, 'Mauriac's Thérèse: An Androgynous Heroine', in Mary Ann Caws (ed.), *Writing in a Modern Temper: Essays on French Literature and Thought, in Honor of Henri Peyre* (Stanford CA: Anma Libri, 1984).

Flannigan, Arthur, '"The Eye of the Witch": Non-Verbal Communication and the Exercise of Power in *Une vie de boy*', *The French Review*, 56/1 (1982).

Flieger, Jerry Aline, *Colette and the Fantom Subject of Autobiography* (Ithaca NY: Cornell University Press, 1992).

Freadman, Anne, '… You Know, The Enunciation …', *The Canadian Review of Comparative Literature*, 22/2 (June 1995), 301–18.

Freedman, Barbara, 'Frame-Up: Feminism, Psychoanalysis, Theatre', in Sue-Ellen Case (ed.), *Performing Feminisms: Feminist Critical Theory and Theatre* (Baltimore MD: Johns Hopkins University Press, 1990).

— *Staging the Gaze: Postmodernism, Psychoanalysis, and Shakespearean Comedy* (Ithaca NY and London: Cornell University Press, 1991).

Freeman, Barbara Claire, *The Feminine Sublime: Gender and Excess in Women's Fiction* (Berkeley CA: University of California Press, 1995).

Freud, Sigmund, *The Standard Edition of the Complete Works of Sigmund Freud*, trans. and ed. James Strachey with the collaboration of Anna Freud (24 vols) (London: Hogarth Press, 1953–74).

Fried, Michael, *Absorption and Theatricality: Painting and Beholder in the Age of Diderot* (Berkeley CA: University of California Press, 1980).

— *Manet's Modernism, or The Face of Painting in the 1860s* (Chicago IL: University of Chicago Press, 1996).

Gallagher, Edward, *Textual Hauntings: Studies in Flaubert's* Madame Bovary *and Mauriac's* Thérèse Desqueyroux (Lanham MD: University Press of America, 2005), vii, p. 134.

Garfitt, J. S. T., 'Clés pour *Thérèse Desqueyroux*: Onomastique et Calendrier Liturgique', *Présence de François Mauriac*, in *Actes du colloque organisé à Bordeaux pour le Centenaire de Mauriac* (10–12 October 1985) (Pessac: Presses Universitaires de Bordeaux, 1986).

— *Mauriac: Thérèse Desqueyroux* (London: Grant and Cutler, Ltd, 1991).

Geahchan, Dominique, 'Haine et identification négative dans l'hystérie', *Revue française de psychanalyse*, 37 (1973), 337–57.

Geertz, Clifford, *The Interpretation of Cultures* (Chicago IL: Basic Books, 1973).

Genette, Gérard, *Figures III: Discours du récit* (Paris: Editions du Seuil, 1972).

— *Nouveaux discours du récit* (Paris: Editions du Seuil, Collection Poétique, 1983).

Gide, André, *Journal* (2 vols), ed. Eric Marty (Paris: Gallimard, Bibliothèque de la Pléiade, 1951).

— *La porte étroite*, in Y. Davet and J.-J. Thierry (eds), *Romans, Récits et Soties* (Paris: Gallimard, Bibliothèque de la Pléïade, 1958).

— *The Correspondence of André Gide and Edmund Gosse, 1904–1928*, ed. Linette F. Brugman (London: Peter Owen, 1960).

Girard, René, *Mensonge romantique et vérité romanesque* (Paris: Grasset, 1961).

Gilbert, Sandra and Susan Gubar, *The Madwoman in the Attic: The Woman Writer and the Nineteenth-Century Literary Imagination* (New Haven CT: Yale University Press, 1979).

Gasser, Jacques, *Jean-Martin Charcot (1825–1893) et le système nerveux: étude de la motricité, du langage, de la mémoire et de l'hystérie à la fin du XIXème siècle* (Thèse de doctorat, 3ème cycle, 3 vols) (Paris: Ecole des Hautes Etudes en Sciences Sociales, 1990).

Glissant, Edouard, *Poétique de la relation – Poétique III* (Paris: Gallimard, 1990).

— *L'imaginaire des langues, Entretiens avec Lise Gauvin (1991–2009)* (Paris: Gallimard, 2010).

Gopnik, Adam, 'High and Low: Caricature, Primitivism, and the Cubist Portrait', *Art Journal*, 43 (1983), 371–6.

Gosse, Edmund, in Linette F. Brugmans (ed.), *The Correspondence of André Gide and Edmund Gosse, 1904–1928* (London: Peter Owen, 1960).

Göttner-Abendroth, Heide, *Die Göttin und ihr Heros* (Munich: Verlag Munich Frauenoffensive, 1980).

Greenblatt, Stephen, 'Resonance and Wonder', in Ivan Karp and Steven D. Lavine (eds), *Exhibiting Cultures: The Poetics and Politics of Museum Display* (Washington DC and London: The Smithsonian Institution Press, 1991), pp. 42–56.

Greene, Robert, 'Fading (Sacred) Texts and Dying (Guiding) Voices in Gide's Early Récits', *French Forum*, 12/1 (1987).

Gregg, John, *Maurice Blanchot and the Literature of Transgression* (Princeton NJ: Princeton University Press, 1994).

Gubar, Susan, 'Representing Pornography: Feminism, Criticism and Depictions of Female Violation, *Critical Inquiry*, 13/4 (Summer 1987), 712–41.

Guillain, Georges, *J.-M. Charcot 1825–93, His Life – His Work*, trans. P. Bailey (New York: Paul B. Hoeber, 1959).

Harris, Geraldine, *Staging Femininities: Performance and Performativity* (Manchester and New York: Manchester University Press, 1999).

Harrow, Susan, *The Art of the Text: Visuality in Nineteenth and Twentieth-Century Literary and Other Media* (Cardiff: University of Wales Press, 2013).

Hartenberg, Paul, *L'hystérie et les hystériques* (Paris: Alcan, 1910).

Hermann, Anne, 'Travesty and Transgression: Transvestism in Shakespeare, Brecht, and

Churchill', in Sue-Ellen Case (ed.), *Performing Feminisms* (Baltimore MD: Johns Hopkins University Press, 1990).

Heuscher, Julius, *A Psychiatric Study of Myths and Fairy Tales: Their Origin, Meaning and Usefulness* (Springfield IL: Charles C. Thomas Publisher, 1974).

Hewitt, Leah D., *Autobiographical Tightropes: Simone de Beauvoir, Nathalie Sarraute, Marguerite Duras, Monique Wittig, and Maryse Condé* (Lincoln NE: University of Nebraska Press, 1990).

Hill, Leslie, *Marguerite Duras: Apocalyptic Desires* (London: Routledge, 1993).

Hobson, Marian, 'Du théâtrum mundi au Theatrum', *Revue des Sciences Humaines*, 167 (1977).

Hovey, Jaime, '"Kissing a Negress in the Dark": Englishness as a Masquerade in Woolf's *Orlando*', *PMLA*, 112/3 (1997), 393–404.

Huet, Marie-Hélène, *Monstrous Imagination* (Cambridge MA: Harvard University Press, 1993).

Huffer, Lynn, 'The (En)gendered Text: Colette and the Problem of Writing', *French Literature Series*, XVI (1989).

— *Another Colette* (Ann Arbor MI: University of Michigan Press, 1992).

Huyssen, Andreas, *After the Great Divide: Modernism, Mass Culture, Postmodernism* (Bloomington IN: Indiana University Press, 1986).

Irigaray, Luce, *Ce sexe qui n'en est pas un* (Paris: Minuit, 1977).

— *Speculum de l'autre femme* (Paris: Minuit, 1974).

Jameson, Fredric, *The Political Unconscious: Narrative as a Socially Symbolic Act* (Ithaca NY: Cornell University Press, 1981).

Japrisot, Sébastien, *Piège pour Cendrillon* (Paris: Editions Denoël, 1965).

Joubert, André, *François Mauriac et Thérèse Desqueyroux* (Paris: Nizet, 1982).

Jouve, Nicole Ward, *Colette* (Bloomington IN: Indiana University Press, 1987).

Julien, Eileen, 'Of Colonial and Canonical Encounters: A Reciprocal Reading of *L'immoraliste* and *Une vie de boy*" in Josef Gugler, Hans-Jurgen Lusebrink and Jurgen Martini (eds), *Literary Theory and African Literature* (Hamburg: Lit Verlag, 1994).

Kadish, Doris, '"Alissa dans la vallée": Intertextual Echoes of Balzac in Two Novels by Gide', *French Forum*, 10/1 (1985), 67–83.

Kaplan, E. Ann, *Women and Film: Both Sides of the Camera* (New York and London: Methuen, 1983).

Katrak, Ketu H., 'Decolonizing Culture: Toward a Theory for Postcolonial Women's Texts', *Modern Fiction Studies*, 35/1 (1989).

Kavablum, Leah, *Cinderella: Radical Feminist, Alchemist* (Guttenberg NJ: Guttenberg, 1973).

Kelly, Dorothy, *Fictional Genders: Role and Representation in Nineteenth-Century French Narrative* (Lincoln NE: University of Nebraska Press, 1989).

Kidd, William, 'Oedipal and Pre-Oedipal Elements in *Thérèse Desqueyroux*', in John E. Flower and Bernard C. Swift (eds), *François Mauriac: Visions and Reappraisals* (Oxford: Berg Publishers, 1989).

Klein, Melanie, 'Mourning and its Relation to Manic-Depressive States', *Contributions to Psychoanalysis 1921–1945* (London: Hogarth Press, 1948).

Kofman, Sarah, 'Ça cloche,' in Philippe Lacoue-Labarthe and Jean-Luc Nancy (eds), *Les fins de l'homme*, (Paris: Galilée, 1981).

Kristeva, Julia, *Des Chinoises* (Paris: Editions des femmes, 1974).

— *Soleil Noir: Dépression et mélancolie* (Paris: Gallimard, 1987).

Laplanche, Jean, and J. B. Pontalis, *Vocabulaire de la psychanalyse* (Paris: Presses Universitaires de France, 1967).

Lacan, Jacques, *Les Quatre Concepts fondamentaux de la psychanalyse*, in Jacques-Alain Miller (ed.), *Le Séminaire de Jacques Lacan* (Paris: Editions du Seuil, 1973).

Langbauer, Laurie, *Women and Romance: The Consolations of Gender in the English Novel* (Ithaca NY: Cornell University Press, 'Reading Women Writing' Series, 1990).

Lionnet, Françoise, Rev. of Leah Hewitt, 'Autobiographical Tightropes', *SubStance*, 21/2, issue 68 (1992), 131–7.

Litvak, Joseph, *Caught in the Act: Theatricality in the Nineteenth-Century English Novel* (Berkeley CA: University of California Press, 1992).

Londe, Albert, 'La photographie en médecine', *La nature*, 523 (1883).

Lottman, Herbert, *Colette: A Life* (Boston MA: Little, Brown, 1991).

Lukàcs, György, *The Theory of the Novel: A Historico-Philosophical Essay on the Forms of Great Epic Literature*, trans. Anna Bostock (Boston MA: MIT Press, 1971).

Lydon, Mary, 'Calling Yourself a Woman: Marguerite Yourcenar and Colette', *Differences*, 3/3 (1991).

— 'Myself and M/others', *SubStance*, 32 (1981), 6–14.

— 'The Forgetfulness of Memory: Jacques Lacan, Marguerite Duras, and the Text', *Contemporary Literature*, 29/3 (1988).

— '"L'Eden cinema": Aging and the Imagination in Marguerite Duras', in Kathleen Woodward (ed.), *Aging – Literature – Psychoanalysis* (Bloomington IN: Indiana University Press, 1986).

Mannoni, Octave, *Clefs pour l'imaginaire ou l'autre scene* (Paris: Seuil, 1969).

Marty, Eric, 'A propos de *La porte étroite*: Répétition et remémoration: Le nouvel Abelard', *Revue des sciences humaines*, 70/199 (1985).

Mauriac, François, *Thérèse Desqueyroux* (Paris: Bernard Grasset, 1927).

— *Oeuvres romanesques et théâtrales* (vol. 2), ed. Jacques Petit (Paris: Gallimard, 1979).

Maurois, André, *Lélia, ou la vie de George Sand* (Paris: Hachette, 1952).

McPherson, Karen, *Incriminations: Guilty Women/Telling Stories* (Princeton NJ: Princeton University Press, 1994).

Mei, Huang, *Transforming the Cinderella Dream* (New Brunswick and London: Rutgers University Press, 1990).

Menke, Anne, '"Boy!": The Hinge of Colonial Double Talk', *Studies in Twentieth-Century Literature*, 15/1 (1991).

Mignon, Maurice, *Willy, Colette et Polaire* (Clamecy: Imprimerie générale de la Nièvre, 1960).

Miller, Christopher, *Blank Darkness: Africanist Discourse in French* (Chicago IL: University of Chicago Press, 1985).

— 'Francophonie and Independence', in Hollier *et al.* (eds), *A New History of French Literature* (Cambridge MA: Harvard University Press, 1989).

— *Theories of Africans* (Chicago IL: University of Chicago Press, 1990).

Moi, Toril, *Sexual/Textual Politics: Feminist Literary Theory* (London and New York: Routledge, 1988).

Moore, David Chioni, 'An African Classic in Fourteen Translations: Ferdinand Oyono's *Une vie de boy* on the World Literary Stage', *PMLA*, 128/1 (January 2013).

Mortimer, Armine Kotin, *Plotting to Kill* (New York: Peter Lang Publishing, 1991).

Mulvey, Laura, 'Visual Pleasure and Narrative Cinema', *Screen*, 16.3 (1975), 6–18.

— *Visual and Other Pleasures* (Bloomington IN: Indiana University Press, 1989).

Newmark, Kevin, 'Love's Cross in *La porte étroite*', *MLN*, 99/5 (1984).

Ngai, Sianne, 'Theory of the Gimmick', *Critical Inquiry*, 43 (Winter 2017), 446–505.

Norindr, Panivong, *Phantasmatic Indochina: French Colonial Ideology in Architecture, Film and Literature* (Durham NC: Duke University Press, 1996).

O'Connell, David, *François Mauriac Revisited* (New York: Twayne Publishers, 1995).

Offord, Malcolm, 'Imagery in Colette's *Le blé en herbe*', *Nottingham French Studies*, 25/1 (1986), 34–62.

— 'Colours in Colette's *Le blé en herbe*', *Nottingham French Studies*, 22/2 (1983), 32–52.

Okolie, Maxwell, 'Le regard et le drame de Toundi dans *Une vie de boy*', *Ethiopiques*, 5/1 (1988).

Owen, A. R. G., *Hysteria, Hypnosis and Healing: The Work of J.-M. Charcot* (London: Dennis Dobson, 1971).

Oyono, Ferdinand, *Une vie de boy* (Paris: Juillard,1956).

Parry, Benita, 'Resistance Theory/Theorising Resistance, or Two Cheers for Nativism', in Francis Barker, Peter Hulme and Margaret Iversen (eds), *Colonial Discourse/Postcolonial Theory* (Manchester and New York: Manchester University Press, 1994).

Paulson, William, 'Closing the Circle: Science, Literature, and the Passion of Matter', *New England Review and Bread Loaf Quarterly*, 12/4 (Summer 1990).

Perrault, Charles, *Histoires ou contes du temps passé: Avec des Moralitez* (1697), in Jean-Pierre Collinet (ed.), *Contes* (Paris: Gallimard, 1981).

Petit, Jacques, 'Notice', in *Thérèse Desqueyroux* (vol. 2) (Paris: Gallimard: Bibliothèque de la Pléiade, 1978), pp. 918–27.

Poe, Edgar Allen, 'The Purloined Letter', in *Tales* (London: Wiley and Putnam, 1845).

Polaire [Emilie Marie Bouchard], *Polaire par elle-même* (Paris: Figuière, 1933).

Prelli, Lawrence, 'Rhetorics of Display: An Introduction', in Lawrence Prelli, *Rhetorics of Display* (Columbia SC: University of South Carolina Press, 2006).

Ramas, Maria, 'Freud's Dora, Dora's Hysteria', in Charles Bernheimer and Claire Kahane (eds), *In Dora's Case: Freud – Hysteria – Feminism* (New York: Columbia University Press, 1985), pp. 149–80.

Rea, Annabelle, 'The Siren and the Witch', in Janis Glasgow (ed.), *George Sand: Collected Essays* (Troy NY: The Whitson Publishing Co.,1985).

Reid, Roddey, 'Modernist Aesthetics and Familial Textuality: Gide's Strait is the Gate', *Studies in Twentieth-Century Literature*, 13/2 (1989).

Rémy, Tristan, *Georges Wague, Le Mime de la Belle Epoque* (Paris: Girard, 1964).

Resch, Yannick, *Corps féminin, corps textuel: essai sur le personnage féminin dans l'oeuvre de Colette* (Paris: Klincksieck, 1973).

Richardson, Joanna, *Colette* (London: Methuen, 1983).

Richer, Paul, *L'étude descriptive de la grande attaque hystéro-épileptique et de ses principales variétés* (Paris: V. Adrien Delahaye, 1879).

Richet, Charles, 'Les Démoniaques d'aujourd'hui et d'autrefois', *La revue des deux mondes*, 37 (1880), 532–87.

Riviere, Joan, 'Womanliness as a Masquerade', *International Journal of Psychoanalysis*, 10 (1929).

Russo, Mary, *The Female Grotesque: Risk, Excess and Modernity* (New York: Routledge, 1995).

Said, Edward, 'Representing the Colonized: Anthropology's Interlocutors', *Critical Inquiry*, 15/2 (1989), 205–25.

Sartre, Jean-Paul, 'Orphée noir', *Situations III* (Paris: Editions Gallimard, 1949).

Schapiro, Meyer, 'On Some Problems in the Semiotics of Visual Art: Field and Vehicle in Image-Signs', *Simiolus: Netherlands Quarterly for the History of Art*, 6/1 (1972–3), 9–19.

Schechner, Richard, 'From Ritual to Theater and Back', *Essays on Performance Theory, 1970–1976* (New York: Drama Book Specialists, 1977).

— 'Performers and Spectators, Transported and Transformed', *The Kenyon Review*, 3/4 (Autumn 1981).

Schor, Naomi, *Bad Objects: Essays Popular and Unpopular* (Durham NC and London: Duke University Press, 1995).

— *Breaking the Chain: Women, Theory, and French Realist Fiction* (New York: Columbia University Press, 1985).

— 'Female Fetishism', *Poetics Today*, 6 (1985).

— *Reading in Detail: Aesthetics and the Feminine* (New York: Methuen, 1987).

Schuster, Marilyn, *Marguerite Duras Revisited* (New York: Twayne Publishers, 1993).

Selous, Trista, *The Other Woman: Feminism and Femininity in the Work of Marguerite Duras* (New Haven CT and London: Yale University Press, 1988).

Serres, Michel, *Hermès I: La communication* (Paris: Minuit, 1968).

Shapiro, Meyer, 'On Some Problems in the Semiotics of Visual Art: Field and Vehicle in Image-Signs', *Simiolus: Netherlands Quarterly for the History of Art*, 6/1 (1972–3), 9–19.

Sheridan, Alan, *André Gide: A Life in the Present* (London: Hamish Hamilton Ltd, 1998).

Shohat, Ella, 'Imaging terra incognita', *Public Culture*, 3/2 (1991), 41–70.

Sonnenfeld, Albert, 'On Readers and Reading in *La porte étroite* and *L'immoraliste*', *Romanic Review*, LXVII, 3 (1976).

— 'Strait is the Gate: Byroads in Gide's Labyrinth', *Novel*, 1/2 (1968).

Sonolet, Jacqueline, *Charcot et l'hystérie au XIXème siècle* (Paris: Catalogue de l'exposition à la Salpêtrière, 1982).

Stafford, Barbara Maria, *Body Criticism: Imaging the Unseen in Enlightenment Art and Medicine* (Cambridge MA: MIT Press, 1991).

Stewart, Joan Hinde, *Colette* (Boston MA: Twayne Publishers, 1983).

Stone, Kay, 'Feminist Approaches to the Interpretation of Fairy Tales', in Ruth B. Bottigheimer (ed.), *Fairy Tales and Society: Illusion, Allusion, and Paradigm* (Philadelphia PA: University of Pennsylvania Press, 1986).

— 'The Misuses of Enchantment: Controversies on The Significance of Fairy Tales', in Rosan A. Jordan and Susan Kalcik (eds), *Women's Folklore, Women's Culture* (Philadelphia PA: University of Pennsylvania Press, 1985).

Straub, Kristina, *Sexual Suspects: Eighteenth-Century Players and Sexual Ideology* (Princeton NJ: Princeton University Press, 1992).

Suleiman, Susan Rubin, 'Writing and Motherhood', in S. Garner, C. Kahane and M. Sprengnether (eds), *The (M)Other Tongue* (Ithaca NY and London: Cornell University Press, 1985).

— *Subversive Intent: Gender, Politics and the Avant-Garde* (Cambridge MA: Harvard University Press, 1990).

Tilburg, Patricia A., *Colette's Republic: Work, Gender, and Popular Culture in France, 1870–1914* (New York: Berghahn Books, 2009).

Todorov, Tzvetan, 'Typologie du roman policier', *Poétique de la prose* (Paris: Seuil, 1971).

Toepfer, Karl, *Theatre, Aristocracy and Pornocracy* (New York: PAJ Publications, 1991).

Virmaux, Alain, and Odette Virmaux (eds), *Colette au cinéma: chroniques, dialogues, scénarios* (Paris: Flammarion, 1975).

Waelti–Walters, Jennifer, *Feminist Novelists of the Belle Epoque* (Bloomington IN and Indianapolis IN: Indiana University Press, 1990).

Went-Daoust, Yvette, 'L'écriture au féminin singulier: *L'amant* de Marguerite Duras', *French Literature Series*, XVI (1989), 149–63.

Williams, Linda, 'When the Woman Looks', in Linda Williams (ed.), *Re-Vision: Essays in Feminist Film Criticism* (Frederick, Maryland: University Publications, 1983).

Williams, Timothy J., 'Thérèse and Anne: Mauriac's Mimetic Rivals', *Romance Quarterly*, 48/2 (Spring 2001), 75.

Willis, Sharon, *Marguerite Duras: Writing on the Body* (Urbana IL and Chicago IL: University of Illinois Press, 1987).

Zipes, Jack, *Fairy Tales and The Art of Subversion* (New York: Wildman Press, 1983).

Zola, Emile, *Oeuvres complètes* (Paris: Cercle du Livre Précieux, 1968).

—— *Nos auteurs dramatiques* (Paris: Fasquelle, 1923).

Index